This book will be of value not only to those interested in post-Dreyfus France and its culture, politics and history, but also to those interested in theatre *per se.* As a specialist in *fin-de-siècle* European culture, I would recommend it to teachers of the period. As someone who has been involved with student productions of French theatre, I would also recommend it as an excellent choice.

– Dr Richard Hibbitt, Senior Lecturer in French, University of Leeds

These two remarkable plays belatedly re-introduce the comic world of Octave Mirbeau to the theatrical canon. Mirbeau's theatre is firmly in the mould of the French comedy of manners, but is savage in its condemnation of the hypocrisies that underpin his – and our – society. These plays are subversive, political, and above all, very funny.

– Sean Foley, Olivier-award-winning playwright and director

T0345335

Octave Mirbeau: Two Plays

OCTAVE MIRBEAU

Woodcut of Octave Mirbeau by A. Delannoy.

Octave Mirbeau: Two Plays
Business Is Business & *Charity*

Translated & Adapted by Richard J. Hand

intellect Bristol, UK / Chicago, USA

First published in the UK in 2012 by
Intellect, The Mill, Parnall Road, Fishponds, Bristol, BS16 3JG, UK

First published in the USA in 2012 by
Intellect, The University of Chicago Press, 1427 E. 60th Street,
Chicago, IL 60637, USA

Performance permissions: Anyone wishing to perform either of the
plays should contact Richard Hand for his permission at the following
address: Prof Richard J. Hand FRSA, Cardiff School of Creative and
Cultural Industries, University of Glamorgan, The Atrium, 86-88 Adam
Street, Cardiff, CF24 2FN, Wales

A catalogue record for this book is available from the
British Library.

Series: Playtext Series
Series editor: Roberta Mock
Series ISSN: 1754–0933

Cover designer: Gareth Hughes
Copy-editor: MPS India
Typesetting: Planman Technologies

ISBN 978–1–84150–486–5

Printed and bound by Hobbs, UK.

Dedicated to Sadiyah, Shahrazad, Danyazad and Jimahl

Loin de vous
Je suis perdu

Contents

Acknowledgements

I would like to thank the Arts and Humanities Research Council for a small grant in the performing arts to support the research and publication of this volume.

A very special debt of gratitude is owed to Marie-Hélène Grosos for permission to include illustrations by Gus Bofa. Bofa (1883–1968) was a major French cartoonist of the twentieth century, and his drawings for the 1935 French edition of Mirbeau's plays remain the definitive illustrations of Mirbeau's theatre. For further details of Bofa's achievements and more examples of his work, readers are directed to the Bofa website: www.gusbofa.com I would also like to express special thanks to Emmanuel Pollaud-Dulian, custodian of the Bofa website, for his dedication and efficiency in securing the Bofa images.

Professor Sharif Gemie (University of Glamorgan) who proposed this volume and gave invaluable advice and Mirbeau expertise.

Pierre Michel (founding president of the Octave Mirbeau Society and editor of *Cahiers Octave Mirbeau*) who greeted this project with such enthusiasm and encouragement.

The late Claude Schumacher (emeritus professor of theatre studies at the University of Glasgow) who offered, as he always did, brilliant advice on the translations and their theatricality.

Laure Humbert (University of Exeter) and Andrea Beaghton (Victor Hugo Society) for reading through the final versions.

Professor Graham Ley (University of Exeter) and Professor Roberta Mock (University of Plymouth) for their constant belief in this project.

Students of drama at the University of Glamorgan who helped to bring early drafts of these translations to life in the studio.

Introduction

Octave Mirbeau: A biographical sketch

Octave Mirbeau was born in Trévières, Normandy, on 16 February 1848. He had a quiet childhood, which seemingly came to an abrupt end when he was sent to a Jesuit college at Vannes in 1859. The next four years were a miserable experience for the young Mirbeau, and the barbarity, tyranny and snobbery he encountered there – which seemed to him a microcosm of French society – would never be far from his writing for the rest of his life. Mirbeau registered to study law at university in 1866 but in 1868 would claim that 'he had been eating nothing and smoking up to 180 pipes of opium a day' (Levi, 1992, 437). When the Franco-Prussian War broke out in 1870, Mirbeau could finally abandon his studies completely and join the army as a lieutenant. In December 1870 he was wounded, and in 1871 he was accused of desertion (he was acquitted of this charge in 1872). Just as his life in the Jesuit college had been traumatic, Mirbeau's experiences in the army made him develop 'a passionate loathing for the absurdity of war' (Levi, 1992, 437). After the Franco-Prussian War, Mirbeau became a journalist specializing in art criticism (he was a pioneering advocate of Paul Cézanne, Claude Monet, Auguste Rodin and Vincent Van Gogh) and then theatre reviewing. He established and edited his own satirical journal *Les Grimaces* in the 1880s. Mirbeau was always a colourful figure and was involved in at least twelve duels in his life, several on account of the provocative opinions expressed in his journalism. The life and work of Mirbeau remain a remarkable reflection of an extraordinary time.

Although primarily a journalist, Mirbeau was a versatile writer producing some significant fiction, including *L'Abbé Jules* (*Father Jules* 1888), and two vitriolic masterpieces of the erotic-grotesque, satires of contemporary France which have never lost the power to shock or provoke universally: *Le Jardin des supplices*/*Torture Garden* (1899) and *Le Journal d'une femme de chambre*/*The Diary of a Chambermaid* (1900). By no means a prolific playwright, Mirbeau nonetheless wrote six one-act plays (published together as *Farces et moralités* (*Farces and Morality Plays* in 1904) and three full-length plays – one of which, *Les affaires sont les affaires*/*Business Is Business* (1903), enjoyed international acclaim and is the work that made Mirbeau, as Pierre Michel (1999, 25) reveals, 'un millionaire'. In terms of his politics, too, Mirbeau offers an astonishing reflection of a dynamic epoch, moving steadily to the left through his career. Starting as a Bonapartist with anti-Semitic views, he became, by turns, a monarchist and then a republican before becoming, most famously, an anarchist. As an anarchist living through a fascinating and tumultuous epoch of French history, Mirbeau strove to be as provocative and incendiary as he could through his writing. Indeed, despite this radical shift in his political opinions, Mirbeau was always consistent in presenting – in his fiction, plays and journalism – an acerbic critique of what he perceived as the widespread hypocrisy and corruption in French society. Given his shift in political opinions, it is not surprising that the one-time anti-Semite Mirbeau would, like Émile Zola, be outspoken in his support of the Jewish army officer Alfred Dreyfus in the notorious and protracted Dreyfus Affair of the 1890s onwards. Mirbeau developed many important artistic friends in his career, including Camille Pissarro, Stéphane Mallarmé and Anatole France. Compatriots such as Guillaume Apollinaire regarded Mirbeau as 'the sole prophet of our age' (Lemarié and Michel, 2011, 1182), and his international standing is reflected in Leon Tolstoy's assessment that Mirbeau is 'France's greatest contemporary writer' and the pre-eminent example of French culture's 'secular genius' (Lemarié and Michel, 2011, 1181). Afflicted by poor health and demoralized by the horror and futility of the First World War, the once prolific Mirbeau wrote less and less and died on his sixty-ninth birthday in 1917.

Octave Mirbeau: The novelist

Today, Mirbeau's reputation lies most significantly in the area of fiction. Among his semi-autobiographical novels are *Le Calvaire* (*Calvary* 1886), *L'Abbé Jules* (1888) and *Sébastien Roch* (1890), which feature damning assaults on the Church in France, sexual relationships and morality, and the army. Later, Mirbeau would write some ambitiously experimental travel writing such as *La 628-E8* (1907) – the title of which is the registration number of Mirbeau's car – which is a fictionalized account of a journey across the Low Countries and Germany and includes experiential descriptions of the act of motor travelling as well as Mirbeau's characteristically radical political commentary. However, Mirbeau's reputation as a novelist persists, most tangibly, with the two novels *Le Jardin des supplices/Torture Garden* (1899) and *Le Journal d'une femme de chambre/The Diary of a Chambermaid* (1900).

    Torture Garden has been described, according to V. Vale and Andrea Juno, as 'the most sickening work of art in the nineteenth century' (quoted in Mirbeau, 1989, 7), and it has lost none of its power to shock or disturb. The novel is predominantly a first-person narrative account of an anonymous man as he makes a journey in the East. The decadent protagonist meets a young English widow Clara on a ship, and she leads him into a taboo world of erotic-grotesquery, culminating in the Chinese torture garden of the title where indigenous criminals are mutilated or executed in horrifically inventive – and meticulously described – ways while the European pleasure-seekers watch. Mirbeau's narrator sometimes watches aghast, but the thrill of arousal inexorably crawls into him. When the narrator declares in despair, 'There is nothing real, then, except evil!' (Mirbeau, 1989, 47), he is not only objectively denouncing the omnipresent forces of sadism and colonialism but also acknowledging the presence of these forces within himself. The institutionalized horror and sadism in the novel make it a forerunner to Franz Kafka's *In der Strafkolonie/ In the Penal Colony* (1919). Moreover, in its unremitting disturbing journey into the atrocities and psyche of Western colonialism it is not dissimilar in structure or theme to a contemporaneous work of fiction: Joseph Conrad's 1899 novella *Heart of Darkness* (see Hand, 2005, 114–116). Mirbeau's unstinting focus on sexual depravity and decadence, however, makes *Torture Garden* the sadistic and sexualized *Heart of Darkness* of the *fin de siècle*. 'The horror, the horror' pervades Mirbeau's world as much as Conrad's, but it is, first and foremost, an explicitly *sexual* horror.

Published the following year, *The Diary of a Chambermaid* (1900) also remains an unsettling masterpiece of the erotic and is a devastating critique of bourgeois France. The novel is presented as the diary of Célestine and her descriptions of her various employers, who are sadistic and fetishistic and subject her to trials both bizarre and humiliating. But that is not to say that Célestine is a naïve victim: what makes the book so powerful is Célestine's wisdom and manipulation of the situation. She is a servant and a woman with an indomitable spirit, and her every decision – when to resign, when to have sex – is calculated to be to her advantage. On the rare occasion when Célestine actually falls in love it is with a man dying of consumption, and Célestine describes how 'his lips were stained with bloodstained froth, and I took a clot of blood in my mouth and swallowed it as if it were the elixir of life' (Mirbeau, 2001d, 116). In a typical move, Mirbeau compounds eroticism and death and, by doing so, follows in the tradition of another classic of Decadent fiction – Rachilde's *La Marquise de Sade* (*Marquis de Sade* 1887) – in casting an iconoclastic bomb into the romantic idealism of 'true love'. Mirbeau's novel paints yet another damning portrait of *fin de siècle* France and its values and realities. It is testament to its power as a novel that *The Diary of a Chambermaid* has had the privilege of being adapted to the screen by directors as celebrated – and dissimilar – as Jean Renoir (1946) and Luis Buñuel (1964).

Octave Mirbeau the dramatist: The short plays

Following the descriptions in the previous section, what should we expect to find when we turn to Mirbeau's plays? Onstage sadism, violent death and disease? Such expectations are not only understandable but also increased when we realize that four of Mirbeau's six one-act plays were performed at the Théâtre du Grand-Guignol, Paris's legendary Theatre of Horror which thrived in Montmartre from 1897 until it closed in 1962. Indeed, after his death, Mirbeau's *Le Jardin des supplices* was performed at the Grand-Guignol in 1922 in a stage adaptation written by Pierre Chaine and André de Lorde (see Hand and Wilson, 2002, 195–230). Although the dramatization essentially transforms Mirbeau's decadent novel into an espionage thriller, the play does put atrocity centre stage, with a prostitute skinned alive and Clara getting her eyeballs burned out with red-hot needles (significantly, there is no 'just' retribution delivered on the sadistic Englishwoman at the end of Mirbeau's novel). However, when it came to writing plays for the theatre himself, Mirbeau regarded the worlds of fiction and drama as completely different, and his plays for the Grand-Guignol would seem, at first glance, remarkably restrained for that most notorious of popular theatres and that most notorious of writers. Nevertheless, we must acknowledge that the comedy genre was as important to the Grand-Guignol as horror, and Mirbeau's plays for the Grand-Guignol are all masterful examples of the genre of Grand-Guignol comedy. In short, they may be comedies but they are nonetheless extremely brutal in their ruthless satire of contemporary relationships and morality. For example, Mirbeau's first play, *Vieux ménages/The Old Couple*, was premiered at the Théâtre d'Application in 1894 and revived extremely comfortably at the Grand-Guignol in October 1900. In this play we are presented with a portrait of a long-married couple and their loveless, cruel relationship. The couple are as vindictive as any dysfunctional couple in the plays of August Strindberg, Tennessee Williams or Harold Pinter. In terms of French theatre, one is reminded of the bitter encounter between Lucrèce Borgia and her husband, Don Alphonse, in *Act 2* of Victor Hugo's *Lucrèce Borgia* (1833), an act that Hugo subtitles 'Le Couple'. Mirbeau's bourgeois couple are both in their sixties and are marred by self-pity and resentment of each other. Not much of a comedy, it would seem. Yet, for Mirbeau, the comic intention is grounded in satire. The old couple represent the bourgeoisie and should be contented and self-satisfied, and yet their mutually dependant cruelty in a hermetically sealed hell of their own construction (this is a hell of other people decades before Jean-Paul Sartre's *Huis Clos* (*No Exit* 1944)) makes them less figures of tragedy than those worthy of ridicule. This sense of ridicule is politically motivated and is unabashedly provocative, a stance suitable for Grand-Guignol comedy at its best.

Mirbeau could deploy other dramatic styles. For instance, *L'Épidémie/The Epidemic* – which premiered at the legendary experimental studio Théâtre Antoine in May 1898 – is a farce that rather than using the distinctive Grand-Guignol hybrid of naturalism and melodrama, exploits stark archetypes and stereotypes. Mirbeau's caustic satire concerns an outbreak of typhoid fever and lampoons a local council's response to the crisis and is a resonant critique of bureaucracy and government. It is a work not dissimilar in style to examples of proto-Expressionist and Expressionist drama by writers such as Frank Wedekind, Georg Kaiser or Ernst Toller. *L'Épidémie* is also precursive to examples of Epic theatre in the Brechtian mould, agitprop drama and even to the Theatre of the Absurd by writers like Eugène Ionesco. Although there is a hint of *L'Épidémie*'s comic stereotypes in Isidore Lechat's dinner guests and Baron Courtin's lady charity workers in the first acts of the two plays in this volume, it is Mirbeau's Grand-Guignol repertoire that proves most influential on his major drama. *Vieux ménages* and his other brutal comedies for the Grand-Guignol – ruthlessly satirical and witty plays with richly detailed characterization that nestled comfortably between horror plays – inaugurate the style that will be fully developed when he comes to creating his two greatest plays.

Octave Mirbeau the dramatist: The full-length plays

Mirbeau's first full-length play was the five-act *Les Mauvais Bergers/The Bad Shepherds*, which premiered at the Théâtre de la Renaissance in December 1897 with Sarah Bernhardt in the central role of Madeleine. The play is a realist drama exploration of class division in France with a focus on its working-class characters and their struggle. However, it is Mirbeau's two other full-length plays – the mordant comedies *Les Affaires sont les affaires/Business Is Business* (1903) and *Le Foyer/Charity* (1908) – that embody Octave Mirbeau's greatest achievement as a dramatist.

Les Affaires sont les affaires/Business Is Business (1903) is Mirbeau's masterpiece, enjoying hugely successful productions in France, Germany and Russia, and is the work that made his fortune. The play even made it to production in Britain, although Sydney Grundy's 1905 adaptation of it – to judge by the copy held in the Lord Chamberlain's Office archives at the British Library – was a very much tempered and substantially shortened version, almost certainly because a more accurate translation would have been deemed far too risqué for the British theatre censors of the time. The protagonist of the play, Isidore Lechat, is one of the most diabolical characters in French drama: he is a working-class man made good, a hugely powerful industrialist and newspaper owner with political aspirations who is utterly unscrupulous in his business affairs and his personal life. He is the descendant of several of Molière's despicable yet hilarious anti-heroes and is a forerunner to the newspaper magnate Lambert Le Roux in Howard Brenton and David Hare's *Pravda* (1985). Like Shakespeare's King Richard III, Isidore (Mirbeau consistently uses his first name) is a man whom an audience loves to hate. As we watch the play, we wait for Isidore to get his comeuppance, and yet when it should happen (a shocking personal tragedy happens in *Act 3*), it fails to. Isidore's love of money and his self-aggrandizing aspirations never waver. We see Isidore for what he really is: the victim of a capitalist system detached from human emotion. This is the true tragedy that underpins this three-act comedy. Isidore is a tragic Faust-like figure in love with money, power and desire itself but irredeemably lost in the godless, anarchistic universe created by Octave Mirbeau.

Mirbeau's final play *Le Foyer/Charity* (1908) was ostensibly co-written with the art critic Thadée Natanson, although Pierre Michel reveals that this was an attempt by Mirbeau to raise money, in the form of royalties, for his bankrupted friend (Mirbeau, 1999, 306). The script was instantly controversial and despite being completed in 1906 the play finally premiered at the Comédie-Française in December 1908. *Charity*, another three-act comedy of manners in the Molière tradition, is in the same mould as *Business Is Business* but takes as its theme *charity* rather than *business*. Nonetheless, to Mirbeau both themes are inseparable from the capitalist society they spring from. 'Le Foyer' of the title is the name of a charity home (translated as 'The Haven' in *Charity*) established by Baron Courtin, politician, writer, member of the Académie française and philanthropist. Courtin is a figure almost as gargantuan as Isidore Lechat, although his essence could not be more different. In *Business Is Business*, despite a number of exquisitely drawn characters (including Germaine Lechat, Lucien Garraud and the

Marquis of Porcellet), Isidore unequivocally dominates the play. In *Charity*, there is a more acute balance between Courtin and the other characters, in particular Courtin's wife Therese and her erstwhile lover, the millionaire Armand Biron. The Baroness's past, ongoing and projected adultery is deliberately provocative when juxtaposed with the seeming humanitarian idealism of her husband. However, despite habitually taking the moral high ground, Courtin is a complex figure who ultimately teeters on the precipice of doom because of his own corruption. Mirbeau creates Courtin's depth of character partly through the care with which he creates those who encounter him: the idealistic Robert d'Auberval, the austere Miss Rambert or the loathsomely expedient – and anti-Semitic – Celestin Lerible. Although one empathizes with Courtin, when his redemption is orchestrated there is a sudden dissatisfaction at the lack of justice. After all, although lip service is given to the miseries instigated by capitalism (as Therese declaims, 'money poisons our very existence'), this is offset by Courtin and the ruling class's desire to preserve the status quo at all costs.

The focus of the play is the charity home. Although established ostensibly in good faith, the stories which seep into the play from The Haven are increasingly disturbing, and one realizes that far from offering salvation to the destitute adolescent girls it houses it creates greater problems: financial corruption, physical and sexual abuse, and death. Mirbeau originally set a whole act in The Haven but cut it due to length and redeployed the material into the rest of the play. The omitted act would have presented an audience with rich material that is described but absent from the final play, including characters like the girls who live in the charity home and the Duchess's much anticipated visit. It was a bold decision on Mirbeau's part but a justified one: in *Charity*, as it stands, by being perpetually offstage, The Haven is horribly distant from the people and forces that rule over it and decide the fate of the poor souls within it.

The dramatic principles of Octave Mirbeau's drama

Prior to becoming a playwright himself, Mirbeau's interest in theatre had been manifest in his journalism where, with characteristic passion, he attacked stage censorship, championed the realist drama of Henrik Ibsen and defended the symbolist theatre of Maurice Maeterlinck. In 1885 he denounced the Comédie-Française (which two decades later would present *Le Foyer*) for placing more importance on the actors than the plays they were actually performing (Lemarié and Michel, 2011, 546). Eventually, Mirbeau followed in the footsteps of Émile Zola: both believed French theatre to be moribund, and this compelled these accomplished writers to turn to the stage to try what was, for them, a new art form. Unlike Zola, who found making forays into theatre from fiction problematic, Mirbeau metamorphosed himself into a successful and accomplished playwright. Mirbeau's preoccupations with themes such as institutional and systemic failings, human weakness and expediency, and social injustice and hypocrisy are animated on stage with scathing, penetrating wit. At times Mirbeau's drama recalls the work of his

European contemporaries or near contemporaries such as Ibsen, Gerhart Hauptmann or Carl Sternheim, but Mirbeau remains a distinctive and scintillating dramatist in his own right.

Pierre Michel draws on an interview Mirbeau gave to Paul Gsell in *La Revue* (15 March 1907) in order to clarify the three key principles in Mirbeau's theatre (Mirbeau, 1999, 12–14). The year 1907 was an interesting time for Mirbeau to take stock of his dramatic practice, coming as it does after he has had eight plays staged and *Charity* is slowly heading towards production.

First of all, Mirbeau believed that stage characters must not be made out of 'cardboard' but must be real people. Although the caricatures in his short play *L'Épidémie/The Epidemic* (1898) are an audacious exception to this, it is a recurrent feature to the rest of his plays; despite the satirical humour with which his dramatic personae are created (whether this is Isidore's demonic fits of rage or Biron's trousers which are 'always too short') they are still feasibly *real*. That is not to suggest that Mirbeau does not enjoy being archly playful with his situations (we might consider, again, the bourgeois dinner guests in *Business Is Business*) or even his characters' names: in *Charity*, the former member of parliament is Arnaud Tripier ('tripier' is French for a butcher who specializes in tripe) and Courtin's anxious charity ladies include Mrs Rature ('rature' means to cross or scribble out) and Mrs Pigeon (as in the bird but also a dupe or 'stool pigeon').

Second, Mirbeau believed that stage characters should be preoccupied with recognizably modern hopes, dreams and attitudes, and this is starkly placed in the context of a contemporary, hypocritical society. This principle lies at the heart of the satirical irony in Mirbeau's drama.

Finally, Mirbeau believed that dialogue should be as real as possible. Although Mirbeau is a political playwright, the expression of ideas is modulated through a natural discourse complete with silences, pauses and, as the reader will discover, countless … carefully … placed … ellipses.

With these principles in mind, what we discover in the plays of Octave Mirbeau is a body of drama that can offer rounded characters, vibrant ideas and realistic dialogue. The resulting theatre is very rich for actors, directors, audiences and readers. Like some other-world playwrights of the same era, Mirbeau has been one of the most neglected world dramatists on the British stage. This is probably because he was too risqué for Britain in his own time but was swiftly superseded in more liberal times. Indeed, when *The New York Times* reviewed a production of *Les Mauvais Bergers* in 1918, it reflected on how Zola's work and the plays of John Galsworthy have 'been shoved into the background by the greater struggle in which the workmen and employers now find themselves' (21 February 1918); in other words, the First World War changed politics, art and theatre.

It is hoped that this volume of translations/adaptations is timely. The reason they have been described as adaptations as much as translations is partly because certain historical details and rhetoric (especially in *Charity*) have been edited or streamlined and, throughout, the dialogue has been developed with an eye – and ear – on theatricality rather than some assumed notion of 'the literal'. It is hoped that the scripts will 'flow' coherently and entertainingly for anglophone actors and audiences. Moreover, the twinning of adaptation with translation reflects a guiding principle effectively articulated by Friedrich Kittler when he writes that to 'transfer messages from one medium to another always involves reshaping them … every transposition is to a degree arbitrary, a manipulation' (Kittler, 1990, 265). Translation and adaptation are intertwined processes that (re)shape, (re)create and (re)invent.

As for these examples of Belle Époque theatre, let us hope that the time of being 'superseded' has passed and Octave Mirbeau may, like his contemporary Edwardian playwrights in Britain, begin to enjoy a revival of fortune in the English-language theatre. Certainly Mirbeau's rediscovery in France with recent high-profile and award-winning productions makes this seem possible. Mirbeau the playwright may remind us of Galsworthy (especially *Strife* (1909) and the 1920 play *The Skin Game*), but Mirbeau's aptitude for comedy combined with an impassioned and politically informed contempt for the capitalist system make him particularly similar to George Bernard Shaw. When one reads *Charity* and *Business Is Business*, one may well think of the contemporaneous plays of GBS, especially *Mrs Warren's Profession* (1902) and *Major Barbara* (1905). By interrogating the most serious of issues with humour, Mirbeau, like Shaw, demonstrates a faith in the revolutionary power of laughter. Moreover, the targets in Mirbeau's drama – the injustices, ironies and hypocrisies that imbue capitalist society – seem as frighteningly relevant in the twenty-first century as they were in the early twentieth.

Earlier, the question of whether Mirbeau presents the same material on the stage that he does in his fiction was posed: namely sadism, violent death and disease. Although never centre stage, such things are never far away in Mirbeau's theatre. The abused children in *Charity*, including one death, and the fatal car crash in *Business Is Business* (perhaps the first car accident in the history of drama) may not be centre stage, but their very presence just in the wings does not diminish their potency in determining the dramatic trajectory of the plays. As Robert Ziegler says, in his appraisal of *Le Jardin des supplices*, 'Murder, whose prevention is the pretext for forming governments, is the practice that these governments most assiduously engage in' (Ziegler, 2007, 230). The brutal practices and cant of so-called civilization and society appals Mirbeau the anarchist, and they are never far away in any of Mirbeau's plays, no matter how humorous the treatment may be. In short, Mirbeau may not skin anyone alive on his stage, but – as suggested in Gus Bofa's masterful caricature of the writer – his scalpel-sharp satire eviscerates the hypocritical morality, culture and politics of a French civilization and society. One is never sure if we are witnessing a life-saving procedure or a post-mortem. Either way, Octave Mirbeau, the skilful surgeon, cracks jokes as he inserts the blade.

Bibliography

Baines, Roger, Marinetti, Cristina and Manuela Perteghella (eds), *Staging and Performing Translation: Text and Theatre Practice*, Houndmills: Palgrave Macmillan, 2010.

Brenton, Howard and David Hare, *Pravda*, London: Methuen, 1985.

Esslin, Martin, *The Theatre of the Absurd* (revised and enlarged edition), Harmondsworth: Penguin, 1968.

Galsworthy, John, *Five Plays*, Methuen: London, 1999.

Hand, Richard J. *The Theatre of Joseph Conrad: Reconstructed Fictions*, London: Palgrave, 2005.

Hand, Richard J. and Michael Wilson, *Grand-Guignol: The French Theatre of Horror*, Exeter: University of Exeter Press, 2002.

Hugo, Victor, *Oeuvre Complet: Théâtre I*, Paris: Robert Laffont, 2002.

Hugo, Victor, *Victor Hugo: Plays* (edited by Claude Schumacher), London: Methuen, 2004.

Ibsen, Henrik, *Ghosts and Other Plays*, Harmondsworth: Penguin, 1964.

Ibsen, Henrik, *A Doll's House and Other Plays*, Harmondsworth: Penguin, 1965.

Ionesco, Eugène, *Rhinoceros/The Chairs/The Lesson*, Harmondsworth: Penguin, 1962.

Ionesco, Eugène, *Théâtre complet*, Paris: Gallimard, 1991.

Kittler, Friedrich, *Discourse Networks 1800/1900* (translated by Michael Metteer), Paolo Alto: Stanford University Press, 1990.

Lemarié, Yannick and Pierre Michel (eds), *Dictionnaire Octave Mirbeau*, Lausanne, Switzerland: L'Age d'Homme, 2011.

Levi, Anthony, *Guide to French Literature 1789 to the Present*, Chicago: St James, 1992.

Mirbeau, Octave, *The Torture Garden* (translated by A. C. Bessie), San Francisco: Re-Search, 1989.

Mirbeau, Octave, *Théâtre Complet* (edited and introduced by Pierre Michel), Saint-Pierre-du-Mont, France: Eurédit, 1999.

Mirbeau, Octave, *Oeuvre Romanesque 1* (edited and introduced by Pierre Michel), Paris: Buchet Chastel, 2000a.

Mirbeau, Octave, *Oeuvre Romanesque 2* (edited and introduced by Pierre Michel), Paris: Buchet Chastel, 2001b.

Mirbeau, Octave, *Oeuvre Romanesque 3* (edited and introduced by Pierre Michel), Paris: Buchet Chastel, 2001c.

Mirbeau, Octave, *The Diary of a Chambermaid* (translated by Douglas Jarman), Sawtry, UK: Dedalus, 2001d.

Mirbeau, Octave, *Théâtre Complet tome 1: Les Mauvais Bergers* (edited and introduced by Pierre Michel), Cazaubon, France: Eurédit, 2003a.

Mirbeau, Octave, *Théâtre Complet tome 2: Les Affaires sont les affaires* (edited and introduced by Pierre Michel), Cazaubon, France: Eurédit, 2003b.

Mirbeau, Octave, *Théâtre Complet tome 3: Le Foyer* (edited and introduced by Pierre Michel), Cazaubon, France: Eurédit, 2003c.

Mirbeau, Octave, *Théâtre Complet tome 4: Farces et moralités* (edited and introduced by Pierre Michel), Cazaubon, France: Eurédit, 2003d.

Pinter, Harold, *Plays 1*, London: Faber and Faber, 1996.

Pinter, Harold, *Plays 2*, London: Faber and Faber, 1996.

Pinter, Harold, *Plays 3*, London: Faber and Faber, 1997.

Raab, Paul (ed.), *German Expressionism: The Era of German Expressionism*, London: Calder and Boyars, 1974.

Ritchie, McPherson J. (ed.), *German Expressionism: Seven Expressionist Plays*, London: Calder and Boyars, 1968.

Sartre, Jean-Paul, *Huis Clos*, Paris: Gallimard, 1947.

Shakespeare, William, *The Complete Works of William Shakespeare*, London: Oxford University Press, 1964.

Shaw, George Bernard, *Major Barbara*, Harmondsworth: Penguin, 1960.

Shaw, George Bernard, *Plays Unpleasant: Widowers' Houses; The Philanderer, and, Mrs Warren's Profession*, Harmondsworth: Penguin, 2000.

Sternheim, Carl, *Scenes from the Heroic Life of the Middle Classes: Five Plays*, London: Calder and Boyars, 1970.

Strindberg, August, *Plays: 1*, London: Methuen, 1982.

Strindberg, August, *Plays: 2*, London: Methuen, 1982.

Strindberg, August, *Plays: 3*, London: Methuen, 1993.

Toller, Ernst, *Seven Plays*, New York: Liveright, 1934.

Wedekind, Frank, *Wedekind Plays One*, London: Methuen, 1993.

Williams, Tennessee, *Cat on a Hot Tin Roof and Other Plays*, Harmondsworth: Penguin, 1990.

Ziegler, Robert, *The Nothing Machine: The Fiction of Octave Mirbeau*, Amsterdam: Rodopi, 2007.

Octave Mirbeau: A Theatre Chronology

1894
20 December: *Vieux ménages* (a comedy in one act), Théâtre d'Application.

1897
14 December: *Les Mauvais Bergers* (a play in five acts), Théâtre de la Renaissance.

1898
14 May: *L'Épidémie* (a farce in one act), Théâtre Antoine.

1900
29 October: Revival of *Vieux ménages* (a comedy in one act), Théâtre du Grand-Guignol.

1901
25 May: *Les Amants* (a comedy in one act), Théâtre du Grand-Guignol.

1902
19 February: *Le Portefeuille* (a comedy in one act), Théâtre de la Renaissance-Gémier.
2 June: *Scrupules* (a play in one act), Théâtre du Grand-Guignol.

1903
20 April: *Les Affaires sont les affaires* (a comedy in three acts), Comédie-Française.

1904
1 February: *Interview* (a farce in one act), Théâtre du Grand-Guignol.

1908
7 December: *Le Foyer* (a comedy in three acts), Comédie-Française.

Business Is Business

A Comedy in Three Acts
(*Les Affaires sont les affaires*, 1903)

ISIDORE LECHAT, newspaper owner and businessman, 57
MRS LECHAT, ISIDORE'S wife, 57
GERMAINE LECHAT, ISIDORE'S daughter, 25
MARQUIS OF PORCELLET, 60
XAVIER LECHAT, son of ISIDORE, 21
LUCIEN GARRAUD, chemist employed by ISIDORE, 30
PHINCK, electrical engineer, 35
GRUGGH, electrical engineer, 35
VISCOUNT OF FONTANELLE, intendant of Vauperdu chateau, 64
HEAD GARDENER
MAGISTRATE
TAX INSPECTOR
DOCTOR
YOUNG GARDENER
CAPTAIN
MAGISTRATE
MAGISTRATE'S WIFE
DOCTOR
DOCTOR'S WIFE
TAX INSPECTOR
TAX INSPECTOR'S WIFE
JULIE, a servant
FOOTMAN
SERVANTS

Act 1

The gardens of the Vauperdu chateau.

To the right, a monumental staircase, adorned with golden torches, leads to the chateau which is unseen but lies to the rear of the stage. To one side of the steps is a huge line of rosebushes; on the other side, there are enormous flowery shrubs. To the left, in the background, are the French-style grounds which are enormous and magnificent with flowerbeds, ornamental lakes, delicately trimmed yew trees, marble balustrades and so on. Also on the left, a green marble statue of a sinisterly laughing fawn stands in the overgrown shade of a large tree. The forced regular lines of avenues, sunlit and dusty, can be seen in the distance. Through them, one can see the open plain, the fields and the wooded hillsides. It is a sumptuous backdrop.

When the curtain rises, MRS LECHAT *sits, dressed in lace, in a large chair stuffed with cushions. She is knitting, wearing large, round glasses. Within reach of her on the table is her knitting bag. She is a large woman, plump and vulgar, wearing an excess of make-up. To her left is her daughter,* GERMAINE, *sitting on a garden chaise longue with an open book on her lap.* GERMAINE *gazes dreamily through the gardens to the countryside beyond. She is twenty-five, with a lithe figure and her eyes passionate yet sad. She is beautiful yet is dressed very simply and neglectfully. Here and there are tables and other wicker furniture. It is the end of a beautiful September day.*

Scene One

MRS LECHAT:	*(Without looking up from her knitting)* Germaine? …
GERMAINE:	Yes, mother? …
MRS LECHAT:	You're very quiet this evening …
GERMAINE:	I obviously have nothing to say.
MRS LECHAT:	You're normally reading something …
GERMAINE:	I have nothing to read.
MRS LECHAT:	Are you daydreaming? …
GERMAINE:	I have nothing to dream about …
MRS LECHAT:	Well … what *are* you doing? …
GERMAINE:	Nothing … I'm completely bored …
MRS LECHAT:	*(Shrugging)* Yes … yes … I realize that … Well … listen to me … Maybe this will distract you … What's the time?
GERMAINE:	Six o'clock …
MRS LECHAT:	Six o'clock … Already? … Doesn't time fly! … *(A* FOOTMAN *enters from the hall and comes down steps carrying a letter on a tray)* What is it?
FOOTMAN:	A telegram, madam.

MRS LECHAT:	*(Stops knitting)* A telegram? … Whoever can have sent me a telegram? … *(Confused)* It's funny … Whenever I receive a telegram I get butterflies in my stomach … *(She takes the telegram and opens it. The* FOOTMAN *withdraws)* Wait! *(Looks at the telegram)* It's from Ostend … It's your brother … *(Reads)* 'Coming for lunch at Vauperdu tomorrow … Xavier' *(To the* FOOTMAN*)* Why are you standing there? … Off you go … *(*FOOTMAN *exits)* Tomorrow … A day for racing, Xavier? … *(She turns the telegram over and over in her hands)* Something's not right … as usual … *(Pause)* Anyway … he won't be coming here out of the goodness of his heart … And I bet he hasn't paid for the telegram either … *(Looks at the telegram)* Of course! … I knew it … *(Puts the telegram on the table and sighs)* Anyway … *(Picks up her knitting)* What time is it?
GERMAINE:	I've already told you … six o'clock …
MRS LECHAT:	Oh, yes! … Doesn't time fly! … What about your father? … I'm worried … You know what he's like, bringing anyone home … What on earth has he gone to Paris for? … Any idea? …
GERMAINE:	How on earth would I know?
MRS LECHAT:	He might have said something to you …
GERMAINE:	I didn't see him this morning … Besides … my father never tells me anything …
MRS LECHAT:	Well, what do you expect? … You always give him the cold shoulder …
GERMAINE:	Do you honestly think that at nine o'clock this morning he knew where he'd be at six o'clock this evening? …
MRS LECHAT:	That's true … that's just like him … *(Short silence)* The journalists who work on his papers … Heaven knows they don't bother me … But those five or six strangers he dragged in the other day! He didn't warn me … And it's always people I don't know … And today is Saturday of course … Sunday tomorrow … We'll be expected to put everyone up for the night and lend them clean nightshirts … Just like last weekend … Oh! What a fine business! *(She heaves a long sigh)* You see, I thought we'd just have a bite to eat tonight … last night's leftovers, no more than that … I'm afraid there won't be enough … *(Reacting to a movement by* GERMAINE*)* Yes … Yes … Mock your own home, why don't you … Ah! You'd be wise not to get married … What a lovely household you'd run … I'd give you two years before being totally ruined … *(*GERMAINE *laughs and relaxes on a chaise longue)* I don't know why you're laughing … There's nothing to laugh at, you know, there really isn't …

GERMAINE:	Shall I cry instead? … *(She readjusts her hair where a pin came out)* That'd suit me better …
MRS LECHAT:	It's impossible to talk to you … seriously … for more than two minutes. *(A silence)* It's so annoying that your father never warns me when he's bringing someone over! … All he'd have to do is telephone … Well … of course not … *(She sighs again)* Maybe I'd better have one of the chickens killed … just in case … What do you think?
GERMAINE:	You know that he always brings someone home … It's obvious, isn't it? … You'd better have a dinner ready … *(GERMAINE stands up while talking. She walks beside the rosebushes in an obvious state of annoyance)*
MRS LECHAT:	You get things ready then … You do it! … It's clear that the burden of running this house is not on your shoulders … And just think … if for some reason he doesn't drag anyone back with him – after all, that might just happen – what a waste of a chicken … No matter how rich we are … I can't bear to squander food … Waste fills me with horror …
GERMAINE:	The dogs could always have it …
MRS LECHAT:	Heavens above! …
GERMAINE:	What about the poor people? …
MRS LECHAT:	Poor people? … Ah, of course … the poor … don't think I've forgotten them … I have never seen a place with so many poor people as around here … *(GERMAINE stops in front of a rosebush to trim off some flowers)* It's obscene …
GERMAINE:	Have you ever noticed … how when there's an extremely rich person … there are always many more extremely poor people living nearby? …
MRS LECHAT:	We can't do anything about it … And that's no reason to feel obliged to feed them … certainly not with chicken … If they got off their backsides and found a job they'd find themselves a lot less hungry …
GERMAINE:	If they worked? … Doing what exactly? …
MRS LECHAT:	What do you mean? …
GERMAINE:	We've taken everything away from them … their fields … their cottages … their gardens … all in the name of my father's property … Those who could go went as soon as they could …
MRS LECHAT:	Didn't we pay them? …
GERMAINE:	Those who stayed … *(She crushes an insect against her thumbnail)* Got you, you little wretch!

MRS LECHAT:	Germaine! Anyway … your father offered them seasonal labour … They declined … They preferred to beg … Well, that's their business, isn't it! …
GERMAINE:	My father offered them seasonal starvation … They …
MRS LECHAT:	*(Interrupting)* Oh that's enough! … I should know better than try to have a serious conversation with you … Come on, what is it then?
GERMAINE:	Nothing …
MRS LECHAT:	Unbelievable … I don't know where you get such ridiculous ideas in your head … *(Vindictive)* From Mr Lucien Garraud … no doubt?
GERMAINE:	What's Mr Garraud got to do with anything?
MRS LECHAT:	Good God! The man never says a word …
GERMAINE:	If Mr Garraud never says a word … how could he have put ideas in my head? …
MRS LECHAT:	I look and listen, my girl … People who never say a word … they say more than the loudest chatterbox … Besides … I don't like the look of him … your dear Mr Garraud …
GERMAINE:	'Dear' Mr Garraud? … Why 'dear' Mr Garraud …
MRS LECHAT:	Good lord! You're always together … A young lady like you … The daughter of a man who owns an historic estate like this … mixing with one of your father's *employees* … almost a servant! …
GERMAINE:	That's right – a servant! …
MRS LECHAT:	Almost, I said, almost … Is that decent? It'd be better if he spent a little more time in our distillery making chemical fertilizer … Oh, I've no idea where your father dug him up, really I haven't … A chemist … Him? Don't make me laugh! … The inventor of chemical fertilizers? *(She shakes her head)* A swindler more like … Before he came here he hardly had a shirt on his back … Huh! … *(Silence. GERMAINE is evidently irritated)* From University? … Yes … the University of Life, that is …
GERMAINE:	Mother … why are you so beastly?
MRS LECHAT:	I'm not beastly … Besides, every word I've said is true … When I think of the money we've squandered building him a laboratory … it cost an arm and a leg! … Yet for three months now your father hasn't given me enough money to pay the greengrocer! … It's too much, it really is! … *(She stops knitting and removes her glasses)* What time is it?
GERMAINE:	Quarter past six …

MRS LECHAT:	Doesn't time fly! … Your father will be home soon … Who will he bring home with him today, I wonder? … The devil knows … Good grief … I don't know … I won't kill a chicken … They'll just have to make do with what we've got … Germaine?
GERMAINE:	*(Irritated)* What? …
MRS LECHAT:	You need to go into the cellar … we need some wine …
GERMAINE:	I've already told you … I'm not going down the cellar … You've got servants, haven't you?
MRS LECHAT:	Servants who rob me blind, yes I have … Yesterday another five bottles went missing from the middle wine rack … How on earth does it happen when I'm the only one with the key?
GERMAINE:	If you only made it clear that you trusted them more maybe they'd steal less? … What do you expect in a house where the only topic of conversation is how to swindle all and sundry! Calm down … they've never stolen as much wine as … some people I know … who have earned millions …
MRS LECHAT:	*(Angry)* Germaine! …
GERMAINE:	Why are you upset? … I said earned …
MRS LECHAT:	I will not let you talk like this … Some of the things you say these days … and your attitude! … Honestly … I cannot understand it! …
GERMAINE:	I can … ever since I was old enough to understand it and feel it … When I see everything that goes on here … God knows that …
MRS LECHAT:	*(Violently interrupting)* Shut up! Don't say another word … *(She goes to the table and stuffs the knitting into her basket, angrily)* It's your father, isn't it? … *(Silence while GERMAINE trims off a rose, sits down in the chaise longue and sniffs the flower)* Well … for once … tell me …
GERMAINE:	*(Irritated)* Oh, *please* …
MRS LECHAT:	Yes … yes … I want to … Your father is not without his faults … some large faults, admittedly … I am the person who has had to suffer them most and who has done more than anyone to reproach him for them … He is vain … a wastrel … insolent … inconsiderate … a liar … yes, he is a liar … and sometime even a fool … it's true … He often repudiates what he's said … He likes to swindle people … Of course … and he does all of this, *in the name of business*. Really he is an honest man … understand? An honest man … And even if he wasn't … even if he was at the bottom of the heap … it'd be none of your business … Your father is your father … it is not for *you* to judge him …
GERMAINE:	*(Coldly)* Who can then?

MRS LECHAT:	What did you say? … *(A short silence)* Yes … that's right … shrug your shoulders … *(Pause)* Remember that he owes no one for his fortune … No one … Understand? He made his fortune through hard work … And a little luck … He was in the right place at the right time … I should know … But he is a man of skill and courage … So what if he's been bankrupt twice … He received his certificates again, didn't he? So what if he's been in prison … So what, I say? He was acquitted eventually, wasn't he? Oh, he's had his tough times, the poor boy … Other men, lesser men than he, would've blown their brains out … Not your father … Every time he's been down on his luck he's picked himself up again … And climbed back to the top … He is the founder of a major newspaper … and he himself can hardly write … You see? … If your father was really such a crook … how come he's friends with a government minister? …
GERMAINE:	*(Ironically)* Surely he's friends with the entire cabinet …
MRS LECHAT:	*(Glancing at her daughter)* The 'entire cabinet' … the cheek of it … Huh! … *(Enthusiastically)* And what about me, hmm? … With my orderliness … my sense of economy … my advice … I have played my part in securing this fortune which you're so quick to dismiss … And I am not ashamed to boast about it … Is it because we come from the common people, both me and him? Is it because we were once poor … that this young lady is so ashamed of us today? Have you seen her? A little fool … a little arrogant fool … spending her time judging her parents! …
GERMAINE:	It's just as well I'm judging you …
MRS LECHAT:	It's obscene … You *unnatural* girl, you … If anyone should hear you … we'd have to lock you away …
GERMAINE:	I don't think it's decent of you to reproach me for the things *you* do all the time …
MRS LECHAT:	Me? That's not the same thing …
GERMAINE:	Of course not …
MRS LECHAT:	I'm lost for words … What is wrong with you today? You want to incite the servants to pillage … It's unbelievable … Now are you or are you not going to go down the cellar? …
GERMAINE:	No …
MRS LECHAT:	Very good … *(She stands up)* I'll go then … me … I'll go despite my rheumatism … *(With a defiant air)* I'll go despite my rheumatism … you heartless child … *(She goes up the steps with difficulty)* It's unbelievable! Ha! You're wise never to have married … *(She stops, turns and leans on the balustrade)* What are you

doing now? … At least go and get dressed … If everyone comes home now … I don't want you looking like a scarecrow! … My word … It looks like we don't give you clothes to wear! … (GERMAINE *is silent*) Do you hear? … Do you understand? …

GERMAINE: I'm just fine …

MRS LECHAT: (*Shrugging*) Well … whatever you want … You want to look ridiculous? … It is unbelievable … *unbelievable*!

MRS LECHAT *exits from the terrace and walks towards the mansion.* GERMAINE *looks across the gardens, the woods, the fields. The* HEAD GARDENER *enters stage left. He is dressed in his Sunday best.*

Scene Two

In front of GERMAINE, *the* HEAD GARDENER *removes his hat and turns it around nervously in his hands. His face is weather beaten and his hands are brown and calloused, deformed by years of hard work. He is timid and his expression is troubled.*

HEAD GARDENER: Miss Germaine …

GERMAINE: (*Startled by* HEAD GARDENER'S *appearance*) How fine you look today! … Are you going to a wedding, Jules? …

HEAD GARDENER: A wedding? … Oh, Miss Germaine …

GERMAINE: I mean it! … But why do you look so sad? … Why do you seem so awkward? … Come on … Tell me … What is it? …

HEAD GARDENER: You mean … you don't know, Miss? …

GERMAINE: No … What is it? …

HEAD GARDENER: It makes sense … I said as much to myself … It's not right that I haven't seen you, until today of all days … in the garden.

GERMAINE: Today? What's special about today? …

HEAD GARDENER: Because … with all respect, Miss … It pains me to say it … I've come to say my goodbyes …

GERMAINE: Your goodbyes? … What is it, what's wrong? …

HEAD GARDENER: (*Looking up towards the sun with unsteady balance*) I've handed in my notice … to sir, this morning …

GERMAINE: You?

HEAD GARDENER: Yes, Miss …

GERMAINE: But that's impossible …

HEAD GARDENER: No, Miss … It's true … It had to happen … Oh, it makes me so very sad, Miss …

GERMAINE: You're not happy here anymore?

HEAD GARDENER:	*(Awkward)* It's not that ... no, not that ... *(A little more energetically)* I had no choice – none at all! ...
GERMAINE:	Why? ...
HEAD GARDENER:	With all due respect, Miss, your father is not an easy man to work for ... And sir would always be looking for fault ... When a row of vegetables are on the right ... well, sir wants them to be on the left ... If they are on the left ... they have to be replanted on the right ... It's just a pointless task ... Sir certainly has some funny ideas! ... For ages ... I never said a word ... because ... I didn't want to leave you, Miss ... You've always been so kind to me and the wife. But eventually ... You can't take it anymore ... It's time to go ... *(GERMAINE looks very sombre and pensive)*
GERMAINE:	*(After a pause)* Tell me exactly what happened between you and my father ...
HEAD GARDENER:	Nothing really happened, Miss ...
GERMAINE:	*What happened? ...*
HEAD GARDENER:	Words were said, Miss ... and it got worse from there ... And then, well, we agreed to part company ... And he insisted that I get out tonight ... But, you see, when you leave a place ... it's better to go at once ... It's better for all concerned ...
GERMAINE:	Do you think that maybe you're being ... a little oversensitive? ... Or maybe, by mistake, you misunderstood something that my father said?
HEAD GARDENER:	Sensitive? ... After working for your father for four years? ... Oh, Miss ... *(Pause)* I know I haven't had much education ... But ... I know my job ... The soil ... the plants ... the conservatories ... I love it all ... You've been happy with me, haven't you, Miss Germaine? ...
GERMAINE:	You know I have ...
HEAD GARDENER:	*(Emotional)* These gardens ... the clematis ...
GERMAINE:	Always so beautiful! ...
HEAD GARDENER:	And it caused a lot of trouble for us, remember Miss? And the Japanese iris ... beside the great lake? ... That was your idea too, Miss ...
GERMAINE:	Yes ... yes ...
HEAD GARDENER:	The florist you went to see ... everyday ... to get bouquets and bouquets of flowers! ... *(Pause)* Bouquets ... seeing that was what taught me how to make them, Miss ... And the roses? ... And the seedlings? ... And everything else ... God knows, sir would not waste a drop of compost on flowers ... We used to manage ... *(A short silence)*

GERMAINE:	Have you thought of what you'll lose by leaving all this …
HEAD GARDENER:	*(Making a sad gesture)* But if Miss has always been happy with me … I can go … with a happy heart …
GERMAINE:	Come on … It must be a misunderstanding … It can all be cleared up … I'll talk to my father this evening …
HEAD GARDENER:	Thank you, Miss … But what's done is done … That's the end of it! …
GERMAINE:	But what if …
HEAD GARDENER:	It would be back to square one tomorrow … the same problem or one just the same … No … enough is enough … *(Very serious)* Besides … *(He is silent)*
GERMAINE:	What? … Tell me …
HEAD GARDENER:	Well … *(He fidgets nervously with his hat)* Oh God! … I must tell you everything, the whole story … You know that my wife is, er, expecting … Begging your pardon, Miss …
GERMAINE:	Please, carry on …
HEAD GARDENER:	The baby's due in two months now …
GERMAINE:	Yes.
HEAD GARDENER:	Well … You see … Sir has strictly forbidden children in the house … He said to me this morning 'No children; they'd ruin the lawns … mess up the garden paths … frighten the horses …' *(Silence in which GERMAINE shakes her head, emotional and uncomfortable)* Of course … it wasn't deliberate … Life is difficult enough as it is for me and the wife … But when children come along … Well, we can't kill the poor thing, can we, Miss Germaine? …
GERMAINE:	*(As if to herself)* So that's the reason … But what will you do now?
HEAD GARDENER:	I'll look for another job … It's not the best time of the year, though … In work like mine … the best jobs are already gone … And with a pregnant wife, Miss … we'll have to go from house to house! … It won't be easy … heaven knows … It won't be easy …
GERMAINE:	Have you got any savings you can use? …
HEAD GARDENER:	Just my arms, Miss …
GERMAINE:	*(Emotional)* My poor Jules … there's nothing I can do … All I can give you is my deepest sympathy and my love. *(She stands up and takes his hand)* Goodbye …
HEAD GARDENER:	*(He stands still, silent and very troubled for several moments)* Miss Germaine … I want to tell you something … *(He points at his throat)* Something in here … Oh, I can't …

GERMAINE:	Please … I beg you …
HEAD GARDENER:	*(In a trembling voice)* Miss Germaine … you're … you're not happy either …
GERMAINE:	You are mistaken. Of course I am happy … Very happy …
HEAD GARDENER:	*(Shaking his head)* No, Miss … I know you only too well … With a heart like yours how could you be happy in this place? … *(He takes a few steps)*
GERMAINE:	*(With her head lowered)* Where's your wife?
HEAD GARDENER:	She's in town … She's gone to find a carriage so that we can pack and move out …
GERMAINE:	Why? There are plenty of carriages here.
HEAD GARDENER:	It's every man for himself now, Miss … I think it's for the best …
GERMAINE:	But I want you to …
HEAD GARDENER:	Of course, Miss … but since this morning … and all that happened … you understand … there's no time …
GERMAINE:	*(Very sad)* Goodbye.
HEAD GARDENER:	Goodbye, Miss …

The HEAD GARDENER *slowly exits. He stops and, by force of habit, straightens a plant cane which is not perfectly straight.*

Scene Three

The HEAD GARDENER *has gone.* GERMAINE *has sat down on the* chaise longue *looking very sad. Mechanically, she flips through the book that is there. She closes it and leans her head in her hands staring at the sun. Suddenly the yapping voice of* MRS LECHAT *can be heard coming from the antechamber.*

MRS LECHAT:	*(Appearing at the stairs and turning back towards the hall)* Where on earth are they? … What the hell are they doing? Not a single servant in the antechamber? … Unbelievable! *(She starts to descend the steps)* The more servants you have, the less gets done … *(Noticing* LUCIEN *enter stage right she stands still)* Ah, Mr Garraud, now … *(*GERMAINE *stands up on hearing* LUCIEN. MRS LECHAT *speaks in a hostile, dismissive tone)* My husband is not home yet, Mr Garraud …
LUCIEN:	Oh, I beg your pardon, madam … I thought I heard his car …
MRS LECHAT:	Well, you thought wrong, didn't you … *(She descends one step and stops again)* You wish to speak to my husband, do you?
LUCIEN:	Yes, madam.

MRS LECHAT:	*(To GERMAINE)* You can't even lift a finger to help your poor mother down the stairs … *(GERMAINE goes over and helps her mother)* A fine state of affairs … *(Walking past LUCIEN)* The servants … have you seen any of them? … Oh, I *do* hope your father sorts out this jolly state of affairs …
GERMAINE:	He certainly sorted out poor old Jules.
MRS LECHAT:	*(Mimicking her daughter's voice)* Ah, poor old Jules … Of course … You only have pity for slugabeds, drunkards … and thieves.
GERMAINE:	Mother, I don't …
MRS LECHAT:	*(Looking angrily at GERMAINE)* Huh! … All it takes is one year and the servants act like masters … They make themselves at home alright … *(Mimicking her daughter)* Poor old Jules! … *(Led by GERMAINE she has reached her armchair and has sat down)* Ugh! … *(She catches her breath and takes up her knitting)* Can you please tell me why – at my age and in my condition – I'm forced, myself, alone, to go down to the wine cellar every day? … Hmm? What is the world coming to, I ask you! *(She knits viciously)* Well … Mr Garraud? …
LUCIEN:	Madam …
MRS LECHAT:	It seems to me that you fill my husband's head with fine ideas … fine ideas that prove to be the stupidest idiocies … As if he didn't have enough stupid ideas of his *own*, for God's sake! …
LUCIEN:	Me, madam? …
MRS LECHAT:	What do you want now, anyway? … These days all he can talk about is revolutionizing agriculture … Oats … Wheat … Beetroot … He believes that the traditional crops are old-fashioned and need replacing … After talking to you, that is … To sow … and plant … God knows what!
LUCIEN:	You're right, madam … But it is not my fault, I swear. On the contrary, I've done everything I could to show him the error of his ways … But he doesn't want to listen … He dismisses me as a commoner … *(Laughs)* A 'dirty commoner', no less!
MRS LECHAT:	You … are you trying to suggest that my husband is a fool?
LUCIEN:	*(Protesting)* No, madam! … But Mr Lechat is audacious … innovative … and very stubborn …
MRS LECHAT:	Yes … and it has cost us a fortune in fertilizer and in pointless and ridiculous experiments … thousands and thousands of francs! …
LUCIEN:	I'm afraid so …

MRS LECHAT:	Oh, thank you! … And as well as his experiments in cultivation we have the elections in two months … Oh, what a fine year this will prove to be! …
LUCIEN:	*(Very gently)* Madam … do you remember last month, for Bastille day your husband wanted to paint the elms on the grand avenue – those magnificent and beautiful specimens – he wanted to paint the trunks red, white and blue … And you dissuaded him, happily … Perhaps you could – I beg you – encourage him *not* to continue with his agricultural plans …
MRS LECHAT:	*(Thoughtful, stopping knitting)* Our gorgeous elms … painted like a tricolour! The very idea! … There's never a moment's peace with a man like him … *(Short silence)* Tell me, Mr Garraud, you are evidently a highly intelligent man … Why do you think my husband has such bizarre notions? … After all, Isidore is extremely intelligent … a very strong man too … He has a reputation – well deserved, of course – as a pre-eminent entrepreneur, the most exceptional businessman in Paris …
LUCIEN:	No one would argue with that …
MRS LECHAT:	And yet outside of business … he talks nothing but hogwash … *(LUCIEN protests)* No … no … nothing but hogwash! …
LUCIEN:	*(Awkward)* Good heavens, madam … It's very difficult for me to answer that … Mr Lechat is in many ways a typical figure of the modern business world … His extreme self-confidence … His habitual drive for success and domination … His constant desire to innovate … The intoxicating joy of conquering obstacles … I don't know … *(Timidly)* A little arrogant too … in need of an 'ideal' … maybe. *(Makes a vague gesture)*
MRS LECHAT:	*(Ironic)* In need of an 'ideal' indeed! …
LUCIEN:	Each to their own, but one shouldn't treat the earth like you can treat the poor … The earth is less flexible and more resistant …
MRS LECHAT:	*(Sighing)* Let me ask you something … *(Pause)* Am I right to think you have some influence over my husband? …
LUCIEN:	Not at all, madam …
GERMAINE:	Mr Garraud is too poor … he has too many principles …
MRS LECHAT:	*(Looks at GERMAINE severely)* I wasn't talking to you … *(At this moment the klaxon of a car can be heard approaching. She listens)* There's the car … It must be him …
LUCIEN:	I'll go and greet him.
MRS LECHAT:	*(Imploring)* Please try to make him understand … *(LUCIEN bows and exits)*

Scene Four

MRS LECHAT:	*(Very agitated. She puts her knitting in the basket)* I wonder what he'll have brought back from Paris for us … What time is it? … *(GERMAINE is silent)* What time is it?
GERMAINE:	*(Curtly)* I don't know.
MRS LECHAT:	Typical … *(She slightly readjusts her lace and her dress)* My gloves! … Ah! … *(She sees them on the table, snatches them up and puts them on)* You … do something with your hair … Just look at you! God knows what a state you're in! Your blouse is all puffed up at the back … Come here … *(She readjusts her daughter's blouse)* Unable to dress yourself, at your age … You should honour your mother, my dear … *(Upset)* Oh God, the dinner … I just hope he hasn't brought anyone back with him … That's the least he could do … Honestly, with this devil of a man every night is pandemonium! …

The car is silent. VOICES *can be heard through the window.*

VOICES:	*(Through the window)* Long live Isidore Lechat! … Man of the people Lechat! …
MRS LECHAT:	*(Sarcastic)* Oh, wonderful – the farm workers are backing their man again! He's *bound* to get elected now! … Then he can be Minister of Agriculture at long last – just imagine! … My God …
VOICES:	*(Through the window)* Long live Isidore Lechat! …
VOICE OF ISIDORE:	Thank you … Thank you all … Now clear off … *(The VOICES increase. ISIDORE appears in profile in the distance stage right, stepping backwards, making appeasing gestures)* For Christ's sake, put a sock in it will you! … It's not the man but *what he stands for* that matters! His principles – celebrate the principles! …
VOICES:	*(Through the window)* Long live Isidore Lechat! …
ISIDORE:	*Get out of it!* … Hold on a minute … Here you are … *(He chucks down some small change)* You've had your money, now clear off … Give me strength … *(He turns around)* Ah! … My beautiful ladies! … A picture of rural bliss! … One of those Watteau paintings! … Good evening, my darlings …

He enters followed by LUCIEN. *Then* PHINCK *and* GRUGGH *enter followed by two of* ISIDORE's SERVANTS *each carrying a bag and an overcoat.*

Scene Five

ISIDORE wears a straw hat and a black jacket, which is very long and spacious, and has newspapers in the pockets. He has a waistcoat which has a large gold chain emerging from one of its pockets. He has grey trousers and yellow shoes. He is a large, pot-bellied man with a somewhat vulgar air. He has a suspicious and duplicitous look in his eyes, which are constantly shifty in stark contrast to the spring in his step and his constantly restless movement. His greying beard, short and severe, emphasizes the scowl on his lips – which, when parted, reveal teeth as white as a wolf's fangs. His jaw looks formidably strong; the man is evidently a carnivore. MRS LECHAT has stood up to receive her husband's guests. At the beginning of the scene, MRS LECHAT's eyes look uneasily at PHINCK and GRUGGH and their luggage.

ISIDORE:	*(To PHINCK and GRUGGH with a lightly contemptuous arrogance)* They are wildly enthusiastic, the people round here … You see, progress, progress – even in a place like this … *(Brusquely, he pulls out his watch)* Fifteen minutes … How about that – the station to the house in exactly fifteen minutes … Ha, ha, ha! … Not bad, eh? Nice ride for the horses! Ha, ha! *(PHINCK and GRUGGH agree. He turns to LUCIEN)* Fertilizer? …
LUCIEN:	No progress I'm afraid, sir.
ISIDORE:	For Christ's sake! Come on lad … work … work … I've already announced our developments to the Society of Agriculture and even to Jules Méline, the Minister of Agriculture … Everyone … I've started a campaign in *The Little Tricolour* … then … well … there's the elections … For God's sake, lad … get on with it … Work! Work! *(He presents PHINCK and GRUGGH to his wife)* Mr Phinck and … Mr … *(He struggles to remember the name)*
GRUGGH:	Gruggh … Wilhelm Gruggh.
ISIDORE:	Gruggh – of course! Good old Gruggh! … I forgot your name … very well then … *(Ceremoniously)* Mr Gruggh! … *(Various greetings occur)*
MRS LECHAT:	Gentlemen …
ISIDORE:	Electrical engineers … my friends … my old friends … *(He slaps both of them on the shoulder and all three laugh)* Just look at these fellows … Together they represent ten thousand horsepower …
PHINCK:	Um, *twenty thousand* horsepower …
ISIDORE:	Twenty thousand horsepower … in the form of a waterfall suitable for hydroelectric development … Oh, you fine fellows you … *(Presents his wife)* Allow me to present my wife … Mrs Isidore Lechat. *(Another round of greetings)*

MRS LECHAT:	Gentlemen …
ISIDORE:	Germaine … my daughter … *(Greetings.* GERMAINE *merely nods her head)* She's a good girl, really … Has some odd ideas sometimes … but a heart of gold … just like her father! … She's a bluestocking too, I'll have you know! … What is wrong with society today? … Go on, ask her what's wrong with society today! Bankrupt aristocrats and royalty without a penny to their name … that's right isn't it, sweetheart? *(Pointing at* GERMAINE*)* A real little American, ha, ha! …
GERMAINE:	Father, *please* …
ISIDORE:	Modest too … Good … Good … *(He pulls the newspapers out of his pockets, which he hands out to* MRS LECHAT, GERMAINE *and* LUCIEN*)* An historic issue today … There's a major article … A virulent condemnation of agricultural policy … I won't say anymore … *(To* LUCIEN*)* Go on, read it! … *(*LUCIEN *opens the paper)* Second page … three columns … signed 'Parsifal' … *(To* MRS LECHAT*)* He's your protégé … little Rampon … He's going places, I can tell you … little Rampon … Wonderful chap … and he can write too! …
MRS LECHAT:	I always said that he'd go far …
ISIDORE:	*(To* PHINCK *and* GRUGGH*)* Just think … The chap started on my newspaper last year … Weather reports first of all … Then I made him theatre reviewer … And now … He's our expert on political economy … It is completely unheard of … extraordinary! … You see … in my newspaper … no 'literature' or any of those over-educated writers and all that dross! … No … Just clear and simple ideas … facts … honest-to-goodness facts … There you have it! …
GRUGGH:	A newspaper … that must be a delightful enterprise …
ISIDORE:	I don't know about that – it's the *influence* it allows me to exert that is more important … *(He puts other newspapers on the table and notices the telegram)* Who's this from?
MRS LECHAT:	Xavier …
ISIDORE:	Good, good, good … *(Reads it)* Wonderful! … *(Holds up the telegram)* Allow me to introduce you to my son Xavier Isidore Lechat of Vauperdu … my son … A fine fellow … a thoroughly modern chap … First heir to the Vauperdu estate … Anyway, you'll meet him in person tomorrow …
MRS LECHAT:	*(Sadly)* So … these gentlemen are staying the night? …
ISIDORE:	Of course … We're not booting these fellows out … *(To* PHINCK *and* GRUGGH*)* Do you know my son? …

PHINCK:	No …
GRUGGH:	No …
ISIDORE:	Really? That's most peculiar … he's very well known … He's in the sports papers all the time … He owns a stable for race horses … He has a yacht … an automobile … it's worth fifty thousand francs … He's a member of the Society of Artists … He's got pals in the highest society … including the most beautiful leading ladies in Paris … And he's scarcely twenty-one! … He's also been caught up in two or three of the most fantastic scandals …
MRS LECHAT:	He's too many things … He gives us no end of trouble … well, gives *me* no end of trouble that is … You see, his father would do anything for that boy … He can get away with murder … (*ISIDORE rubs his hands gleefully*) And the little rogue takes advantage of it, God knows! …
ISIDORE:	He's just having a bit of fun, that's all … Like any lad of his age should!
MRS LECHAT:	Of course he should enjoy himself … but why does it have to be so very expensive?
ISIDORE:	You worry too much, my poor old dear. Why? You know I'm rich enough to afford the glories of a son thrown headlong into Parisian society … You mean you don't glow with pride when you see your son in the papers, driving his car in the Ostend races or riding a horse at the Jockey Club? … That's a mother's love for you … Huh! I ask you!
MRS LECHAT:	But it's not just the money …
ISIDORE:	Enough! … (*To PHINCK and GRUGGH*) She doesn't understand that Xavier's antics are a constant boost to my business – a living advert! … (*To MRS LECHAT*) God knows, you have never understood that all the money you think I've squandered on him has been more than paid back to me! Huh! Women! Sentiment by the bucket load … But as for business sense … (*He merely shrugs his shoulders and walks around energetically rubbing his hands. He looks at his watch*) Look at the time … You remember that lanky fellow I pointed out to you at the station – the Duke of Maugis – and later we overtook his carriage … well, I see he still hasn't arrived home yet … Aren't my horses great! What do you think of my horses? …
PHINCK:	Quite stunning …
ISIDORE:	(*Slapping his shoulder*) Worth their weight in gold, old boy, almost literally! …
PHINCK:	Quite stunning …

GRUGGH:	Besides, madam, we ran over a sheep on the road …
ISIDORE:	(*Arrogantly*) Two sheep! Two of them! (*He rubs his hands*) Last week, I knocked down a cow and her calf … Once I almost killed a child … some kid belonging to a road labourer …
MRS LECHAT:	That's nothing to *boast* about now, is it? …
ISIDORE:	What's wrong with you? … I paid the fellow off, didn't I? … I had to! … (*He rubs his hands*) It's true … There are three squires in the area – nasty bits of work, every one of them – they scarcely have a hundred and fifty thousand francs to their name and they are determined to mess with my horses! … (*To* GRUGGH, *catching hold of his waistcoat*) Listen … It was last Sunday, old boy … You don't mind me being informal with you, do you? …
GRUGGH:	On the contrary …
ISIDORE:	Good man! … You're a good chap, you are! … People like us prefer informality … None of those stuffy old traditions for us, oh no … All those old dukes and counts … We're not like them … We are democratic Frenchmen … isn't that right!? … We're the *real* working class, aren't we? … (*He taps* GRUGGH's *belly*) Anyway, it was last Sunday … I was coming back from Saint Gauberge … I had decided to take a little road through the forest … hardly another carriage … When suddenly … guess what I saw fifty metres ahead of me? … The Duke of Maugis … That prize idiot you saw at the station and who has had the audacity to stand against me in the elections … (*Shrugs his shoulders*) Yes – him! I don't get out of the way for anyone, least of all for the Duke of Maugis … Understand? So I said to my coachman, 'Get them the hell out of *my* way!' … The coachman replied, 'There ain't enough room, sir!' So I said, 'You just go forward – knock the duke, carriage and horses into a ditch for all I care! Otherwise you'll be out of a job tonight, my lad!' Anyway, this will make you laugh … The coachman made the horses charge forward – Crash! I was out one side, the duke on another and the coachman was ten meters away in a bush! … What a bloody mess! … All the same, the carriage was fine – my carriage is *always* fine – and so I got to my feet, sorted out the horses, got in the carriage and rode past … The duke, however, his horse was lying there with its hooves in the air … Ha, ha, ha! … That's the way to treat them, isn't it? … Those silly old aristocrats … What do you think of that!? …
GRUGGH:	Great! …

ISIDORE:	It's only fair … I mean, I've got about fifty million francs … That's what I've got. And the duke? Scarcely two to his name … A tramp, that's all he is … Huh! And they want to mess with me? …
PHINCK:	But would you say that you're a *popular* man? …
ISIDORE:	Popular? Didn't you hear them just then? Fine fellows – they love me! Just think, in the elections you will see just the same thing … *(Mimes a carriage crashing into a ditch)* It will be just like that, mark my words! … Do you know what they call me round here? Tiger Lechat! … *(Long laughter from ISIDORE, PHINCK and GRUGGH)* Who will win the election, eh? Tiger Lechat – obviously! *(Rubs his hands)* Never mind all this … come on … *(To one of the SERVANTS)* Take this bag into the Francis the First room … *(To GRUGGH)* Will that suit you? …
GRUGGH:	But of course …
ISIDORE:	*(To other SERVANT)* Take that bag into the Louis XIV room …
MRS LECHAT:	Ah, my dear … I'm afraid the Louis XIV room is not free at the moment …
ISIDORE:	What do you mean it's not free? …
MRS LECHAT:	I'm using that room to dry out lime-blossom at the moment …
ISIDORE:	Oh, very well … That's fine … the Louis XV room will do … *(To PHINCK)* Or would you prefer the Henry II, Henry III, Henry IV, Louis XIII or Louis XVI … Take your pick. There are as many rooms in my house as there are kings in the history of France! … *(Rubs his hands)* Great touch, isn't it!? …
PHINCK:	Especially for a *democrat* …
ISIDORE:	Deliberate irony. Antimonarchist *contempt* … Come on, take your pick …
PHINCK:	Louis XV will suit me fine, I'm sure …
ISIDORE:	Louis XV? … I knew it … ! What a scoundrel *he* was! … Ha, ha, ha! *(To SERVANT)* The Louis XV room it is …

The SERVANTS carry the bags up the stairs and exit.

MRS LECHAT:	The gentlemen must excuse me … We only have a rather humble dinner to offer tonight … *(To ISIDORE)* It's your fault … You could've at least telephoned … *(To PHINCK and GRUGGH)* You see, gentlemen, my husband never warns me when he's bringing all and sundry back home …
ISIDORE:	These aren't all and sundry! These are friends – Phinck and, er … Gruggh!

MRS LECHAT:	Even if they are friends, you should still have the decency to telephone me …
ISIDORE:	Very well … They haven't come here to eat anyway!
PHINCK:	Please, madam, you mustn't put yourself to any trouble on our account …
ISIDORE:	They're here for business purposes.
GRUGGH:	That's right …
ISIDORE:	Business – potentially enormous. Business to the tune of twenty thousand horsepower. *(He shoves PHINCK and GRUGGH downstage. Quietly)* Pay no attention to my wife … She's a good woman at heart … but completely useless. *(Returning centre stage)* Ah! Business! Major business! The kind of business that will affect the lives of millions! Change their lives forever! Ha! Gigantic construction programmes … Bridges … Docks … Mines … Tramways … I love all that. That's what my life is all about … *(To PHINCK)* Do you reckon we'll get your lot, the Swiss, on board? *(To GRUGGH)* And what about your lot, the Germans? They think they're the kings of electricity, don't they? Well, they haven't heard of me yet … Look at my chateau … It was built by Louis XIV … For the whole court and all its foppish entourage … Everyone dressed in silk and velvet … Where did that get them in the long run? Who owns this royal chateau now? A prince? … No … A duke? … No … It belongs to a proletarian! A socialist! …
PHINCK AND GRUGGH:	Isidore Lechat! …
ISIDORE:	The People's Revenge – that's what I am! Ha, ha, ha! Glory to the people! …

The VISCOUNT OF FONTANELLE, the intendant of Vauperdu chateau, enters stage left, running. He stops, timidly and out of breath. He is an old man, very red in the face with greying hair and a short white beard. He wears a hat, a velvet jacket and dusty gaiters. He has a shoulder strap which carries a gardening hatchet in a yellow leather sheath.

Scene Six

ISIDORE:	*(Going over to FONTANELLE)* Well, have you decided? … And why on earth weren't you here for my arrival? …
FONTANELLE:	*(Breathless and stuttering)* Sorry I'm late, sir … I was trimming the oaks …
ISIDORE:	Trimming the oaks isn't an excuse … in fact, *nothing* should ever prevent you from being here, at your post, when I return … This

is the last time I'm going to warn you, got it? *(He looks up and down with a look of disdain)* Tell me … Is it now the fashion for you to wear a hat in front of me … *(FONTANELLE snatches his hat off)* No, no … don't worry about it … I mean if you are used to servants wearing their hats in front of their betters that is just fine … Just fine! … *(Turns to his guests)* Allow me to present to you the Viscount of Fontanelle … He is the intendant of my estate … An aristocrat, no less … He had a run of bad luck, the poor fellow – women, horses, cards … *(Pointing at FONTANELLE)* The rest, as they say, is history …

FONTANELLE: *(Raises his hand angrily)* Sir! … *(ISIDORE stares at him fixedly. FONTANELLE is quiet and lowers his hand)*

ISIDORE: Very good … *(Laughing)* Come on, you old monarchist you, put your hat back on … in fact, why not dig out the old coronet – or did you sell that with everything else? … *(FONTANELLE looks caught between humiliation and fury and puts his hat back on. A painful atmosphere. Everyone looks uncomfortable. GERMAINE, extremely angry, can hardly contain herself. ISIDORE sits in a chair near the table and crosses his legs. PHINCK and GRUGGH walk away talking quietly to each other)* So … what's new?

FONTANELLE: *(Speaking with difficulty)* Hippolyte Gouin – one of your farmers in Villejeu – has requested a further extension on the rent …

ISIDORE: Not a day more … Arrange for bailiffs tomorrow …

FONTANELLE: He's a good chap, sir … He's had an awful run of misfortune … If I could just …

ISIDORE: *(Interrupting with a critical look)* What? … *(FONTANELLE is silent)* Anything else? …

FONTANELLE: I'm afraid I haven't been able to settle things with the Head Gardener … He refuses to agree to a pay cut …

ISIDORE: What? … He *refuses*? … An idiot like him? … He doesn't even know how to grow a bean … and yet happily gets his wife up the duff under my roof *without my permission* … Huh! … Get rid of him … Get me a new gardener tomorrow … Sort it out, will you? … Anything else? … I haven't got all day you know …

FONTANELLE: I've seen the decorator … He's none too happy … He claims that you authorized him to tell the ironsmith to remove the bells from the main tower …

ISIDORE: Can he prove it in writing? … Did I sign anything? … No, of course I didn't … He's such a nuisance … *(Emphatically)* Anyway, what I may have said is neither here nor there … it's

	what I put in writing that counts … Tell the decorator to put them back himself … What else? …
FONTANELLE:	I sorted out the forage, as you requested …
ISIDORE:	The alfalfa?
FONTANELLE:	Distributed amongst the deserving …
ISIDORE:	Very good … Any poachers today?
FONTANELLE:	Not to my knowledge … The stewards haven't come to see me to report anything …
ISIDORE:	Why ever not? What on earth are they doing?
FONTANELLE:	*(Holds out his watch)* It's not even seven o'clock, sir … However … I must report that I think I saw old Mrs Motteau picking up dry twigs …
ISIDORE:	In the reserve?
FONTANELLE:	No, in the grounds …
ISIDORE:	For Christ's sake! … What about the fences … the barbed wire … the iron railings … I suppose she thinks that's to stop slugs and snails! … Give her a written warning – legal action … Yes?
FONTANELLE:	I doubt that would do any good, sir …
ISIDORE:	And why not?
FONTANELLE:	It's a custom, sir … If it went to court, we'd lose …
MRS LECHAT:	*(Pushed by GERMAINE who stands behind her)* The poor do have the right to collect dead wood, my dear …
ISIDORE:	The right? … Don't talk to me about *rights*! … The poor shouldn't have any rights … You see, what they do is exploit rights like these … The vagabonds! … They use it as a pretext to sprawl over my land … They set traps, you see, to poach from me … Chop down my saplings … Devastate my woodland … It's time we put a stop to it … It's outrageous, it really is! … The poor – huh, everyone's poor these days … Some of them are nearly millionaires by now, I'm sure! … No one is more of a democrat than me … But I am no fool … *(To MRS LECHAT)* We did give out bread on Sunday, didn't we?
MRS LECHAT:	Of course, dear …
ISIDORE:	*(Shaking the basket of MRS LECHAT's knitting)* Just look what you spend your life doing … You've nearly ruined your eyes knitting for the poor … vests … hats … socks … True?
MRS LECHAT:	Yes, it's true! …
ISIDORE:	There you are, you see … They *must* be warm … If they really must burn something, they should use coal, not my wood … *(He stands up and walks. To FONTANELLE)* Next time you catch that

	old witch … bring her to me … Got it? I'll give her a lesson she'll never forget … *(Rubs his hands)* Is that all?
FONTANELLE:	The Marquis of Porcellet has requested a meeting with you …
ISIDORE:	*(Triumphantly)* Ha ha! So the Marquis of Porcellet has finally deigned to call on me, has he? The man himself … in person? … It can't be true! … He *must* be strapped for cash! …
FONTANELLE:	He'd like to see you tomorrow if possible … he was rather insistent, sir …
ISIDORE:	How interesting! … Pretty urgent, is it? … Telephone him. Tell him I will see him at … two o'clock tomorrow … Get his file ready too … *(Rubs his hands)* This will be a laugh, yes indeed …
FONTANELLE:	There's also your cow, sir.
ISIDORE:	Oh God, I'd quite forgotten! … We should've started with that … How is the poor beast? …
FONTANELLE:	Not at all well.
ISIDORE:	What on earth do you mean by that? …
FONTANELLE:	The vet examined her … He spent a long time looking at her … He said she has infectious pneumonia … There's no hope for her, I'm afraid …
ISIDORE:	*(Erupting)* No hope for a cow that cost me eighteen hundred francs! … Is he mad!? … What utter nonsense! … This vet of yours is an imbecile … You might as well have brought me a boy from the knacker's yard for all the good he's done! … I'll have a look at the creature myself … *(To his guests)* May I be excused? … I'll only be two minutes …
PHINCK:	Of course …
GRUGGH:	Please …
ISIDORE:	Garraud! …
LUCIEN:	Sir! …
ISIDORE:	Come with me … We can have a chat on the way down … *(To FONTANELLE)* You go ahead … Get a move on, my noble lord! … *(FONTANELLE exits)* I'll be back in two minutes … *(He indicates that they should not listen to his wife)* Now, my boy, about this fertilizer …

ISIDORE and LUCIEN exit.

VOICES:	*(Through the window)* Long live Isidore Lechat! Man of the people Lechat! …
ISIDORE:	*(Through the window)* Will you *shove off*! … And I've told you all before – it's not the man but what he stands for! …

The VOICES fade. Silence.

MRS LECHAT: *(To PHINCK and GRUGGH, rather disconcerted)* He's just a big baby, really ...

Scene Seven

Throughout the previous scene GERMAINE has become increasingly agitated: she has stopped just short of being confrontational or aggressive. She always has a melancholic irritation which she just struggles to contain. Her father gone, GERMAINE goes to the table and picks up the various objects belonging to her.

GERMAINE: *(To MRS LECHAT)* Do you mind if I go to my room ... I'm not feeling too well ...
MRS LECHAT: What's wrong? Don't you want dinner?
GERMAINE: No thanks ... I really don't feel very well ...
MRS LECHAT: *(Shrugs)* Fair enough ... off you go ...
GERMAINE: *(As she passes PHINCK and GRUGGH)* Please excuse me, gentlemen ...
PHINCK: Of course, mademoiselle ...
GRUGGH: I'm sorry we won't have your company ... *(GERMAINE climbs the stairs and exits)*

Scene Eight

PHINCK: Nothing serious I hope.
MRS LECHAT: No ... No ...
GRUGGH: A little migraine, perhaps?
MRS LECHAT: That's right ...
GRUGGH: Such a charming young lady! ...
PHINCK: Something of a thinker too, I'd guess! ...
MRS LECHAT: She never says much, that's true ... Please sit down, gentlemen ... I'm so embarrassed ... with Isidore blustering away like that you haven't even had chance to sit down ...
PHINCK: That's fine ... Doesn't matter ... *(PHINCK and GRUGGH grab a seat and sit)* Ah! ... Er, Mr Lechat is a very lucky man, isn't he?
MRS LECHAT: *(Sadly)* Too lucky in some ways ...
PHINCK: He's got it all ... Successful business ... A wonderful family ... Social status ... *(With a gesture that indicates the chateau, the grounds and the horizon)* You've got a magnificent home, madam ...

GRUGGH:	Quite extraordinary … These buildings … The pathways … The grounds … I don't think I've ever seen anything quite so beautiful or imposing … Was it really built for Louis XIV?
MRS LECHAT:	So they tell me …
GRUGGH:	Marvellous! …
MRS LECHAT:	*(Dismissively)* It's too big … I can't live in such a rambling house … I get lost in it! …
PHINCK:	Oh! …
MRS LECHAT:	I'm not joking … And the running of it … the servants … the thousand things you have to see to in a house this big … *(Sighs)* If you only knew the *worry* of it all! … It's too much, really it is … It's simply too much … *(Sad, her head drooping)* You see, gentlemen, this came to us … all too late …
GRUGGH:	What can you mean, madam?
PHINCK:	You are much too modest, madam. I would be only too proud to have secured all this, through the sweat of my labours, through my unmitigated talent … It's admirable, that's what it is …
MRS LECHAT:	No … no … One has to be born to a life like this … Or at least come to it at a very early age … One gets used to one's ways and it's impossible to change … It's so strange … I've never felt at home here … I feel like I'm in a hotel in a foreign country … I feel like I'm homesick! …
GRUGGH:	Ha, ha!
MRS LECHAT:	I'm not joking … God knows, it's not so bad outside … The trees … the lawns and flowers … But *inside* … in those rooms … Those countless rooms … All those huge portraits on the walls … Princesses staring down at me, intimidating me … Suits of armour in the hallways … holding weapons … I dare not look at them … Whenever I walk past them I seem to hear them whisper: 'Who on earth is this plump little woman? … She does not belong here … What right does she have to walk these corridors?' *(Hangs her head melancholically)* It's true, all true! …
GRUGGH:	You're not being fair on yourself … or on your good fortune …
MRS LECHAT:	Fortune? My good fortune?
PHINCK:	Of course … And besides, a fine lady deserves a home becoming to her station …
MRS LECHAT:	You're too kind, sir … But no … You see, I don't think this place will ever suit me … I need a small house … with one maid and a little garden … That'd be just perfect … If my husband was like everyone else, once more … if he could only be happy to live a

humble life again ... Happy with his lot! Is he sensible? I ask you, do you think that a man like that, with all his business affairs in Paris ... all kinds of enterprise ... the stock exchange ... his newspaper ... God knows what! Do you think that he'd be happy only coming here in the evenings and in the summer? ... Waste is everywhere ... It's here ... it's there ... machines that don't work ... failed experiments ... let alone the personal cost ... and it's eating us up ... The money disappears ... it floods away! ... Nothing to show for it ...

GRUGGH: But Mr Lechat must have his pleasures ...

MRS LECHAT: Pleasures that just throw money away and bring nothing back to us ... That's no pleasure, that's torment ... what can you do? That's the way it is ...

GRUGGH: Well, the business affairs of Mr Lechat, which are already so vast, will be improved enormously when he is elected.

PHINCK: Yes, yes, that will be very helpful for his business interests.

MRS LECHAT: Elected? Elected?

GRUGGH: It's in the bag – he's told us so himself ...

MRS LECHAT: Oh, for heaven's sake ... He's always *saying* that ... It's the third time he's stood and he hasn't won yet, has he? ... (*Sighs*) I'm dreading it! Look, I'm trembling at the very prospect ... and the chaos of it all! My God ... If you only knew ...

Enter ISIDORE *followed by* LUCIEN.

Scene Nine

ISIDORE: (*Looking at* MRS LECHAT, PHINCK *and* GRUGGH) Ah, I've caught you red handed, you scoundrels! ... Talking about me while my back is turned ... Enjoying the gossip, are we?

MRS LECHAT: How's the cow? ...

ISIDORE: (*Rubbing his hands*) Nothing to it! ... I gave her a bottle of strong rum and the illness just vanished ... isn't that right, Garraud?

LUCIEN stays silent.

MRS LECHAT: Rum? To a cow? ... Are you trying to kill the poor beast? ...

ISIDORE: Now, now, dear ... You don't know a thing about animal husbandry, do you? ... Where's Germaine? ...

MRS LECHAT:	She's retired to her room … She wasn't feeling too well …
ISIDORE:	More hot flushes? … I don't know, these intellectuals! … *(He walks over by the* chaise longue *and sees* GERMAINE's *book. He picks it up, flicks through it and it makes him shudder)* Reading … always reading … *Poetry* even! … All this rubbish goes straight to her head … She stuffs herself with a barrel of stupidity … *(He opens his mouth with comic disgust. To* PHINCK*)* Poetry … Lamartine … Hugo … Musset … Who the hell are they, anyway?
PHINCK:	But, er, poetry is …
ISIDORE:	A crock of manure … *(They both laugh)* What do you read, eh?
PHINCK:	Business news … Train timetables …
ISIDORE:	Very good! … *(To* GRUGGH*)* What about you? …
GRUGGH:	Occasionally … when travelling … I read short stories … I quite enjoy–
ISIDORE:	*(Slapping* GRUGGH's *shoulder)* You bloody poet, you! … Well … As for me … I never read anything – never have, never will … Proud of it too … Look where it's got me! Isidore Lechat … Lord of Vauperdu … Personal fortune of fifty million … I own a major newspaper over which I control all opinion … political, literary and philosophical, you name it … I own and control *the lot* … *(He moves with agitated glee, rubbing his hands, coming to a standstill downstage. He looks all around himself. He tucks his thumbs into his waistcoat pockets, and his face broadens into an enormous grin)* Phinck! And you … er … er … er …
GRUGGH:	Gruggh! … Wilhelm Gruggh!
ISIDORE:	That's it … Gruggh … I simply can't get that beastly name in my head … Come here … both of you … *(With a large gesture he takes in all the eye can see)* What do you think of the view I've got here?
PHINCK:	Superb! …
GRUGGH:	We were just admiring it with Mrs Lechat …
ISIDORE:	*(Low)* With the wife? What does she know about it? She's good for nothing, I tell you! *(Loud)* Everything that you can see … to the right … to the left … in front of you … behind you … all these fields … the prairies … and … look … over there … that river … that large windmill … and … that way … on the hillside … all the woods … Well … it's mine … all of it … And there's also all that you *can't* see … I own seven thousand hectares … I own two districts, eight cantons and twenty-four communes … I have four hundred and nineteen fields and

	meadows, together they form my territory … But you'd get an even better impression if you looked at my map … Garraud? …
LUCIEN:	Sir! …
ISIDORE:	Don't panic … Go and fetch my map from the antechamber … It's on the left … on the Marie Antoinette desk … next to the royal heron … (LUCIEN *goes up the steps. To* PHINCK *and* GRUGGH) The royal heron was killed on the fifth of December 1898 … in the Valdieu prairie … I get everything here, you see … and it's all *royal*, of course! (He moves upstage again) It takes eight hours to see all my property … But you can just look at the map today … Tomorrow I'll show you my sixty dairy cows … my hundred and thirty beef cattle … You'll see my drainage system … my seed nurseries … my fish-breeding lakes … my flocks of sheep … you'll see the lot …
PHINCK:	Do you have a lot of wildfowl? …
ISIDORE:	An enormous amount … but just partridges and pheasants … apart from them you won't find any other birds …
PHINCK:	That's a shame …
ISIDORE:	What do you mean, a shame!? Didn't you know that birds are the biggest enemy to agriculture? They're vandals … But I'm even more ruthless than they are … I kill the lot of them. I pay two sous for every dead sparrow, three for every robin and greenfinch … five for a warbler … six for a goldfinch or nightingale … they're rare you see … In spring, I give twenty sous for a nest with eggs … People bring them from ten leagues all around … At this rate, I'll have killed every bird in France in a matter of years … (Rubs his hands) You'll see some wonders here, my friends …
PHINCK:	(Pointing at something to the left) I beg your pardon, but unless I'm mistaken …
ISIDORE:	What?
PHINCK:	A bird!
ISIDORE:	(Laughing) Ha, ha, good one!
PHINCK:	I'm not joking! I can really see one … look over there …
ISIDORE:	A robin … I don't believe it … the little bastard! … (LUCIEN *returns with a rolled up map*) Here … Put it on the table … (ISIDORE *takes the map from* LUCIEN *and rolls it out on the table*) Look at this map … (ISIDORE, PHINCK *and* GRUGGH *look at the map together.* ISIDORE *traces details on the map with his finger*) Pretty good, eh? My fields … meadows … forests … you can see it as if you were there in person, with a walking stick in your hand … Ah, look! … These red patches … these are my eight farms … The yellow

	patches with black stripes … those are my reserves! … Look … that's where I killed that royal heron I was telling you about …
PHINCK:	And what is that, er, thing, the green one …
ISIDORE:	That's my lake at Culoisel … like the old kings of France did at Fontainebleau, I breed huge carp – big as whales some of them – the lake covers one hundred and fourteen hectares … It's lovely there …
MRS LECHAT:	I think you're tiring your guests, my dear … Maybe they'd like to retire to their rooms before dinner?
ISIDORE:	Am I … boring you with my map?
GRUGGH:	Not at all … not at all …
ISIDORE:	*(Low)* She's good for nothing I tell you … *(Loud, to* PHINCK*)* Shall I take your hat for you? You'll see better … *(He snatches* PHINCK'S *hat and puts it on the table)* Look at this big white space here … bulging into my property? *(Sneers)* Hmm … That's Porcellet … It belongs to the Marquis of Porcellet … He's a debauched old fool … I've lent him loads of money and eventually … Well, it would be good to see Vauperdu and Porcellet united under one owner, wouldn't it?
PHINCK:	I should say so! …
ISIDORE:	Well, it's all in the bag, friends … Well, it'll be in the bag *tomorrow*, at any rate … Tomorrow you will see how yours truly, Isidore Lechat, can make the old aristocrats hop to it … yes, indeed … It'll be such a laugh, I promise you! …
MRS LECHAT:	Another estate … another chateau! … Haven't you got enough for God's sake? … Do you want to drive me completely to despair?
ISIDORE:	*(Shrugs)* Who could tell? You're always moaning anyway …
PHINCK:	What are all these little men on the map … In different colours in each area of the map?
ISIDORE:	You can't tell?
PHINCK:	No …
ISIDORE:	It's me … Little pictures of me on my land … Good, isn't it? Leaves you in no doubt as to who owns it all! … *(He traces the map with his fingers)* Look … that little violet square … that's my distillery … I've installed the very latest in laboratories … *(He turns to* LUCIEN*)* And here's my chemist … charming lad … clever, too … With him I'm making magnificent discoveries in the field of … of … Garraud! …
LUCIEN:	Sir!
ISIDORE:	Well, what do you call it?
LUCIEN:	Vegetable biology.

ISIDORE:	That's it! Vegetable biology! Have you ever heard the like? Of course you haven't! I think I'd better explain my discoveries … Here goes! *(He rolls up the map and uses it to gesticulate)* I am not an agriculturalist … I am … please note the difference … an *agricultural economist* … What this means is that I cultivate in the mind of intelligent man … in the economist, in the modern thinker … Well? … Wheat … barley … oats … They're all finished … They won't be needed anymore … They won't sell anymore … We need something else … Progress marches ever forward! … New needs and new wants … And yet the world doesn't even know it yet … The world is behind the times, stuck in a rut … All the world … except Isidore Lechat! … Me … the revolutionary agricultural economist … the socialist economist … Just watch me! … I will plant paddy fields of rice … tea plants … coffee beans … sugarcane … *(PHINCK and GRUGGH look dumbfounded)*
MRS LECHAT:	*(Shaking her head weakly)* God help us!
ISIDORE:	*(To MRS LECHAT)* What do you mean, 'God help us'? What would you know about it – get on with whatever you should be doing … *(More precisely)* Sugarcane … *(Pause. To PHINCK and GRUGGH)* What about you … Do you know what I'm talking about? …
MRS LECHAT:	Isidore, please …
ISIDORE:	Shut up, woman! … What do women know about contemporary social questions, hmm? It's only too simple. With my system, not only will I change traditional agriculture, but I will also do away with the colonies … Imagine … no more wars … costly and far-flung expeditions … brutal conquests and occupations … The colonies will be free at last! … *(Rubs his hands and roars with laughter)* India … China … Africa … Tonkin … Madagascar … independent – the lot of them! You look terribly upset! … It's something you didn't expect to see, is it?
PHINCK:	Well, I have to say that initially …
GRUGGH:	It *is* a rather astonishing proposal …
ISIDORE:	Like all great discoveries … You just wait and see … Oh, I know all the arguments … Those crops won't grow … Well … we shall see … *(Arrogant and ferocious)* Everything that I want comes to pass … I wanted to be a millionaire … I became one … I wanted to own a chateau … Here I am, living in one … I want the Marquis of Porcellet's estate … It'll be mine tomorrow … I want sugarcane to grow in my back garden … It will! … Isn't that right, Garraud? … Manure – that's what it's all about … chemical fertilizers … It will work – I stake my fortune on it … Is that how

I am promoting my candidature in the election? ... No ... But have you seen my campaign posters plastered everywhere? ... Isidore Lechat ... agricultural economist ... neo-colonialist ... anticlerical ...

MRS LECHAT: *(Shrill voice)* Six hundred votes! ...

ISIDORE: What are you on about?

MRS LECHAT: Six hundred votes which will cost you six hundred thousand francs, as usual ... *(Growing in anger)* Anticlerical, you? ... When you have the slightest graze on your knee you scream for a priest ... *(To* PHINCK *and* GRUGGH*)* The poor priest is forced to come here all the time prepared to administer the last rites to Isidore ... Yes ... Six hundred votes! ...

ISIDORE: *(Laughing caustically and pushing* PHINCK *and* GRUGGH *downstage)* Ha ... ha ... She's so funny ... She doesn't know what she's saying half the time! ... It's hilarious, really ... She's always blathering away ... And the priests ... and the monarchists ... they are always sticking their noses into my business ... *(Gong sounds for dinner)* Ah, dinner is served! *(They return upstage.* MRS LECHAT *takes* PHINCK*'s arm and mounts the steps)*

MRS LECHAT: You wouldn't believe we had a telephone would you? He's always inviting people without a word of warning ...

ISIDORE: *(taking* GRUGGH*'s arm. Sincerely)* You must excuse my wife. She's good for nothing, she really is ... *(At this moment seven guests arrive ceremoniously:* THE CAPTAIN, THE MAGISTRATE, THE MAGISTRATE'S WIFE, THE DOCTOR, THE DOCTOR'S WIFE, THE TAX INSPECTOR, THE TAX INSPECTOR'S WIFE*)*

Scene Ten

MRS LECHAT: *(Eyes bulging with apprehension)* Who on earth are all these people?

ISIDORE: *(Slaps his forehead)* Oh, I don't believe it ... It's the people from Marecourt ... I remember now ... I invited them for dinner ... Didn't I tell you?

MRS LECHAT: *(Utterly flabbergasted)* You invited them? ...

ISIDORE: Yes, yes, of course!

MRS LECHAT: And you forgot? ... I'm sorry – they can't stay.

ISIDORE: Oh, come off it!

MRS LECHAT: *(Hurrying down the steps)* How on earth do you expect me to feed this bunch of people?

ISIDORE:	My friends, dear … my *electorate* … (ISIDORE *hurries over to the new arrivals and shakes each one by the hand firmly*)
MRS LECHAT:	(*Aghast*) God in heaven! (*She looks over at the guests in a stupor*)
ISIDORE:	(*Milling amongst his new guests*) My dear Doctor … My dear Magistrate … Madam …
MAGISTRATE:	I'm sorry we're a bit late.
ISIDORE:	Not at all … not at all … We're a bit early, ha ha …
MAGISTRATE'S WIFE:	(*To* MRS LECHAT) We couldn't wait to get here, madam …
DOCTOR'S WIFE:	I thought the omnibus would never arrive! … (*A flurry of polite protests and apologies.* ISIDORE *continues to be energetic, shaking hands and slapping shoulders*)
ISIDORE:	(*To* CAPTAIN) Well, Captain … How's your rheumatism?
CAPTAIN:	Don't even talk about it! (*He bends his knee*) Aagh! Jesus Christ!
ISIDORE:	Get yourself an exercise bicycle, Captain. That'll do the trick. By the way, I saw the Minister of War.
CAPTAIN:	Really? And?
ISIDORE:	I'll tell you … (*He leads the* CAPTAIN *away. To the* TAX INSPECTOR) By the way, I saw the Minister of Finance.
TAX INSPECTOR:	Really? And?
ISIDORE:	I'll tell you … (*He leads the* TAX INSPECTOR *away. The women flock around* MRS LECHAT. *The* TAX INSPECTOR *and* DOCTOR *chat with* LUCIEN. *During the hubbub,* PHINCK *and* GRUGGH *stand aside*)
GRUGGH:	He's an utter thug …
PHINCK:	Perhaps …
GRUGGH:	An idiot … I think it'll be only too easy to get him to do anything we want.
PHINCK:	Maybe … But I think we should be very careful with this idiot … Look at his eyes … He is a nasty bit of work … Frightful!
GRUGGH:	So what! …
PHINCK:	No, we should be careful. I've come across his sort before. They're the most dangerous.
GRUGGH:	You're always the same. You lose your nerve …
PHINCK:	What about you? No gut reaction … Just look at him …
GRUGGH:	A man completely incapable of being elected, with a fortune like his!
PHINCK:	He could really do us over if we're not careful …
GRUGGH:	Huh! I'd like to see that!
ISIDORE:	(*From amidst his group*) The Duke of Maugis is a prize idiot … Just watch as I take him to the cleaners! (*Laughter*)
MRS LECHAT:	(*Very troubled, to the women surrounding her*) I am so sorry … We've hardly any food to offer …

ISIDORE:	A modest, homely dinner … A simple, family dinner …
DOCTOR'S WIFE:	They're the best! …
MRS LECHAT:	I'm sorry, but …
ISIDORE:	Very well … very well! … These ladies haven't come here to eat, they've come here to see you, my dear! *(To LUCIEN)* Will you be available for dinner tonight?
LUCIEN:	I'm afraid not, sir.
ISIDORE:	You busy chap you, the folly of youth, eh!? Anyway … remember the fertilizer, yes? … Keep your mind on that … now off with you! *(Dinner gong sounds again)* Time to escort the ladies! *(Foot SERVANTS appear at top of the steps and present themselves beside the ladies ceremoniously. A procession with pleasantries and simpering)*
MRS LECHAT:	*(Mounting the steps with the MAGISTRATE)* Can you believe that my husband is impossible to contact when he's out of the house … He never telephones me …
MAGISTRATE:	Mr Lechat is an extremely busy man.
ISIDORE:	*(At the back of the line accompanying the MAGISTRATE'S WIFE. In front of him is the TAX INSPECTOR who looks back when ISIDORE taps him on the shoulder)* Today's issue of *The Little Tricolour* has a fantastic article in it … Criticizing wheat production … You must read it. *(To MAGISTRATE'S WIFE)* It's written by my protégé … little Rampon. I think you met him here once …
MAGISTRATE'S WIFE:	Mr Rampon? Little blonde chap, very amusing fellow …
ISIDORE:	That's the one.
MAGISTRATE'S WIFE:	Does a wonderful imitation of Sarah Bernhardt?
ISIDORE:	That's right!
MAGISTRATE'S WIFE:	Plays the piano … with his toes … and his nose? …
ISIDORE:	Believe me, he can play the piano with any part of his anatomy … His *nom de plume* is Parsifal … charming lad … And a famous economic theorist! … *(All exit except LUCIEN)*

Scene Eleven

LUCIEN remains onstage. The day darkens. Lights above the steps are switched on. LUCIEN looks at the chateau. Just when he is about to exit, GERMAINE comes on quickly from around the corner of the chateau and dashes over to LUCIEN.

GERMAINE:	It's you! Are you alone? *(LUCIEN moves over to GERMAINE eagerly)* Alone at last! … I thought they'd never go inside! … *(She throws herself into his arms)* Lucien … my darling! …

LUCIEN:	(*Embracing* GERMAINE) Germaine, my love … I was so miserable … so worried that I wouldn't see you … Look at me … look into my eyes … (*He holds her head*) Are you unwell? …
GERMAINE:	(*Leaning her head on* LUCIEN'*s shoulder and caressing him*) No … no …
LUCIEN:	You've been crying …
GERMAINE:	No … no … really I haven't …
LUCIEN:	Why did you leave so quickly? …
GERMAINE:	(*Sighing*) I couldn't stay … I couldn't stop myself … It all makes me so ill … this life here … it's killing me … I'm dying of shame … of anger, I just want to rebel against this house where every second of every day another crime or injustice is committed … I can't stand it anymore … (*With a deep sigh*) I can't stand it anymore …
LUCIEN:	(*Looking around him*) Be careful … someone might see us, someone might hear us …
GERMAINE:	Oh, for God's sake! … So what if someone does? What would happen? … What would you do? … (*With nervous agitation*) While we are still here …
LUCIEN:	(*Very gently and tenderly*) Calm down, darling … I will help you! …
GERMAINE:	(*Upset*) How? (*Pause*) Yes … yes … You are here for me now … That's wonderful … (*She snuggles up to* LUCIEN *who hugs her*) That's so nice … (*Pause*) You can't imagine the good this does me, just being near you does my heart good … just having you close to me … talking to you … having you to comfort me … (*Pause*) You see, I'm not anxious anymore, not stressed … I am not sad anymore … I am happy now … (*Pause*) Very … very happy … (*Imploringly*) You want me, don't you Lucien … (*Her voice more intense*) You want me … (*She stares at him deeply*) Lucien …
LUCIEN:	Germaine, my darling!
GERMAINE:	Take me away from all this … set me free … (LUCIEN *moves*) Yes … yes … I beg you … have mercy on me! Take me away from all this … far away from this place … Oh, that'd be wonderful – such freedom!
LUCIEN:	Careful!

A SERVANT *comes down the steps looking for something* MRS LECHAT *has left behind. He finds a shawl on the table and picks it up. During this time,* GERMAINE *and* LUCIEN *have concealed themselves by the tree. The* SERVANT *exits and* GERMAINE *and* LUCIEN *come back. They hold hands and exit stage left, slowly, silently like shadows.*

Act 2

The next morning. A Louis XVI-style lounge richly decorated with antique furniture, the various styles of which clash painfully. The walls to the back are decorated with ancient silk tapestries. To the left, a large door opens onto another lounge, equally lavish. Another door connects to ISIDORE's study. To the right, a large window looks out onto the sunlit estate. Upon an antique and evidently extremely valuable table sits a hideous and ridiculous terracotta vase which is outrageously modern and which has a rose shoved on top of it. Mixed in with various fine objects are tacky pieces of bric-a-brac which clash appallingly. On the walls to the left and right numerous antique oil paintings represent princesses and aristocrats of the past. A full-length portrait of ISIDORE flanked by two electric spotlights enjoys a prominent position in the room.

Scene One

When the curtain rises, GERMAINE sits at a table. She flicks through a magazine absent-mindedly. She rises, walks over to the window, stares out, nervously, impatiently, as she is waiting for someone. FONTANELLE emerges from ISIDORE's study with a briefcase under his arm. He acknowledges GERMAINE in silence without stopping and heads for the door at the back.

GERMAINE:	Mr Fontanelle? …
FONTANELLE:	Yes, miss? …
GERMAINE:	Have you just come from my father?
FONTANELLE:	Yes, miss …
GERMAINE:	I thought he was out.
FONTANELLE:	He has gone out just this moment … He left through the gallery … He's visiting the stables, I believe …
GERMAINE:	How is he this morning?
FONTANELLE:	Very well indeed … Very happy …
GERMAINE:	Very happy? … Has he said anything to you?
FONTANELLE:	Nothing out of the ordinary, miss. He made a long telephone call … something to do with those two engineers. After that we just talked business … *(A silence)*
GERMAINE:	Would you do me a favour, Mr Fontanelle?
FONTANELLE:	I'd be delighted to, miss.
GERMAINE:	The gardener – Jules – has he left Vauperdu yet?
FONTANELLE:	Last night …
GERMAINE:	Do you think he'll come back?

FONTANELLE:	I'd be astonished if he's not waiting outside my office bright and early tomorrow morning … The poor chap … They're all the same … Their resistance doesn't last for more than a day before they come back, cap in hand … Poor devils!
GERMAINE:	*(Handing FONTANELLE an envelope)* Could you give this to him? It's just a little money.
FONTANELLE:	Of course, miss …
GERMAINE:	Don't tell him where it's come from …
FONTANELLE:	I'm sure he won't be fooled, miss …
GERMAINE:	Are you going to the summer house?
FONTANELLE:	Yes …
GERMAINE:	Would it inconvenience you to tell Mr Garraud that I'd like to speak with him?
FONTANELLE:	Not at all …
GERMAINE:	I have a few matters I need to discuss with him.
FONTANELLE:	I'm at your service, miss …
GERMAINE:	Thank you so much … *(FONTANELLE bows and makes to leave)* Mr Fontanelle? … *(Pause)* Last night … something awful happened … something terrible … *(FONTANELLE makes a gesture to indicate that GERMAINE should not speak of it)* Sorry … *(She takes his hand)*
FONTANELLE:	*(Very moved)* Oh, miss! … *(He takes her hand and kisses it. He drops his briefcase and GERMAINE immediately picks it up and hands it back to him. He stammers)* Mi-Miss! … Miss! …
GERMAINE:	Glad to help …
FONTANELLE:	*(Evidently moved)* I don't deserve your kindness, miss … I had such a terrible life before I came here … Before I met your father I had no life or hope … Without your father where would I be now? … And without you, miss … what ever would become of me now? *(He wipes away a tear)* You'll never know …
GERMAINE:	*(Soothingly)* You are sad … that's all I need to know … *(PHINCK and GRUGGH appear at the door)*

Scene Two

GRUGGH:	Good morning – it's only us, miss.
GERMAINE:	*(With a rather distant politeness)* Are you looking for my father, gentlemen?
GRUGGH:	Yes, miss …
GERMAINE:	My father's gone out …

PHINCK:	I'm delighted to see that you've recovered from your indisposition last night.
GERMAINE:	Completely. *(To* FONTANELLE*)* Mr Fontanelle … would you escort these gentlemen? *(*PHINCK, GRUGGH *and* FONTANELLE *exit)*

Scene Three

GERMAINE starts to walk again, extremely impatient and nervous. Enter MRS LECHAT, *dressed to go out with a prayer book in her hands.*

MRS LECHAT:	*(At the door)* Well, Germaine? Are you ready?
GERMAINE:	Ready?
MRS LECHAT:	*(Coming into the room)* It's time.
GERMAINE:	Time for what?
MRS LECHAT:	Time to go to Mass … *(She sits down on an armchair and buttons her gloves)*
GERMAINE:	I'm not going.
MRS LECHAT:	Oh, I see … What nonsense has got into your head now?
GERMAINE:	It isn't nonsense … I just don't want to go to Mass … I can't stand it …
MRS LECHAT:	Your father will be furious … You know what he's like if anyone misses Mass …
GERMAINE:	I couldn't care less … It's time I started doing what I want … and this morning I want to stay here …
MRS LECHAT:	*(Trying to dissuade* GERMAINE*)* Here we go again! …
GERMAINE:	Since my father suddenly loves Mass so much, why on earth doesn't he go?
MRS LECHAT:	Your father can't go to Mass because he's anticlerical … this year … However, it is extremely useful for his business and for his election prospects that *we* are seen at Mass … It probably doesn't make much difference in actual fact. But if it keeps your father happy …
GERMAINE:	Marvellous …
MRS LECHAT:	It's just a *political activity* …
GERMAINE:	Good. I'm not going.
MRS LECHAT:	Besides … it's a chance to get out … a little distraction … It'd be good for you. Better than sitting around here …
GERMAINE:	*(Curtly)* I don't need a distraction …
MRS LECHAT:	*(Looking sadly at* GERMAINE*)* My poor girl, I have no idea what goes on in your head, I really don't … For quite a while now …

Something has happened to you, something that is no good at all, I know that much … You seem feverish, anxious … And you are more and more aggressive towards your parents … You don't want to see anyone … And when someone's here … you are so rude … you make your excuses and leave … How pleasant for us, having a daughter like that! We can't even say a word to you … You say things that frighten us … And you are astonished when we sometimes snap back at you … Sometimes I ask myself … I have to ask myself … if perhaps you are not right in the head … Seriously, I sometimes worry that you are a little … in the head … Come on, Germaine, tell me. What is wrong?

GERMAINE: Nothing.

MRS LECHAT: Are you unwell?

GERMAINE: No …

MRS LECHAT: If something's making you suffer … tell me what it is … *(Slowly)* I am your mother, after all …

GERMAINE: *(Her voice is slightly gentler)* Nothing is wrong, really …

MRS LECHAT: You make me so sad … Sometimes it's like you are making a martyr of yourself … you refuse everything … Is something – or someone – worrying you? …

GERMAINE: No … No … Really …

MRS LECHAT: It's unbelievable … You are as free as the air here … You can come and go as you please … You can do whatever you want … You are a girl but you are as free as a boy … This morning, for instance, you asked for three hundred francs and I gave them to you … Did I ask what they were for? Why you wanted them? No. I just gave you the money … No question … Do you think all mothers are like that? … After all, three hundred francs is quite a sum, you know … And with your habit of being overgenerous towards people who don't deserve a thing … Yes … Quite … Well … What do you want? …

GERMAINE: Nothing … Please, mother … Stop asking me …

MRS LECHAT: Oh God, what did I do to deserve this? … I have two children … A son who I never see and causes me nothing but worry … A girl I see all the time and who acts as if I ignore all her feelings and her ideas … a girl who never smiles … never shows any warmth towards me … *(With a long sigh)* Is this where money gets you? …

GERMAINE: Mother … it's not my fault …

MRS LECHAT: *(Shakes her head)* It's my fault, obviously! I know it is … of course it's my fault! I'm just a simple woman, that's all … I can't talk

	about the things you talk about … all those intellectual things … the kind of thing you and Mr Garraud talk about, no doubt! …
GERMAINE:	*(Rather curtly)* Please, mother, stop! …
MRS LECHAT:	I wasn't raised to be like you, you see … I'm just an ordinary, commonsense woman … *(Pause)* I'm no good at conversation, am I? … I'm much better at getting on with everyday things …
GERMAINE:	No one's saying that, mother.
MRS LECHAT:	Yes … Yes! Oh, my God … *(She stands up)* Decision? … Are you coming to Mass with me?
GERMAINE:	I think it's best if I stay here …
MRS LECHAT:	*(Worrying)* But … So I'll have to have the carriage changed, will I? *(She rings a bell)* Do you see the hassle that your ridiculous whims cause everyone? … *(SERVANT enters)* Tell the stables that I will need the old carriage and just *one* horse …
SERVANT:	I was just coming to tell you, ma'am, that the carriage is ready for you …
MRS LECHAT:	The Victoria carriage?
SERVANT:	Yes, ma'am …
MRS LECHAT:	With two horses?
SERVANT:	Yes, ma'am …
MRS LECHAT:	I don't need that one … Just tell them to get me the old carriage with just one horse …
SERVANT:	Very good, ma'am … *(Exits)*
GERMAINE:	You'll be late … By the time you get there Mass will be over …
MRS LECHAT:	It'll be alright, it always is … But … it's more than I can bear … I simply can't go … on my own … in a carriage with *two* horses. I just wouldn't be comfortable like that! … It's a dreadful thought … Is that what you really want to put me through? … I'd be ashamed to be seen on my own like that … I must have someone with me … or at least some luggage … Honestly! … *(Pause)* I must sort a few things out while I'm waiting … *(She pauses for thought for a few seconds)* I think those two fellows will be off tonight …
GERMAINE:	I don't know.
MRS LECHAT:	I don't know what it is … I've no idea where they've come from … but I have to say they're a funny pair! …
GERMAINE:	No more than any of the people father drags here … They're all the same.
MRS LECHAT:	Good heavens! These are businessmen … Of course it's only right that they should visit your father … but I really don't trust them …
GERMAINE:	That's exactly what they must be saying about him! …

MRS LECHAT:	Come on … don't be mean … Haven't you got a kiss for your mother?
GERMAINE:	Of course, mother … (*She kisses* MRS LECHAT, *rather weakly*)
MRS LECHAT:	Huh! Don't let me force you to do anything against your will! … You are such a stubborn, naughty girl! … Come on, give me a smile, at least … Put a bit of sunshine in my day! … (GERMAINE *forces a sad and weak smile*) By the way, what *did* you need three hundred francs for? …
GERMAINE:	Mother … you promised you wouldn't ask! …
MRS LECHAT:	Very well, very well … (*She starts to leave but as she gets to the door she returns*) My prayer book … (GERMAINE *picks up the prayer book from the table and gives it to* MRS LECHAT) Oh … if your brother arrives before I'm back … make sure you give him a lecture about his lifestyle – you never know, he might even listen to you! … Oh dear, I wonder what delights today has in store for us! …
GERMAINE:	Mother, I have no influence over Xavier … He does exactly what he wants to …
MRS LECHAT:	God help us! (*Entreating*) Dress yourself up a little for lunch … I'd like to see you looking pretty … Promise me?
GERMAINE:	Yes, mother …
MRS LECHAT:	*Very* pretty! …

MRS LECHAT *exits.*

Scene Four

GERMAINE *starts to walk around nervously again. A* YOUNG GARDENER *arrives ready to tend to the plants. Seeing* GERMAINE *he hesitates.*

GERMAINE:	Come in … Please! …
YOUNG GARDENER:	Excuse me, miss … It's all running a bit late this morning now that Jules has gone … (*He replaces old plants with new ones. He replaces the rose in the terracotta vase with a new one, and he stands back and admires the effect*) Pretty, isn't it?
GERMAINE:	Has the new gardener arrived?
YOUNG GARDENER:	He's just moving his stuff into the house right now … Big dark fellow … with a beard … Doesn't seem very polite! … (*He carries on working*) You haven't asked for any flowers this morning, miss.
GERMAINE:	I don't want any, thanks.

The YOUNG GARDENER *finishes and starts to leave, taking the old plants with him.* LUCIEN *enters.*

YOUNG GARDENER:	Good morning, Mr Garraud.
LUCIEN:	Morning, lad! *(The* YOUNG GARDENER *exits)*

Scene Five

LUCIEN:	*(He waits until the* YOUNG GARDENER *is out of earshot)* Is everything alright?
GERMAINE:	No … I wanted to see you … Any news in the post today?
LUCIEN:	No – I wish there was. *(Silence)*
GERMAINE:	Lucien … We've got to go … Today, even … We can't live like this anymore … We can't live in this state of constant indecision … Well, *I* can't live like this anyway …
LUCIEN:	*(Sadly)* You mean you can't be patient a little longer?
GERMAINE:	Be patient! Always be patient! … Days and days of patience … Weeks and weeks of submission … How noble! … It'll all be worth it! … No. No, it won't. This constant restriction is torture … Living a lie like this is humiliating for you and for me … And the burden of this house – the way it hangs on my heart … It's beyond my strength now, I can't bear it! … Please, Lucien … Please … Let's be what we are … Let's face the world as we are and as we want to be … Together …
LUCIEN:	Look, Germaine … Let's not rush … I beg you … Just a few more days, that's all … I showed you those letters …
GERMAINE:	The letters? …
LUCIEN:	They promise all kinds of prospects … serious prospects …
GERMAINE:	Prospects! …
LUCIEN:	Listen, darling … I can't just rush headlong into something … I've got to make sure that I find a position, a serious position, which can provide for all our needs …
GERMAINE:	You don't have to stay here waiting for that to happen … It will happen whether you are here or not … So let's – both of us together – let's just *go* … Just think, Lucien!
LUCIEN:	Tomorrow … maybe …
GERMAINE:	Tomorrow? Why wait until tomorrow? Why always put everything off until tomorrow? No … Let's finish this torture now … If you love me–
LUCIEN:	Of course I love you!

GERMAINE:	Alright, but listen to me … *(She takes his hands)* When I went to bed last night … I couldn't sleep … I was awake all night … My mind was turning over and over … I was wide awake … thinking of your words … your caress … your kiss … I don't want to be alone anymore … I want you. I waited until the sun rose and then I came down … I walked through the fields and the forest … I walked and walked … It did me so much good … It calmed my nerves … I felt the sensation of being alive and free, freshened by the air and a feeling of pure joy … And I thought of you … of us … of our love, so wild and passionate … Wild as the trees and the leaves that brushed against me … wild as the flowers and their fresh perfume all around me … Then I slowly came back home … My heart was at peace and … happy … Yes … I was almost happy … Suddenly, through the clearing of the forest I saw the chateau ahead of me … It struck me horribly … It was as if I could suddenly see death before me … It was a terrifying moment … a ghastly, haunting moment … In that moment I had a terrible vision, more clearly and truthfully than ever I saw what this place has done to me … How it is crushing and killing everything around it: the forest … the fields … the gardens … This hideous lump of rock, merciless as the sun … It is such a crime! … Every pebble … each blade of grass … all of it has been cheated and abused … And as I walked on the earth – *my* earth, I think of it as my earth – I could hear nothing but weeping and see nothing but blood … It seemed that all around me I could hear screams of 'Thief! Thief!' And all the joy in me changed, suddenly, into misery and suffering … and all the love that was in me transformed into hatred and rebellion … No … No … I cannot stand it anymore … I can't stand it. I used to think that I couldn't live without you, Lucien … I used to think that I could stand it all with your love … But now I'm not sure … If I stay here, Lucien … I think I may even begin to detest you too …
LUCIEN:	So … You really want to leave?
GERMAINE:	*(Forcefully)* Yes! Yes! Of course!
LUCIEN:	Where shall we go?
GERMAINE:	It doesn't matter …
LUCIEN:	How will we live?
GERMAINE:	Why don't I get a job? … I have the energy … and the desire to be free and happy …
LUCIEN:	Work? You? Oh, my dear Germaine … You must trust me on this … I know the reality of such things … I have had my share

of miserable times, I can tell you … Spare me the misery of going through it all again, this time with you … Times when I had lost everything, totally washed up … It is utterly wretched and frightening … It robs you of more than just your material wealth … It robs you of pride and dignity, it robs you of your sense of right and wrong … and … even worse … it can rob you of any feelings of love … Woe betides being in love when you find yourself in such a tragic condition … You see … I also … was intelligent … I had energy … I tell you … I had the desire to work … I had a bitter and stubborn desire to succeed … I had all those qualities … but still I couldn't get a job … Yes … for three long years I searched and searched in vain … In vain, I knocked on door after door … None of them opened to me … It's hard to believe, I know … but it is true and it is still the same now …

GERMAINE: Oh, Lucien, my darling! …

LUCIEN: So that I didn't starve to death … *starve to death* … I was forced to make some shameful compromises … I took some humiliating jobs … My God, if I told you what I did … And I am a *man*, in other words I am privileged in our society … Men are protected in this society, all activities, all careers are open to them … But for you, a woman, society will not even recognize you …

GERMAINE: You don't have enough faith in yourself … But the two of us together …

LUCIEN: The two of us … That will only double the suffering … And the thought of being destroyed for the second time … that is what makes me cautious and fearful …

GERMAINE: Well, that is what makes *me* feel determined and hopeful …

LUCIEN: Your boundless optimism frightens me … My darling … I feel responsible for your soul and your existence … And it is my duty to make sure that I show you life as it really is, and not what you dream it to be … You believe in your dreams and your strong will and generosity lead you towards absolute idealism … And absolutes are impossible in real life. It is just fantasy.

GERMAINE: I know for certain that life is filled with absolute crime and absolute suffering … Don't you think that there might also be absolute goodness and absolute purity? …

LUCIEN: I very much doubt it …

GERMAINE: And what about absolute love?

LUCIEN: I'm afraid I doubt that too.

GERMAINE:	Well, it is clear that you don't love me. You can't love me if you really don't believe that there is an absolute love, a blind faith, which can triumph over everything! …
LUCIEN:	Of course I love you. I love you more than anything in the world …
GERMAINE:	Don't argue … Take me … Take me away from here … True love is not based on the crude realities of life, it is about a union of souls … nothing else matters … the rest is nothing …
LUCIEN:	The rest … is the harsh realities of life … It can pound us into dust … It doesn't matter to me, I'm used to it … But you? … And because my love for you is so passionate, deep and all-consuming … I'm scared of risking all this precious happiness … I want to safeguard this happiness … and protect it against your impulsive idealism …
GERMAINE:	What do you mean?
LUCIEN:	You doubt my motives?
GERMAINE:	No … No … Oh, no … it's only you look at the world with a man's rational mind and experience … Whereas I scream aloud with the heart of a woman … Really, it's you who is in a world of fantasy and dreams … But I'm in the world of nature and the essence of life … Well, tell me … what do you want us to do? …
LUCIEN:	Wait a little longer …
GERMAINE:	But if what you're waiting for doesn't happen or maybe never happens?
LUCIEN:	Impossible …
GERMAINE:	But you are always doubting it, aren't you … Come on … admit it … (LUCIEN is silent) Your silence says it all … (Pause) No … There's something else, isn't there? Something you're not telling me? … I can sense it … For a few days now … your attitude … the things you've said … and the things I have had to say to you …
LUCIEN:	There's nothing else – honestly, there isn't …
GERMAINE:	It's my father, isn't it? … It's to do with your loyalty to my father? …
LUCIEN:	It's nothing to do with your father … It's to do with a loyalty to myself maybe! …
GERMAINE:	It's the same thing … Anyway, what does that matter anymore? … I mean, honestly, loyalty to Mr Isidore Lechat … that's an indulgence you could do without …
LUCIEN:	I owe him so much.

GERMAINE:	*(Shrugs)* So does Mr Fontanelle … My father's a saint in his eyes … one of humanity's greatest benefactors … The irony beggars belief! …
LUCIEN:	Don't be like that. He dragged me out of desperation … I was in the abyss when he reached in and took me by the hand …
GERMAINE:	Only to throw you into deeper humiliation … Using your intelligence … your knowledge … your decent morality … Exploiting everything in you that he could never have … a disgusting masquerade … As you yourself have said, complete mendacity …
LUCIEN:	*(Sadly)* Oh, I only said that in a moment of pride, a moment of disgusting arrogance …
GERMAINE:	*(Savagely)* Well … I can't bear it! … If I love something, I defend it ferociously … I would never let anything touch it … let alone *humiliate* it! … *(Pause)* To love each other don't we need the approval of others, don't we need to make a legal declaration and sign our names to it? … Haven't I learnt from my father that contracts are made to be broken … agreements are made to be denounced? … *(A little less viciously)* What about me? … Will I ever be allowed to escape from desperation? … Who will reach in and drag *me* out of the abyss?
LUCIEN:	*(Tenderly)* Please understand, Germaine … I don't want to defend your father against you … After all, you probably have every right and every reason to dislike him … He has made you suffer terribly … But can't you still find it somewhere in you to love your father regardless? To love him without judging him so mercilessly?
GERMAINE:	My judgement is the measure of my hate. I have no choice. *(LUCIEN moves)* What is it?
LUCIEN:	You make things so difficult for me …
GERMAINE:	Why do you say that?
LUCIEN:	Are you sure that you even know your father? … Are you sure that your father is responsible for all that you condemn him for? …
GERMAINE:	If my father was just a fool … I would help him in his folly … But … he's not a fool … He's a ruthless man who never yields, no matter how extravagant are his wild ideas … He's a man with frightening logic at the heart of his irrationalism … He's not mad …
LUCIEN:	My poor Germaine … *(He pulls GERMAINE against him and caresses her head gently and soothingly)* My little free spirit … Ah! If I could only bring a little understanding and pity into that head of yours … Oh, if only I could … *(He kisses her*

forehead) If only I could put a little reality in here! … *(He stares at her intensely)* You are the cause of your own suffering, much more than your father …

GERMAINE: No … No! …

LUCIEN: Yes … Yes … You suffer because you have a dream in your head, a dream that is impossible … And your belief in absolute justice only means, I'm afraid to say, that you will find yourself trapped in sorrow and despair … I'm no saint, God knows … I am like any other ordinary human being: a mixture of good and bad … Maybe more bad than good … Who's to say that the day you realize that I am just an ordinary man – a poor, unremarkable, ordinary man – you won't hate me with the same unforgiving fury that you have created within yourself? Well … What would you become, Germaine?

GERMAINE: What a stupid thing to ask …

LUCIEN: No, it's not … And you look at all the world with an intensity and judgement based on what you have seen here, in your home … People's material lives may vary but the human soul remains the same … Or at least hardly changes … The poor human spirit has its appetites, its desires, its passionate destructiveness … its incoherencies … its fatal faults … Yes! … But it also has the burden of mortal sorrow … You should pity the human soul sooner than despise it … Besides … Even in the most loathsome man … the most wicked criminal … there is always a glimmer of hope: it may be seen by no one but that is where the road to pity may begin! …

GERMAINE: Pity? It's because my heart is so full of pity that it has become so full of hate! *(LUCIEN has moved away from GERMAINE who follows him)* Please … please … don't go … Come here … *(Pause. With great effort)* I haven't told you everything either … For the sake of my parents and myself … It's wrong of me, I know … Other people can share everything together … their joy … their sorrow … their shame … You know part of my life but you don't know everything … You don't know the details of my most personal and secretive life … Well, listen … There's plenty of pain, I promise you! … My mother. What shall I say of her? She is not an evil person … she loves me, she thinks … but her heart, little by little, has become hardened without her even knowing it, hardened by habit and by example … The little bit of conscience she used to have has vanished in the face of opulence and indolence, and she muddles up what she calls her affection for me with her vulgar and vile preoccupations, so far from the realities of love, that despite my strongest efforts and reasoning I can no longer regard her as a mother, as my mother …

LUCIEN: You ask too much of her.

GERMAINE: *(A little feverishly)* Why do you provoke me like this? Why do you aggravate me? I don't ask for *anything* from her … A smile, maybe, from time to time … some show of emotion, some trust … some goodness … yes, that's right, goodness! Is that really too much to ask? … You don't even know her … She seems to be the saving grace of the house with her superficial kindness … In fact, despite what seems to be natural generosity and her feminine tact – just tell me if I'm asking for too much – does she lessen the wickedness that my father creates all around him? … No, not at all … She knows, perhaps only vaguely, but nonetheless she knows that all his ideas cause trouble … all his desires are vicious and violent … and despite her trivial complaints and half-hearted refusal … thanks to understanding the singular responsibility of a wife to stand by her husband … she defends them and sets them in stone … and, if necessary, adds to them … *(With more bitterness)* I do not hate my father for not loving me … But I do hate myself for not being able to love my mother … And how could anyone love a woman who cannot love her own mother? …

LUCIEN: On the contrary, what you have said, Germaine, fills me with compassion … Everyone has their weaknesses, their absurdities, some even have their virtues … Of course, I know your mother … She is a fragile, delicate woman … she is indecisive and obscure … a woman exiled on an island of affluence … She has no idea … She simply does what she can …

GERMAINE: *(Trembling)* And my father? … Does he also simply do what he can? … All the things he does in the name of business: things that amount to fraud, extortion, theft, abduction, murder! … That's what my father's life amounts to!

LUCIEN: You only see the bad – never the good … the good that is never far from bad … In spite of the fact that he is your father … Yes, this beastly man who is your father … He has done many great things …

GERMAINE: So what? He has done nothing for me … Great things, indeed! … Today you will see me go to the bitter end of my feelings … I will scream my disgust for you to hear … And when I've finished you will understand … Huh, *maybe* you will understand

and you will realize what I have lived through … I have grown up between those two people … I might as well be an orphan … a complete stranger … less than a pet … Our house … our mansion in Paris … the chateau we're in now … You have seen all of them, haven't you? And you've seen me in all of them too … A hell wherein I have never seen a heart at peace or a simple smile … where I have never once heard the music of gentle words or kind laughter … Hatred … Anger … Misery … Cruel and gloating laughter … the triumph of crime! … People always come here and leave never to return … Just think of those two idiots who are here at the moment … who knows where they've come from … They will leave here tonight and find they've lost any fortune they may have had and lost any honour if they ever had any in the first place. *(Pause. In a sad voice)* I see the faces of accomplices sometimes … but usually I see the faces of victims … poor, unknown people … more tragic than I ever could imagine … crying and desperate … ruined by my father … And every night, in front of us and even with complete strangers, he boasts of his triumphs. He boasts away with a sinister glee … with a laugh like a murderer … He tells us how he has destroyed someone … robbed someone … dishonoured someone … And you dare to reproach me for having a lack of pity? Oh, Lucien … My heart has brimmed over with pity throughout these horrible years … I cannot walk past a woman and her children in mourning clothes without saying, 'It must be our fault!' I cannot see anyone cry without saying, 'It must be something my family has done!'

LUCIEN: *(With profound tenderness)* Why do you love to torture yourself like this? …

GERMAINE: It is not without reason, I'm afraid … Have you heard of that banker, Gabriel Dauphin?

LUCIEN: Yes.

GERMAINE: Did you know why he died?

LUCIEN: I know that he killed himself.

GERMAINE: He killed himself because of my family … *(LUCIEN moves)* Yes, he killed himself because of us … I can't explain all the details of this tragedy … I don't understand enough of the business side of things, but I do know what I heard whispered on the streets of Paris … The papers didn't report it, of course – my father owns one of them after all, and so he bought their silence … *(Her voice trembles. Her expression becomes more and more miserable)*

LUCIEN:	Your memories are no good for you … my darling Germaine … Your hands are burning … your voice is beginning to choke with tears … Please … stop!
GERMAINE:	No … No … This is doing me good … This comforts me … It is like a sickness which stifles and racks me … *(Continuing)* Dauphin's business was beginning to fail … Not knowing what to do, he came in desperation to my father and begged him for help … what happened between these two men? I don't know. What secret was there between them? I don't know for sure … But what I do know is that Dauphin, in exchange for some illusory help, some half promise, or maybe nothing at all … gave my father in trust, in trust – understand? – executive power over his few remaining assets … A few days later … These assets were suddenly sold off at the stock exchange … There was a panic in which Dauphin was wiped out … He was livid … distraught … insane … he ran to my father and threatened him, begged him on his knees … *(GERMAINE enacts the dialogue)* 'You have committed a crime! … ', 'It was my right!', 'You've destroyed me!', 'I've advanced!', 'But I've a wife and children!', 'So have I!', 'You're driving me to suicide! … ', 'So what!?' … He went home and blew his brains out … Business is business …
LUCIEN:	How dreadful! … But Dauphin was no angel, you know …
GERMAINE:	He was humiliated … destroyed … annihilated … Oh, Lucien!
LUCIEN:	Maybe it's just gossip?
GERMAINE:	Oh, stop it! It's the truth. I went to see Mrs Dauphin … She told me everything … I threw myself at her feet … We held each other and cried … Dauphin is not the only one … There are many others … hundreds … thousands! … And you still think I have no right to judge my father? … *(LUCIEN is silent)* Do you understand why I must leave this house where every stone and patch of earth is stained with someone's tears? *(LUCIEN remains silent)* I told you that my parents have never thought about me … That's not true … You have seen how devoted and loyal is my father's love for me: trying to find me the best person to marry … In other words, marrying me off to the highest bidder or the best deal … He has used me as bait or as a lump sum; it doesn't matter as long as it is to his greatest advantage … I don't really exist to him … I am not a human being in his eyes … I am merely a commodity that changes in value … Not even that … He often drags me out to parade me around in front of eligible clients, showing me off like a butcher does a piece of meat, carving me up, weighing me …

LUCIEN:

Who knows, at this moment he's probably trying to hawk me off to Phinck or Gruggh … In fact … I bet he is! …

LUCIEN: Your passion is misleading you, my darling … Why condemn your father for a fault that all society is guilty of? … After all, as soon as two lovers want to be together, there are contracts to be signed on official paper, a pretty much brutal process altogether … humiliating for anyone if you think about it … But that is how society sanctifies marriage … You've said so yourself … But should that matter to us? Our love is pure and free … we have pledged our love to each other … We have given each other nothing but the gift of ourselves … Forget everything else, Germaine, I beg you …

GERMAINE: I will forget everything … if you can, so will I. If you want me to forget everything, I will … What I want to say to you is that I can accept living like this instead of rebelling against it … In the end I would be fighting no one but myself if no one would stand by me, if no one would help me, support me … Loneliness … moral isolation … have given me such a strong sense of right and wrong … I have never been a young, naïve girl … In this mire of shame and crime, I believe I have somehow managed to avoid being contaminated, unlike my brother … What has spared me from this disease? … I really don't know … Maybe first of all it was because of my spirit of rebellion … and then later it was because of love … Who knows, but I have been able to resist the disease of this house … Oh, Lucien! … If I told you that many times I have thought of shocking my parents, humiliating them for revenge, I have thought of giving myself to a clerk or a stable boy! *(Her voice breaks and she sobs)*

LUCIEN: Germaine! *(He takes her hands in a burst of passion)* Germaine! Be quiet … don't say anything more … never say that again … it's not true! …

GERMAINE: Of all the people who have wandered into this dreadful house, those ugly and cynical faces seem to me the most genuine … *(She sobs)*

LUCIEN: Germaine … Germaine … I beg you! … Your faith … your sense of right … the generosity of your spirit … all your unmitigated sense of purity and idealism … your desperation for freedom and justice … and your suffering … I love all of these more than I love your beauty! … The same things make me tremble … tremble all the time … Well … Listen to me … Yes … We shall leave … We shall leave whenever you want … We can leave today if you want to! …

GERMAINE:	Yes … yes … But not like thieves creeping away in the night … We must leave in broad daylight with our heads held high … with peace in our hearts … Everyone must see us go …
LUCIEN:	Yes …
GERMAINE:	And you must let me do it Lucien … I understand your principles and your conscience … I don't have any … so you must let me act … Go back to the summer house, my darling. You must clear everything … put the books in order. I don't want my father to have any reason to speak to you again … Kiss me … take me in your arms … *(They embrace)* No regrets now … Go and get ready! … When we are together at last … far from here … you will see how happy I will be … happy again at last … happy forever! … Never again will you see these sad eyes that upset you so … We will love each other, equal and forever … Just see how happy we'll be! …
LUCIEN:	Yes … we will be happy … just don't forget the realities of life and the realities of love …
GERMAINE:	*(Slightly annoyed)* Ssh, Lucien … *(Pause)* Will our happiness finally conquer your sadness and cynicism? *(Silence)* How are you for money? …
LUCIEN:	*(Awkwardly)* I've got … enough … for now … In Paris I'll find more … I'll really start earning …
GERMAINE:	Off you go! … Get ready! … My poor love! … And don't leave the chateau until we're ready! *(LUCIEN exits. GERMAINE watches him with a newfound joy)*

Scene Six

GERMAINE rings a bell. A MAIDSERVANT appears.

GERMAINE:	Could you tell Julie that I need to speak to her at once? *(MAIDSERVANT exits. GERMAINE moves over to a vase and removes a flower. She sniffs it and then looks out of the window. JULIE enters)* Julie … I want you to pack a trunk … Put some of my clothes in there … And some of my other things … Essential things …
JULIE:	Yes, miss.
GERMAINE:	*(After a moment's thought she makes a firm decision)* Yes, my jewellery too … All my jewellery! …
JULIE:	Yes, miss. *(Pause)* Are you going on holiday, miss?
GERMAINE:	I'm not sure …

JULIE:	Well … are you leaving, miss? …
GERMAINE:	Why do you ask me? … Julie?
JULIE:	Oh, because …
GERMAINE:	Not a word to anyone. Do you understand?
JULIE:	And, miss, what about me? …
GERMAINE:	*(Looks at* JULIE *for a moment)* Go … Hurry up, my dear! *(*JULIE *exits)*

Scene Seven

Just as GERMAINE *is about to exit,* ISIDORE, PHINCK *and* GRUGGH *enter the room.*

ISIDORE:	What the? … Oh, it's you, Germaine. Why on earth aren't you at Mass? …
GERMAINE:	I was with Mr Garraud.
ISIDORE:	Garraud?
GERMAINE:	Yes …
ISIDORE:	*(Looking around)* Where is that fine fellow? …
GERMAINE:	He's gone back to his summer house.
ISIDORE:	Was he looking for me?
GERMAINE:	Not in the slightest …
ISIDORE:	Well, what the hell was he doing lurking around here?
GERMAINE:	*(Pauses. She looks at* ISIDORE *arrogantly)* You'll see! … *(She exits quickly)*

Scene Eight

ISIDORE:	*(Watches* GERMAINE *exit and remains pensive for a while)* How strange … Very odd … *(Slaps his forehead)* Pretty girl though, isn't she! … A good catch for someone! … *(To* PHINCK*)* Are you married?
PHINCK:	Unfortunately.
ISIDORE:	*(To* GRUGGH*)* And you?
GRUGGH:	I'm afraid so …
ISIDORE:	Oh well … never mind … It's your loss, gentlemen … Well, let's get down to business, shall we? … *(A* SERVANT *enters)*
SERVANT:	You're wanted on the telephone, sir.
ISIDORE:	Who is it?
SERVANT:	*The Little Tricolour*, sir.

ISIDORE:	Oh God! … Oh well, fair enough … *(To* PHINCK *and* GRUGGH*)* I won't be a moment … *(To the* SERVANT*)* Bring the port.
SERVANT:	Port, sir? … *(Looks at* PHINCK *and* GRUGGH*)* The *portfolio*, sir … the business portfolio?
ISIDORE:	No, *port* you idiot … and some cigars …
SERVANT:	You know that I can't get the cigars, sir. There's only one key and I'm afraid Mrs Lechat–
ISIDORE:	Mrs Lechat! … Mrs Lechat! … Who asked your opinion, you idiot? … And when I think of all the cigars you've pilfered from me, you little thief! … Go on, clear off! … *(*ISIDORE *shoves the* SERVANT *who exits rapidly.* ISIDORE *storms into his study)*

Scene Nine

PHINCK:	*(Very nervous)* I feel a bit out of sorts today … I don't think I'm on best form … What shall we do? … I think I'm losing my nerve.
GRUGGH:	What are you talking about? … The man is a complete nincompoop, trust me.
PHINCK:	*(Pointing at the door)* Keep your voice down … If he really is a nincompoop, how come he's made so much money? …
GRUGGH:	He's just a puppet, he's been used by other people before … I mean, come on, *sugar cane*!
PHINCK:	Well, that may have been a flight of fancy … But what about when he told us about the Extra-Centre railway … Remember how clearly he told us the whole story, how eloquent he was … He knew what he was talking about – and what a fantastic success the project was!
GRUGGH:	Luck, that's all.
PHINCK:	Your obstinacy is beginning to frighten me … I tell you, the man has a fantastic sense of business and a sense of the times we live in … We must be on our guard … Let's talk through our plan again …
GRUGGH:	*(Fed up)* For the seventh time …
PHINCK:	So we're going to exaggerate the estimates? That might be too risky. He might immediately take us for … con men.
GRUGGH:	No … He'll think we're extremely canny, that's all … You see we must take control of things, impose ourselves on him and win his trust … He must see how *capable* we are …
PHINCK:	Good! That sounds like a good idea … And the profits to be gained from working with the construction company?

GRUGGH:	Do you think it will occur to him?
PHINCK:	Well what if it *does* occur to him?
GRUGGH:	I'll deny everything; I will deny all knowledge–
PHINCK:	What! Deny all knowledge? Please, I beg you, don't behave like you're defending a trench in the middle of a war … It will just cause more difficulties for us … And it's another one of your bad habits …
GRUGGH:	Oh, give me a break … After all, you're the one who suggested we work together in the first place …
PHINCK:	If we're not careful it's our weak point … He will see that and see how weak *we* are!
GRUGGH:	Well … We'll discuss everything sensibly.
PHINCK:	That's what worries me … I tell you, the man is a devil … What about the aluminium?
GRUGGH:	We *must* tell him about it: it's one of the most attractive possibilities of the venture, and it's certain to get him on board …
PHINCK:	*(Nods)* Absolutely …
GRUGGH:	At the same time … We can't let him have everything …
PHINCK:	*(Energetically)* But we must give him something …
GRUGGH:	Listen to me! We can't let him have everything! …
PHINCK:	At the very least I secured exclusive rights … Let me keep the exclusive rights.
GRUGGH:	*(Comically shrugging his shoulders)* Your exclusive rights … ha ha!
PHINCK:	Yes, the exclusive rights are mine … And I won't let him have them for anything, I can tell you.
GRUGGH:	*(Irritated)* Yes, yes, of course! …
PHINCK:	'Yes, yes, of course' indeed! You always say that but then you give in. Just make sure you don't let him have the name and address … make sure we keep that secret when it comes to the contract … then Lechat won't be able to retract from the agreement!
GRUGGH:	*(Still irritated)* Yes, yes, yes! *(Pause)* And make sure you don't talk all the time … I know what you're like … It's dreadful when you start droning on … God knows what you're talking about … You make the simplest things totally confusing! …
PHINCK:	But that's exactly what we need to do! …
GRUGGH:	Not always …
PHINCK:	So … you think I'm an idiot, do you? …
GRUGGH:	Be quiet … He's coming. *(They take on a confident air and look at the portrait of* ISIDORE *with gestures of admiration.* ISIDORE *enters, joyfully rubbing his hands)*

Scene Ten

ISIDORE:	*(Seeing* PHINCK *and* GRUGGH *admiring the painting)* It's a Bonnat … Heard of him, lads? … He's the painter who does all the presidents … Hold on … *(He switches on the electric lights and steps back to admire the effect)* There you go … Now stand over here … What do you think of that?
PHINCK:	Oh, it's superb … So imposing! …
GRUGGH:	He's really captured you … What a likeness! …
ISIDORE:	*(Slapping* GRUGGH's *shoulder)* Thirty five thousand francs that cost me, old boy! … What a work of art, eh? Ha ha ha! Where's the port? *(At that moment a* SERVANT *carrying a tray enters the room)* Ah, here it is … You took your time … *(Looks at the bottle)* Good stuff, port … don't you think? *(The* SERVANT *puts the tray on the table)* Close the door behind you … I am not at home for anyone … Unless it's my son, of course … Whenever he gets here … *(The* SERVANT *exits and closes the door)* Ah! At least we can talk in peace … *(He pours out the port into glasses)* To your health, lads! … *(They all drink)*
PHINCK:	Mm … Delicious! …
ISIDORE:	1804 this is! … What a work of art, eh! My house is full of art! *(He puts the glass down on the tray)* And now, you'll be very pleased to know that I'm all ears, gentlemen! … *(*GRUGGH *stops in front of the fireplace assuming the attitude of an orator)* Oh, right, so you'll do the talking, eh?
GRUGGH:	If I may?
ISIDORE:	Sure, get on with it! … Nothing to look at then? No paperwork or documents? Oh, do try and keep it brief, won't you? *(*ISIDORE *falls onto a sofa with his head back and his legs raised.* PHINCK *sits on the edge of a desk, and while* GRUGGH *talks he discreetly opens his attaché case and lays some papers out in front of him)*
GRUGGH:	I know that you are well aware of the enormous industrial advancements being made in the area of electricity in countries such as Switzerland and Germany …
ISIDORE:	*(Without moving)* Skip it … Skip anything general … We're not at some opening ceremony … And you're not talking to the dignitaries or the artwork! Come on … Spit your idea out in a sentence if you can …
GRUGGH:	Well, in a sentence then … It is time France was endowed with something equivalent to the Swiss or German models …
ISIDORE:	Leave Switzerland and Germany out of it …
GRUGGH:	*(Continuing)* Only something bigger … Bigger and better! …

ISIDORE:	God, does he ever stop talking?
GRUGGH:	The business venture that I have the honour of presenting to you has a double thrust to it … First of all, it is patriotic …
ISIDORE:	So is all business, it goes without saying …
GRUGGH:	It will also be hugely successful …
ISIDORE:	That remains to be seen! …
GRUGGH:	*(Increasingly awkward and searching for words)* Because I am talking to such a well-informed gentleman … I, er, I needn't explain all the things that electricity is useful for …
ISIDORE:	You're right there …
GRUGGH:	After all, I can explain all the things that electricity is useful for in one word: *everything* … You can do everything with electricity … Er, mechanical traction …
ISIDORE:	Skip it … skip it …
GRUGGH:	*(Becoming dispirited)* Did you want to ask me anything? …
ISIDORE:	No, not at all … *(Carrying on regardless)* Now, you own a waterfall capable of generating ten thousand horsepower …
GRUGGH:	That's *twenty thousand* horsepower …
ISIDORE:	Alright, twenty thousand horsepower … Where is it?
GRUGGH:	Let me explain the overall project and we'll come to the details later …
ISIDORE:	Fair enough … As long as it's not on planet Mars or something! *(Roars with laughter)*
GRUGGH:	The waterfall we're talking of is perfect … It's in a mountain about twenty six kilometres from a city which has a large population and lots of industry … Now, the contract – please note that – the official contract with the gas company expires in three years, and the local government is very wise and very progressive; they will not be looking to renew the contract …
ISIDORE:	I wouldn't count too much on local government if I were you … I know what those swine are like …
GRUGGH:	They want to work with us …
ISIDORE:	Just a couple of favours and they'll be all yours, eh? … Carry on …
GRUGGH:	Three power stations, first and foremost … Of course, other developments will follow around them … Housing, hotels and the like … Finally, and this is one of the most interesting parts of the prospect … The surrounding area is extremely rich in bauxite … And with this rich mineral resource and the energy of the power stations, we will be able to construct a factory for the production of aluminium … We'll be able to take on the Germans in the aluminium industry – possibly overtake them in time!

ISIDORE:	Good. I see what you mean.
PHINCK:	The possibilities are countless!
ISIDORE:	Well, don't bother trying to calculate them now, then … *(He stands and walks around with his arms behind his back)* This waterfall … It's really yours, is it?
GRUGGH:	*(After the slightest hesitation)* Absolutely.
ISIDORE:	I find that a little surprising …
PHINCK:	Why? What's surprising about that?
ISIDORE:	Nothing … You're the owners, are you?
GRUGGH:	Yes … I was just about to explain–
ISIDORE:	That you are *not* the owners …
GRUGGH:	We might as well be. We've got first option on the purchase …
ISIDORE:	From who?
GRUGGH:	From the current owner, obviously …
ISIDORE:	But I thought *you* were the owners? … *(Roars with laughter)* Look, you're nice lads … I like both of you … Me … I'm an idiot, probably … What you're proposing sounds very interesting indeed, but it is just way too complicated … I would never get involved in a project when I don't really know what it is, or where it is or who's involved …

ISIDORE stands in front of his picture and looks at it lovingly and dreamily with his legs wide apart, his hands in his pockets and his head upright. PHINCK and GRUGGH are becoming more and more uneasy, and they look at each other questioningly. ISIDORE occasionally switches the electric lights on and off.

GRUGGH:	You'll be dealing with us … We don't want to hide anything from you … *(irritated)* You didn't let me explain everything … *(ISIDORE is silent)*
PHINCK:	You kept interrupting … *(ISIDORE remains silent)* We're all confused now! …
GRUGGH:	*(After a brief word with PHINCK)* The owner's called Joseph Bruneau …
ISIDORE:	Bruneau? Poor, unlucky chap … *(He moves over and sits on the desk next to PHINCK)* What is the fellow?
GRUGGH:	Part peasant, part bourgeois … Ordinary sort of chap … Not too sharp … but incredibly stubborn … At first he refused to have anything to do with our business proposal … but when we showed him the millions and millions that stand to be made, he decided to let us take over the business on his behalf …
ISIDORE:	So he's rich, is he?

GRUGGH:	He has about three hundred thousand francs … more or less … We gave him an estimate of the works, which he accepted and work began. Ten kilometres of the tunnel has been excavated … Three more kilometres need to be dug, but his three hundred thousand francs is already used … Unfortunately, our estimate was a little inaccurate …
ISIDORE:	*(Sarcastically)* Really?
PHINCK:	Yes, that often happens with estimates …
ISIDORE:	Quite! … *(Laughs with a sneer)* Then what happened? *(ISIDORE scrutinizes PHINCK and GRUGGH)*
GRUGGH:	Bruneau understood the situation at once and was in agreement … We drew up a new private contract by which we took over the business and would completely buy him out at a figure yet to be determined, which will be given by the new partnership when they take over the project …
ISIDORE:	Poor old Bruneau! … What about this wonderful waterfall? Where exactly is it?
GRUGGH:	*(After exchanging a word with PHINCK)* It's in Saint Cerex … near Grenoble …
ISIDORE:	Saint Cerex? … But … hold on, lads … I know Saint Cerex … Correct me if I'm wrong, but isn't Saint Cerex within a military zone? …
GRUGGH:	Yes …
PHINCK:	That's just a minor detail of no importance–
ISIDORE:	Really? Do you think so? … What about all the obstacles and the complications the military authorities might throw at the project? … All the refusals and, yes, all the *details*? … And what if after years of court battles and legal process, squandered money and lost time you are not allowed to do what you wanted and your grand plan is out the window: you call *that* a minor detail? … Honestly, my dear Phinck …
PHINCK:	*(With authority)* Do you really suppose that we have jumped blindly into this enterprise? Don't you think that we might have friends in high places? …
ISIDORE:	Oh, I see..! And no doubt you've got friends with plenty of capital assets as well as influence? … Tremendous! I'm very happy for you … You obviously don't need me then, do you? … Off you go then, lads, and I wish you all the best! … Good luck to you! … How's about another glass of port? … 1804, hmm? … And let's drink to the health of poor old Bruneau, shall we? … *(He pours and they drink)* Whatever's the matter? You don't look too happy for some reason? …

PHINCK:	No! … Quite the opposite!
GRUGGH:	Er … Mr Lechat … We've always felt that you could play a major role in this enterprise … Of course, we have!
ISIDORE:	I see.
GRUGGH:	You own a newspaper … one of the most powerful and formidable forces of modern capitalist society …
PHINCK:	An essential lever in the advancement of capitalism and major business interests …
GRUGGH:	You also–
ISIDORE:	Yes, yes, yes! But don't fool yourselves into believing that you'll be able to use me like a puppet … *(PHINCK and GRUGGH protest)* You've got me wrong if you think that … I am a honest man, I'm loyal, generous – a little too generous – and I always put my cards on the table up front … Understand this: I am not Bruneau. I am not a poor sod like Bruneau … I've got backbone, me … I am thick-skinned too … If someone tries to swallow me down like a fish, I tend to get stuck in their throats … Don't say that I haven't warned you … Now, listen to me carefully … Regarding the business venture you have presented to me, I'm not exactly sure what it is precisely … There's so much you haven't told me, can't tell me, won't tell me … You see? I'm in the dark … However, I'm not averse to looking seriously at the proposal in depth … It might be good … It might be bad … And I have to say that right now I think it is probably a good proposal, and I tend to be right about such things … However, there are a number of conditions that I will need to discuss … *my* conditions … They can be accepted or rejected accordingly … as simple as that … but I simply don't have time to waste on all your petty, childish fiddle-faddle … all these ridiculous vagaries: it's getting us nowhere and it is not just extremely irritating, it is quite *abhorrent* …
GRUGGH:	I'm sorry, but these 'vagaries'–
ISIDORE:	Oh, give it a break, will you? … How much do you estimate the first stage will be: construction, labour, machinery?
PHINCK:	Eight million …
ISIDORE:	Strewth! *(Pause)* I'd like to see that … *(Pause)* I will be expected to come up with this money, that much *is* clear to me … I trust that you will permit me to decide if every detail of the project is acceptable on my terms …
GRUGGH:	That goes without saying …
ISIDORE:	I will also be in charge of all negotiations with the Ministry of Defence … And I promise you that I'll have them completely

outwitted in no time … *(He stands still)* Those are my demands … It's as simple as that! … Now, this Bruneau fellow … I don't know him … I don't want to know him … Get rid of him.

GRUGGH: What? … But poor Bruneau! …

ISIDORE: What is this? Charity or business? I assumed it was business. Am I wrong? … I thought not! Now, you stitched him up once and you don't need me to stitch him up again. He's all yours, the unlucky bastard! *(Roars with laughter)* I also want to make it clear that I expect the estimate you have presented to me to be serious and accurate … Is that clear? … If there are additional costs that transpire later, these will be deducted from *your* part of the profits … *(GRUGGH shows signs of impatience and PHINCK signals that he should stay calm)*

PHINCK: When you say our *part* of the profits, um …

ISIDORE: A simple fifty-fifty split between the two of us, obviously.

PHINCK: Ha ha, you mean between the *three* of us, of course?

ISIDORE: What do you mean, the *three* of us? How do you get that figure? *(To GRUGGH)* You … *(To PHINCK)* And you together … That makes one part … I am one part, you two are one part … Understand? Where on earth do you get this 'third part' business? And obviously I'll be in sole charge of the financial direction of the business with absolute discretion regarding who or what I judge to be beneficial to the development of the venture … You won't be allowed to contravene any of my final decisions … This, of course, won't affect your statutory rights … Mind you, they don't stand for much these days …

GRUGGH: I'm sorry, I don't think I understand …

ISIDORE: Oh, it'll all become clear in due course … Let me finish, please … As I'll be in charge of all the money … there's really no need for me to tell you who I decide to commission and subcontract to undertake the various construction and associated business aspects of the venture …

PHINCK: What do you mean commission and subcontract?

GRUGGH: There is no need to subcontract or commission anyone.

ISIDORE: Is that right, lads? But if there is no commissioning and subcontracting I'd be completely liable … That'd be a laugh … I can also tell you that it won't happen.

GRUGGH: You haven't said anything about how much we'll be earning in all this …

ISIDORE: Let's not trouble ourselves about that for now.

GRUGGH: But this will be a full-time job you know …

ISIDORE:	Let's not worry about that – we're not wretched *employees*, are we?
PHINCK:	Now look … look …
ISIDORE:	Not a word!
PHINCK:	I have secured exclusive rights, you know … What about those?
ISIDORE:	*(Stares at* PHINCK *ironically for a moment)* Your exclusive rights? … What exactly does that mean? … Oh, yes! … *(Slaps him on the shoulder)* I grant you exclusive rights to a seat on the next train to Paris … The next one's at half past six, I believe … It's an express train too; they're the best …
PHINCK:	We simply cannot accept these conditions …
GRUGGH:	You are skinning us alive! …
PHINCK:	Slitting our throats! …
GRUGGH:	It is absolutely unacceptable …
PHINCK:	It's monstrous! I respect the right of capital in any business venture … But capital is not everything, you know … Now what about exclusive rights … *(Fidgets around, looking for a document)* Exclusive rights stand for a lot, you know! …
ISIDORE:	*(Good naturedly)* Good for you! … Off you go with your exclusive rights, lads! … Nothing happened between us, after all … We merely talked … We merely talked business, that's all … And nothing came of it … It happens all the time … No hard feelings, eh? … *(Silence)* You know, the only person who's going to lose out in all this is Bruneau … *(He starts to pace and pace)* Bruneau … The poor fellow! … I find him quite an interesting chap actually … A fine fellow much wronged, if you ask me … Goodness gracious! I've just had a marvellous idea! Why don't I go and visit dear old Bruneau … I could do with a trip … I'll go and see him … and *interview* him … What do you think of that idea? … An interview with Mr Joseph Bruneau in *The Little Tricolour* … Isn't that a *smashing* idea? … Hmm? I really think it could be a most *moving* piece, don't you? … *Dramatic* too, probably? … *(He rubs his hands.* PHINCK *and* GRUGGH *look very troubled)* God, yes! … What a fantastic idea! … And then, the very next day, why don't I go to the Ministry of Defence? *(Emphatically)* It's like a second home to me … I can just wander in and make myself comfortable, any time I like … That's a great idea, it really is! … *(Rubbing his hands)* What do you think, lads? …

GRUGGH:	*(Crushed)* Maybe we could return to the proposal and give it some thought again …
ISIDORE:	Why bother? … You weren't at all happy with the terms I set down … So pass me by … Move on … As agreeable as your company is, you're not obliged to do anything more here … You're free to go! … *(A SERVANT enters)*
SERVANT:	Mr Xavier, sir …
ISIDORE:	Just a moment, I'll be right there! *(SERVANT exits. To PHINCK and GRUGGH)* Sorry, lads, you must excuse me … I must go and see my son … *(GRUGGH takes his hat. PHINCK puts his papers back in his case and closes it. They get ready to leave, looking flustered and confused)*
GRUGGH:	Well, er … we need to … think about it a little more …
ISIDORE:	Whatever you want …
PHINCK:	We need to look at our figures again … do some recalculations …
ISIDORE:	Good idea.
PHINCK:	We would also really like you to reconsider, perhaps–
ISIDORE:	Oh, come off it, lads … Don't ask me to do that … My thoughts on the matter should really not concern you … Besides, they are not negotiable …
PHINCK:	*(Head lowered)* Oh well …
ISIDORE:	I'll give you until six o'clock to make your mind up … Then, when you've had time to reflect, maybe we can get it all wrapped up, eh? …
PHINCK:	Huh! … It's a completely different proposal now …
ISIDORE:	If you accept it … Draw me up a little contract, will you? … It can be provisional and conditional, of course, but it should be unambiguous, understand? Draw it up in relation to what we've already discussed … But it must be unambiguous … Further down the line, when everything's underway, we will look at a few other supplementary conditions … nothing important, just things we haven't had time to discuss yet … *(PHINCK and GRUGGH are startled)* Nothing to worry about, I promise … Mere details, trivial really …
GRUGGH:	*(Deflated and sadly looking down at his feet)* Alright … We'll go and think about it some more …
PHINCK:	*(Grimly)* Of course … God help us …
GRUGGH:	*(Same tone)* That's what we want, after all … isn't it? …
PHINCK:	We'll find a way to agree … as difficult as it may seem …
ISIDORE:	*(He leads PHINCK and GRUGGH to the door with his arms over their shoulders, amicably)* Right then … get on with it … You *are* a funny pair of gentlemen, aren't you? … I am about to make

millionaires of you and you look like you're going to be executed at dawn! … Have a little backbone, for Christ's sake! … Come on … be happy! Smile! Smile! Off you go, lads … (PHINCK *and* GRUGGH *exit.* ISIDORE *calls from the door*) Don't forget the half past six train … (*Enter* XAVIER)

Scene Eleven

XAVIER *wears very stylish clothes for automobile driving. He is tall and thin and his face is already showing signs of aging. He has a rather cold manner.*

ISIDORE:	(*Exuberantly with his arms wide open*) Aha! Here he is at last … the boy racer! …
XAVIER:	Hello, dad. (*He casually raises a hand*)
ISIDORE:	Is that all I get!? Ashamed to give your dad a hug, are you? … Your poor, old man! …
XAVIER:	Fair enough. (*He embraces his father*)
ISIDORE:	Isn't it the done thing anymore? … Not good behaviour in your circles, I suppose? … Come on, look at me … Why the long face … What's worrying you?
XAVIER:	(*Vaguely*) Nothing …
ISIDORE:	The ladies, isn't it? … What have you been up to, eh!? … Come on, tell me! …
XAVIER:	Nothing like that, dad … Not for ages …
ISIDORE:	(*Sarcastically*) Right! … What is it, then? Money?
XAVIER:	You could say that …
ISIDORE:	Don't tell me. Gambling. Did you lose a lot?
XAVIER:	A fair amount …
ISIDORE:	In Ostend?
XAVIER:	Yes …
ISIDORE:	Tell me all about it … A glass of port?
XAVIER:	No thank you! You know that I only drink water …
ISIDORE:	You think I believe that!? … (*He sits down*) Well? …
XAVIER:	(*Sitting down*) Ten thousand louis.
ISIDORE:	I had heard as much … My God! (*He looks at* XAVIER *with a disconcerted air*) Your stories are always to the point, my lad, but they always seem to be expensive …
XAVIER:	Expensive? … What can I say? (*Silence*)
ISIDORE:	Ten thousand louis is quite a sum you know …
XAVIER:	Not for you, it isn't …

ISIDORE:	What have *I* got to do with it? … You are unbelievable! … Besides, no one has more than two hundred thousand francs in ready cash at the drop of a hat for Christ's sake!
XAVIER:	The deadline to pay is tomorrow …
ISIDORE:	Deadline … Tomorrow? … And no way out?
XAVIER:	It's got to be done … My honour rides on this …
ISIDORE:	Honour? … Honour? … Honour be damned! Honour can never exist where money is involved …
XAVIER:	Not in *my* social set …
ISIDORE:	His social set, he says! … Did he really say that? … The nerve … the cheeky little urchin! … Is there any chance of extending the deadline? …
XAVIER:	*(Very dry)* Impossible.
ISIDORE:	Impossible?
XAVIER:	Impossible.
ISIDORE:	Oh … *(Contemplative)* Alright … I can give you two hundred thousand francs … But only on the condition that you can pay me back …
XAVIER:	If I can.
ISIDORE:	You can and you will … Anyway, my head's swimming from the business I've been dealing with this morning … *(He stands up)* And I've got something else to deal with soon … With that nincompoop Porcellet … We're going to have a little chat after lunch …
XAVIER:	A nice pudding, eh?
ISIDORE:	*(Squeezes XAVIER's cheek)* Ha ha, you're a good lad! … Come and see my horses … *(He checks his watch)* We've got time …
XAVIER:	You know I've got to be back in Paris by six?
ISIDORE:	No problem … By the way, don't say anything to your mother, whatever you do …
XAVIER:	Why?
ISIDORE:	I'd only have a fortnight of crying, worrying, nagging …
XAVIER:	She still finds any excuse to drone on and on, does she?
ISIDORE:	If only you knew … *(They head, arm in arm to the door)*
XAVIER:	What about Tartelette Cabri? …
ISIDORE:	*(With conviction)* She's an angel … An absolutely adorable angel! … More and more each day …
XAVIER:	*(Laughing)* At your age, dad? You should be ashamed of yourself!
ISIDORE:	What do you mean? I'm not like you, son … I've got the heart of an eighteen year old, goddamn it! I need love … I need romance …

XAVIER:	*(Ironically)* And a little *idealism*, dad?
ISIDORE:	Yes, that's right! … The kind of thing that's impossible in business! … *(They roar with laugher and exit)*

Act 3

The same day, after lunch. ISIDORE LECHAT's *study.*

At the back, a monumental fireplace surrounded by wooden panelling which frames ancient portraits. On the walls, to the left and right, are splendid sixteenth-century tapestries illustrated with heroic themes. To the right, a door leads to the reception room while a smaller door leads to the private apartments. To the left, a very large glazed door opens onto the terrace from where the gardens and a huge expanse of blue sky can be seen.

In the middle of the room is an immense Louis XIV-period desk covered with papers and antiques. The room is sumptuously furnished with the characteristic LECHAT *mixture of antique and modern leather furniture.*

Scene One

As the curtain rises, isidore *is sat at his desk signing a cheque.* xavier, *with his back to the mantelpiece, smokes a cigar and flicks through a newspaper. Silence.*

ISIDORE:	*(Tearing out the cheque and handing it to* XAVIER*)* Here you go …
XAVIER:	*(Takes the cheque and looks at it)* Ta … *(He casually folds the cheque and puts it into his wallet)*
ISIDORE:	But listen to me, son … You really must get out of the habit of expecting these little lifelines … The fortune of Daddy Lechat is not limitless, you know.
XAVIER:	*(With a wry smile and a little nod of his head)* Right …
ISIDORE:	No … please … I'm not joking! *(A silence in which* ISIDORE *is deep in thought)* I was wondering … You still get on well with that Bragard, yes?
XAVIER:	Which one?
ISIDORE:	The son of the general …
XAVIER:	Henry? … *(Off hand)* Yeah … I'm meeting him tonight in Paris and then we're off to Ostend together …
ISIDORE:	What's he like?
XAVIER:	Oh God, I don't know … Just a friend … Very fashionable too …
ISIDORE:	Is he wealthy?
XAVIER:	Nobody's said he's rich …

ISIDORE:	But what about his family's standard of living?
XAVIER:	Their standard of living? … They seem comfortable enough … Fashionable too …
ISIDORE:	Do you think they're rich?
XAVIER:	I've no idea … It doesn't matter anyway …
ISIDORE:	Oh, I don't know about that … *(Pause)* I'm going to tell you something … I've heard that the Ministry of Defence is planning a complete overhaul of its administration … And General Bragard is going to be named as the new Head of the Military … It's in the bag!
XAVIER:	Really? Henry never told me that!
ISIDORE:	He probably doesn't even know … But I do …
XAVIER:	Crikey! Things are looking up for them!
ISIDORE:	Now, I'm involved in a business project that involves those two idiots you met at lunchtime …
XAVIER:	Nice blokes … But they didn't seem too happy somehow …
ISIDORE:	God knows! *(He gestures tightening a screw. XAVIER laughs)* I could really do with meeting General Bragard in person … You see, if my calculations are correct, we could be talking somewhere in the region of twenty million here … *(XAVIER listens as if a loud whistle has blown)* Yes, that's right, son …
XAVIER:	Blimey? You sure you've got that right?
ISIDORE:	Could be even more than that … It might be even double that amount if I play my cards right … *(XAVIER cannot hide his interest)* But it all depends if I can meet Bragard … I must meet him at all cost …
XAVIER:	What about Porcellet? He's Bragard's first cousin, you know. They're very close.
ISIDORE:	Listen … I need someone really close to him … As for Porcellet … *(Pause)* I'm not sure what I'm going to do with him yet … *(Pause)* Do you know if your pal Henry has any influence over his dad?
XAVIER:	No idea … I expect so … Every son has his dad wrapped around his little finger! …
ISIDORE:	*(Ironically)* Is that right?
XAVIER:	Oh, not you, of course … You always get your way in everything, dad …
ISIDORE:	*(Warmly paternal)* That's right … Feel free to mock now that you've got a cheque for two hundred thousand francs in your pocket! … You little rogue! … Anyway … what do you reckon about Henry?
XAVIER:	It's certainly worth a go …

ISIDORE:	Great … Bring him to see me tomorrow at the newspaper office … We'll have lunch, just the three of us … with plenty of time for a little chat …
XAVIER:	*(After a moment's thought)* That … might be a bit tricky …
ISIDORE:	What do you mean?
XAVIER:	Henry's a good bloke … he's very friendly and all that … but he's really clever … He's also very *formal* …
ISIDORE:	I can be as formal as you want …
XAVIER:	You see, I don't think he'd really like to be seen coming to see you with me …
ISIDORE:	Why ever not?
XAVIER:	Because … you are … a bit … disreputable …
ISIDORE:	What!? Disreputable? Me? What on earth are you talking about?
XAVIER:	I've heard people talk … I know what they say about you … Everywhere … I hear stories at the club, everyday … Stories about you …
ISIDORE:	*(With a beaming smile)* Stories? … About me and the ladies, you mean?
XAVIER:	Not exactly those kind of stories, dad … *(Vaguely)* You see, I think you're great … you know that … But other people think that you're–
ISIDORE:	Well they can get stuffed! Cretins, all of them!
XAVIER:	I think it might be better … You see, I'm very close to Henry's mistress … *(Significantly)* Very close …
ISIDORE:	Who is she?
XAVIER:	You don't know her … She's very sharp and very discreet … She's a bit mysterious … but she has enormous power over her boyfriend …
ISIDORE:	*(Attentively)* I see!
XAVIER:	She's Russian, but can be German or Italian whenever the situation demands … Do you see what I mean?
ISIDORE:	*(Thinks for a moment)* That's not my style … I love ladies, you know that … but outside of romance … I avoid them like the plague … No … no … no women when it comes to business …
XAVIER:	You're wrong … At the end of the day, that's all they're good for …
ISIDORE:	You mean she could be used like a spy?
XAVIER:	*(Cold and dry)* Well … if you want to put it like that … *(Silence)*
ISIDORE:	*(Looks at his son with admiration)* Bless your heart you cunning little fox! … *(Thinks for a moment)* No … No … I think I'll do this business all by myself …

XAVIER:	Don't you trust me?
ISIDORE:	Are you crazy? Of course I trust you! If I didn't trust you do you think I'd have asked you to help arrange the interview?

A SERVANT enters.

SERVANT:	The Marquis of Porcellet has asked if you are ready to see him, sir?
ISIDORE:	Two o'clock exactly! Our Marquis is very punctilious, isn't he? *(To SERVANT)* Ask Mr Porcellet to wait a few moments will you? … *(To XAVIER)* Do you want to meet him?
XAVIER:	No way … *(ISIDORE indicates to the SERVANT who exits)*
ISIDORE:	I'm not bothered if he has to wait a moment anyway … It's only fair as he is not a second late …
XAVIER:	Timeliness is the last refuge of the bankrupt …
ISIDORE:	Ha ha! You're a good lad! *(He stands up)* Anyway, do you understand … Bring him to see me tomorrow … One o'clock?
XAVIER:	I'll do my best …
ISIDORE:	No, it's not a case of 'doing your best' … You *must* …
XAVIER:	*(Silent and then coldly cynical)* How much are you going to give me for this?
ISIDORE:	Now look …
XAVIER:	Come on! If you're going to double your fortune, you can double your generosity towards me … Business is business, after all, eh?
ISIDORE:	Oh, be reasonable now. Just think of all the grief you've given me … Can't I ask you to do anything!?
XAVIER:	Alright, alright … See you tomorrow …
ISIDORE:	Wonderful – don't be late! … Come on, give me a hug … *(They embrace)* How's the automobile, by the way? … Still happy with her?
XAVIER:	She's a beauty!
ISIDORE:	Take care, lad … Don't drive her too fast, eh?
XAVIER:	With a maximum speed of fifty-five per hour? Yeah, right …
ISIDORE:	Even that's too fast … Oh, I don't like those *mechanical* things … Remember to kiss your mother and sister before you go …
XAVIER:	And if I see that 'absolutely adorable angel' in Paris tonight … Can I give her a kiss, too?
ISIDORE:	Off you go, you cheeky rogue! Show your old man a little respect … And whatever you do, make sure you don't tell anyone, least of all her, about the two hundred thousand francs …
XAVIER:	*(Laughing)* Oh, dad!

ISIDORE:	See you tomorrow, my boy …
XAVIER:	See you …

XAVIER exits. ISIDORE walks around the room for a while, deep in thought. He goes back to the desk and opens a dossier. After a moment he sounds a bell and the SERVANT brings the MARQUIS OF PORCELLET into the room.

Scene Two

ISIDORE:	*(Going up to the MARQUIS)* My dear Marquis … It really is a great honour …
MARQUIS:	*(Very elegant with a distinguished air)* Dear Mr Lechat … *(They shake hands)*
ISIDORE:	You must excuse me for keeping you waiting …
MARQUIS:	Think nothing of it! …
ISIDORE:	*(Pulling forward a chair)* Please … I insist … Sit yourself down …
MARQUIS:	Thank you …
ISIDORE:	A cigar? … *(The MARQUIS declines with a gesture of his hand)* A glass of port, maybe? …
MARQUIS:	No, thank you! … A little early for me …
ISIDORE:	*(Sitting at the desk)* My dear Marquis … It is so long since I've had the honour of your visit … We're neighbours, after all … And we're always on the best of terms … I find it really quite curious that we don't see each other more often … It must be three years now, pretty much …
MARQUIS:	Good heavens, you know how it is! … A thousand little obstacles … The thousand petty distractions of everyday life … I never get a moment to myself …
ISIDORE:	Tell me about it!
MARQUIS:	And lately I've been rather preoccupied by my son … He's back home from his travels …
ISIDORE:	You should've brought him along with you … He would've been most welcome … I've always wanted to meet a genuine explorer, a flesh and blood adventurer! … And a heroic companion to the Prince of Orleans, I understand …
MARQUIS:	He's visiting my Aunt Sombreuse in the south-west this weekend unfortunately …
ISIDORE:	Ah … *(Pause)* Did he enjoy his voyage? … Not too exhausting, I hope … and no hideous tropical diseases either, eh?

MARQUIS:	Oh, not at all … He came back singing the praises of Tonkin … He said it is the most marvellous place for hunting wild game …
ISIDORE:	Is that so?
MARQUIS:	Yes … And believe it or not, he said that hunting peacocks of all things is particularly entertaining …
ISIDORE:	Ha ha, fancy that!
MARQUIS:	Surprisingly dangerous, apparently, but extremely entertaining …
ISIDORE:	They're ferocious out there, are they? Peacocks?
MARQUIS:	Peacocks aren't dangerous, obviously. But, you see, you can only find peacocks in parts of the forest that are particularly popular with tigers … In Tonkin, there are deer and where you find deer there are tigers, and where you find tigers there are peacocks …
ISIDORE:	Quite bizarre …
MARQUIS:	Isn't it just? … Robert tells me that there's nothing quite as magnificent as killing a peacock …
ISIDORE:	I can well believe it … Oh! Isn't travel marvellous? … There's nothing like travel to broaden the mind and shape a young man's spirit …
MARQUIS:	And it's good way to fill a young man's time, too … The wilds of Indochina are usually less dangerous than the boudoirs of Paris …
ISIDORE:	You're right there … In a Parisian boudoir there are women and where you find women there are–
MARQUIS:	Dead ducks! *(They laugh)*
ISIDORE:	Or jack rabbits … *(They laugh again)* I'd rather be a jack rabbit than a dead duck, wouldn't you, Marquis!? *(Both men now seem to be comfortable and at ease with each other)*
MARQUIS:	Well, my dear Mr Lechat … it really is a pleasure to see you … *(Pause)* I mean that, it really is a *pleasure* … *(Pause)* Besides the pleasure this visit gives me–
ISIDORE:	*Us,* my dear Marquis, *us.* The feeling's mutual …
MARQUIS:	*(Making a gestures of thanks)* I would like to discuss something with you … a fairly urgent matter …
ISIDORE:	At your service, my dear Marquis …
MARQUIS:	Well, it's this … *(He takes his gloves off)* The financial settlement regarding the liquidation of Gasselin … and the sale of the Melun woods …
ISIDORE:	I know … I know …
MARQUIS:	Hold on … The lawyers have written to me saying that I probably shouldn't expect to see much money …
ISIDORE:	None at all, Marquis.

MARQUIS:	Oh? So that's your opinion too?
ISIDORE:	Yes.
MARQUIS:	That's just what I feared … *(Pause)* This means a huge financial loss for me … It really is rather grim news for me, if truth be told. I have a number of pressing bills that need paying, and yet I do not have ready money … Yes … I am rather indisposed by this … And very, very annoyed … Therefore, I have come to see you again to ask for a loan of two hundred thousand francs …
ISIDORE:	*(Very calmly)* I understand, my dear Marquis, I think I understand …
MARQUIS:	You have no idea how much this would help me, my dear Mr Lechat …
ISIDORE:	Look … I happen to have … Where is it? … Here it is … Your file … *(With a broad smile)* Let's have a little look, shall we? … *(He flicks through the file)* Four loans of two hundred thousand francs … One of four hundred thousand … One million two hundred thousand … The five percent interest remains unpaid … for two years … one million three hundred and … twenty thousand francs … Is that right?
MARQUIS:	Precisely.
ISIDORE:	Yes … Yes … *(He raises his head up and seems to be doing mental calculations)* Well … I'm sorry to say, Marquis, but this time I refuse. It is quite impossible.
MARQUIS:	You … refuse?
ISIDORE:	Sorry. Impossible.
MARQUIS:	But I can give you every possible guarantee …
ISIDORE:	*(Grimaces)* Promises, promises, as usual …
MARQUIS:	I'm sorry? What more can I do than that? … What do you want? …
ISIDORE:	If truth be known, your endless promises are not the only problem that afflicts your property …
MARQUIS:	I beg your pardon? …
ISIDORE:	Your property is in very poor condition … Your land is seriously neglected … Your farms are in ruins … You've allowed your woodlands to be laid waste … It would take a million to sort that mess out …
MARQUIS:	*(Animated)* What? What do you mean? What are you proposing?
ISIDORE:	Oh, for God's sake! *(Silence)*
MARQUIS:	I have other guarantees, you know … I have my honour …
ISIDORE:	Of course, and I respect it completely … Trouble is, when it comes to business, honour is completely irrelevant …

MARQUIS:	There's also my inheritance … My Aunt Sombreuse …
ISIDORE:	Huh!
MARQUIS:	*(Urgently)* She is eighty-three you know! …
ISIDORE:	*(Ironically)* Oh, I know … Inheritances … that ship will come in one fine day …
MARQUIS:	*(Overwhelmed but with dignity)* Very well, sir … *(Stands up)* There's nothing else to be done … Allow me to excuse myself …
ISIDORE:	My dear Marquis … let's not be hasty … Please do me the honour of staying a little longer …
MARQUIS:	But …
ISIDORE:	Please, I insist … *(The MARQUIS sits down. A short silence)* My dear Marquis … You are a man who I admire and respect … I also consider you to be a true friend … All I want to do is save you from what is rapidly becoming a truly disastrous situation …
MARQUIS:	Disastrous? Oh, that's quite preposterous! …
ISIDORE:	Admit it … We're talking about ruin … bankruptcy …
MARQUIS:	*(Feigning confidence)* Tosh! Utter tosh! … Besides, we've all been on the brink of so-called ruin, haven't we, Mr Lechat …
ISIDORE:	Don't lie to me, my dear Marquis … You know as well as I the seriousness of your situation … Or maybe I understand it better than you …
MARQUIS:	Very well, I admit that my situation may not be particularly buoyant right now … But it is not, by any stretch of the imagination, 'truly disastrous'.
ISIDORE:	I'm sorry, Marquis, but it is. It really is. *(Lightly ironic)* Can I tell you something? I have a little confession to make … My secret desire is to unite Vauperdu with the Porcellet estate … *(Speaking over the MARQUIS)* Hear me out, hear me out! … In all honesty, it'd be a dream come true … Just think what a property that would be! *(Short silence)* This little dream of mine … *(He points at the documents open on the table)* Could come true tomorrow … *(viciously) If I want it to. (Convivial once again)* But as I said, I regard you as a true friend … and I am sure we are able to come to some agreement that suits both of us before we find ourselves in a situation that is humiliating for you and distressing for me … We're both respectable, civilized gentlemen, aren't we? There must be some happy medium, hmm? … Some common ground?
MARQUIS:	*(Wisely cautious)* God … I hope so … That's what I want …
ISIDORE:	The ball's entirely in your court …
MARQUIS:	What are you proposing?
ISIDORE:	A mutually advantageous affiliation, my dear Marquis …

MARQUIS:	Carry on …
ISIDORE:	You see … You're a man of principles … high principles … You don't belong very comfortably in the modern world … You're attached to old ideals of an age that's long passed … and … forgive me for saying this … you have all sorts of prejudices which have no place in the modern world … I love the idea of chivalry as much as anyone, but such gallant ideals are simply not practical in this day and age … It's a shame, but we have to face facts …
MARQUIS:	*(With affected dignity)* To remain constant and truthful in a world that is rapidly changing beyond all recognition is not simply the prerogative of the noble class but its overarching glory …
ISIDORE:	Its terminal doom, more like!
MARQUIS:	You are utterly mistaken! In *my* world, Mr Lechat, *honour* is more important than interest rates …
ISIDORE:	Honour, again? … *(To himself pensively)* Honour be damned …
MARQUIS:	I'm sorry?
ISIDORE:	Nothing … I was just thinking of my son … A little coincidence, that's all …
MARQUIS:	*(A little less affected)* Obviously, in politics and even more so in religion I do have certain resolute principles … Principles which I would never, ever transgress … But you mustn't think that I condemn all forms of progress because of that … You may find this hard to believe, but I have an open mind when it comes to certain social necessities … Of course I do … But I will not approve of things that compromise the ideals that I have always lived my life by …
ISIDORE:	The problem is, life is full of compromises …
MARQUIS:	Absolutely not! But, please, tell me about the 'affiliation' you're proposing …
ISIDORE:	*(After a short silence)* I'm sorry, Marquis, I have to say you have made me feel a little discouraged … It's all your grand statements … Honour … Honour, indeed! Of course there is such a thing as honour, but each man interprets it differently … And I am afraid the two of us beg to differ when it comes to an understanding of honour … No, I'm sorry … The affiliation I was proposing must be abandoned …
MARQUIS:	Tell me what it was, all the same …
ISIDORE:	What's the point?
MARQUIS:	Is it really that terrible to tell me what the proposal was going to be? …

ISIDORE:	Sorry, business is business.
MARQUIS:	We are just having a conversation, that's all … It doesn't mean anything …
ISIDORE:	Very well, Marquis, if you insist … *(Pause)* I'm no diplomat … I don't know how to beat around the bush … I am not a man capable of reticence and circumlocution … I call a spade a spade … I always put my cards on the table … Let's put it bluntly … You have a son and he is bankrupt … I have a daughter who is exceedingly wealthy … In fact, you could say she is filthy rich … *(Pause)* Let's make them marry each other …
MARQUIS:	*(Standing up)* I beg your pardon?
ISIDORE:	Let's make them marry each other … And I know how these things work … I know all the usual deals, the dowry and all that stuff … I will cancel your debts of one million three hundred and twenty thousand francs … and you will retain all your property – intact, mind – at Porcellet … *(Pause)* Come on, sit down, my dear Marquis. *(The MARQUIS sits)* You can see that Isidore Lechat – that scoundrel Lechat, as some call me – knows how to be a true gentleman …
MARQUIS:	*(To himself)* Impossible … *(Pause)* You must be dreaming!
ISIDORE:	I beg your pardon, but, yes, I *am* dreaming … I am also 'dreaming' of looking after my daughter's allowance of two hundred and fifty thousand francs … I'm good with money, you see … It's better off in my hands than in hers … Money understands me and I understand money … We're the best of pals … *(He laughs)*
MARQUIS:	So … You're holding me to ransom …
ISIDORE:	Let's just call it business …
MARQUIS:	You want to hold me to ransom; you want to buy me up and take me over!
ISIDORE:	Oh dear, here come all those big words again … No, my dear Marquis, I merely want to help you … I want to save you from inevitable disaster … You'll be old man when you're forced out of your beautiful estate of Porcellet … The lavish lifestyle to which you have become accustomed will be reduced to nothing … You'll be crippled with debt … hunted down by lawyers and bailiffs … You'll see your belongings auctioned off, you'll be dragged from court to court, your once proud coat of arms seized and wrapped up in legal documents … You'll be desperate after all your misery to find some humble position, perhaps becoming the intendant of an estate like the Viscount of Fontanelle is to me … I know what I'm talking about … Don't forget I've been bankrupted

twice … It's no laughing matter … The difference is, I am a man of *resilience* … You, however, are a man of *principles* … And, believe me, principles aren't much use when you're faced with abject misery …

MARQUIS: Buying me up! Buying *me* up!

ISIDORE: Oh, do stop repeating yourself … I am *not* buying you up … This is a deal, an *exchange*, if you like … Business is all about exchange and trade … Trading money, land, property, titles, electoral mandate, knowledge, power and authority, social situation, love … Getting what one person wants in exchange for what the other person needs … Nothing is more legitimate than this and, believe me, nothing is more *honourable* …

MARQUIS: *(Calming a little)* But … my son doesn't want to get married …

ISIDORE: Of course … We all know that … People often don't want to do things … but they realize that they have to do them all the same … Desperate situations call for desperate measures … The twists and turns of life often demand radical actions … Oh, my dear Marquis, if you'd only let me guide you, how marvellous that would be … What superb business we could do … What a team we'd be! Oh, just think, damn it! The Porcellet Mansion, that beautiful stately home that your brother sold off to Prince Kartdoff, is coming up for sale in a few months …

MARQUIS: Really?

ISIDORE: You didn't know?

MARQUIS: Not at all …

ISIDORE: *(With a warm smile)* You see, you should just let me worry about that while you deal with family affairs … I will buy the Porcellet Mansion … all the furniture, art works, the lot … And I will include that as part of my daughter's dowry … A gift fit to set before a king! Where would the marriage put us? We'll be united in bloodline … we'll have common interests … Together we could conquer the world … It's all so simple … *(Silence. The MARQUIS is lost in thought)* You see, in this business we're undertaking, you will be giving as much as I am giving … Everything is matched, fair and equal … In fact, though, if we include all the money that you're contributing – the money that will be coming to you, that is – your contribution is possibly greater than mine … You see, a simple bit of arithmetic and all your problems are solved … *(The MARQUIS lowers his head)* So … if anyone is being 'bought up' in this business deal … it is not you, it's me … *(The MARQUIS stares at ISIDORE with a look of astonishment)* Yes, yes, I mean it, it's

	obvious … Besides, you'll soon have a major boost to your reputation and influence … That exceptional soldier, your first cousin General Bragard, is about to be appointed Head of the Military … Trust me …
MARQUIS:	Do you know everything?
ISIDORE:	*(Modestly)* Just doing my job, my dear Marquis … I'll need the general's full support in a major business project – we're talking something huge here – which depends, a little, on him … It's a project that I'd like to involve you in as well … *(Mysteriously)* We're talking something to do with national defence here, and I am sure the general will give his wholehearted approval … after all, you know only too well what a fine, upstanding patriot I am, don't you? *(Becoming heated)* You are too, damn it! I will tell you all about it sometime … *(Pause)* There's something else …
MARQUIS:	What?
ISIDORE:	You do have some electoral influence … Not very much, granted, but you do have some all the same … And there is no question but I will naturally expect you to use that influence in support of my candidacy … *(The MARQUIS moves abruptly)* Listen, listen … I won't be asking you to distribute pamphlets or go to the hustings shouting, 'vote for Lechat!' No! Heaven forbid! … No, what I want is something more clandestine … I'll tell you what I mean … I've got the support of the revolutionary committee of Paris – an organization that's secretly supported by the government anyway – and just a mere fraction of the Royalist-Bonapartist-Nationalist-Clerical Party … my success is guaranteed.
MARQUIS:	I see … It is not just my good name that you seek to buy but my personal reputation and my political influence … What else?
ISIDORE:	You disappoint me, Marquis, you really do … You treat everything I say as though it is something callous and brutal … Nothing could be further from the truth … You're making it difficult – impossible, in fact – to get the agreement I'm seeking … Very well, I'll stop trying and – believe me – there are no hard feelings on my part … *(Emphatically)* Besides, whatever you decide I'll still get the estate of Porcellet anyway. *(Silence)*
MARQUIS:	But, Mr Lechat, if I am correctly informed, you will be standing for election on a socialist and anticlerical ticket in direct opposition to the Duke of Maugis, who is an old friend of mine and whose ideas have my complete support …
ISIDORE:	We're just talking a political platform here! *(He gestures rejection of something distant)* It's not a pressing issue now!

MARQUIS:	That maybe so … but isn't it likely that by taking an anticlerical stance you will make the Church an implacable enemy?
ISIDORE:	Implacable? You never cease to amaze me, Marquis … Ideals may be implacable, but business never is … Besides … *(He leaps up and walks around animatedly)* do you think that I, as a socialist and anticlerical candidate, will really be less appealing to the Church than your pal the Duke of Maugis with all his belief in miracles and his constant thanks to the Virgin Mary and the host of saints?
MARQUIS:	*(Ironically)* This a new way of looking at things, I must say.
ISIDORE:	Do you know what the Duke of Maugis stands for? I'll tell you. He stands for the past … He's old and dusty … Inert material … Dead on his feet … And what about the Church? The Church drags around behind it the tarnished grandeur of old privileges … It has become paralysed through hierarchy and prejudice and the routines of honour … It has nothing to do with those who created it … A stupid aristocracy has let the Church lose its land and its property and its influence and action … And every day churches become more and more deserted, emptied out by its unpopularity and its impotence …
MARQUIS:	*(Chuckling discretely)* Ha, ha, ha! …
ISIDORE:	No, I'm serious, my dear Marquis … I'm telling it how it is! This is the modern world and far from resisting the forces of change the Church moves with them … And the Church helps to change the world! … The Church expands, transforms, adapts – absolutely admirable – all of it! The Church is still a dominant force and it deserves to be: it works tirelessly … it mobilizes people … ideas … money … it opens up land for development … The Church is everywhere … it has the potential to do anything … it has the potential to *be* everything … It's no longer just an altar where you can buy faith … where you can buy miracles and superstition in bottles … It's no longer a place to offload your confessions and gobble up forgiveness … The Church now has shops where it sells its merchandize … It has filled banks with gold! As well as shops it owns factories … newspapers … *governments*! But until now the Church has been filled with too many feeble, powerless men! And I know how to give it the respect it deserves …
MARQUIS:	*(Ironically)* How admirable! I never knew you could speak with such eloquence …
ISIDORE:	It is so clear to me! In the past, the Church used to arm its nobles with swords and send them into battle in its name – massacring

themselves and others. But warfare is different nowadays. And so are the weapons. The modern weapons of war are money and industry ... And what does the aristocracy know about industry? Nothing. What does the aristocracy know about money? Nothing. So ... people like me have taken over ... You see? The old order is disappearing ...

MARQUIS: In mud and blood.

ISIDORE: That can be cleaned off ... It all can be cleaned ... And all your emblems and symbols and regalia ... *(Pause)* Can't you understand that it is in people like me that the Church finds its natural ally? My dear Marquis, the Church and I are one of the same breed ... The aristocracy is dead. It's dead. And it's dead because it has failed to understand the fundamental law of nature: labour. In other words, the forces of exploitation that exist in every aspect of life ... And it is not because the Church occasionally gives you some meagre, token presence in an administrative meeting because of some charitable donation you have given, an embarrassing token like the State dishes out a pinch of snuff to the widows of men who worked themselves to death ... Don't think that that will offer you salvation!

MARQUIS: That's all well and good, Mr Lechat, but if, as you have so decorously described it, I am dead and obsolete ... what on earth are you doing wasting time with me for?

ISIDORE: That's my business ...

MARQUIS: I am not interested ...

ISIDORE: On your own head be it ... But let me tell you, you are making a serious mistake ...

MARQUIS: You're not expecting me to cleanse the Church of these bizarre, slanderous allegations you have made, which have absolutely no basis in fact ... are you?

ISIDORE: These are not allegations and slanders! I am singing its praises! *(Shrugs his shoulders)* You have absolutely no idea what the Church really is!

MARQUIS: Sorry to disappoint you – I do know what the Church is ... And the picture you have drawn of the Church is unrecognizable, and I am only too happy to disregard it. You see, sir, I am proud to be a member of the aristocracy you so evidently despise and the demise of which you have so arrogantly proclaimed! I am proud, and I will loyally await the aristocracy's triumphant return!

ISIDORE: Yes ... the aristocracy is plotting its return by reviving a civil war and a race war!

MARQUIS:	I am endeavouring to defend the traditions of this nation … And I'm proud to do so!
ISIDORE:	*(Interrupting)* Oh, come on!
MARQUIS:	Heaven defend all of us from the abominable democracy that you stand for! Completely insolent! Brutal! Replacing the traditions of honour, faith and charity in the name of one thing and one thing only: *money*!
ISIDORE:	Now, now, my dear Marquis … calm down, calm down …
MARQUIS:	Your desire is to wield power over everyone. You and your kind want to be the new rulers of the world. And so you will be! For a while … but men who have such an absurd lust for power like you are never blessed with a happy fate … men who've ruthlessly struck a quick fortune like you … Deep down all you have is one dream: you want to imitate *us*. Our houses, our estates, our manners, our vices – that's what you want for yourself … Our ancient, glorious family names … Everything, right down to our chattels and furniture … *(Arrogantly)* But while you can buy all these things, you will never learn how to make use of them …
ISIDORE:	Sorry to disappoint you, but I already 'make use of them' in my own way.
MARQUIS:	You don't have very high standards, I must say!
ISIDORE:	Quite high enough as far as I am concerned.
MARQUIS:	They will never be high enough for all the people you have stripped bare and exploited!
ISIDORE:	Huh! You know nothing! And you don't know me … Right now, the people of France prefer my standards to yours.
MARQUIS:	If you really do want to conquer the world as you say you do, do have the courage to invent something new rather than this ludicrous parody of the past … Create your own traditions, for God's sake! But, no, you haven't the slightest iota of virtue, art or elegance … You haven't the slightest quality of grandeur! …
ISIDORE:	*(Interrupting)* Grandeur! *Grandeur*! Words like that don't mean a thing! There's only one thing that makes a nation or an institution or an individual great … *money*. The Church understands that better than anyone. *(Pause)* Yes … yes … to someone like you we're a bunch of bandits … brigands … terrifying buccaneers … I know that's what you think … and, deep down, it's absolutely true. We *are* bandits, but listen, we are bandits who have achieved something magnificent … buccaneers who have made a great contribution to the force of progress … In other words, a contribution to the good of humanity … filthy scoundrels who

Les Affaires sont les affaires: Madame Lechat by Gus Bofa © Marie Hélène Grosos-ADAGP.

Les Affaires sont les affaires: Le Jardinier by Gus Bofa © Marie Hélène Grosos-ADAGP.

Les Affaires sont les affaires: Isidore Lechat by Gus Bofa © Marie Hélène Grosos-ADAGP.

Les Affaires sont les affaires: Le Vicomte de la Fontanelle by Gus Bofa © Marie Hélène Grosos-ADAGP.

Les Affaires sont les affaires: Phinck et Gruggh by Gus Bofa © Marie Hélène Grosos-ADAGP.

Les Affaires sont les affaires: Lucien Garraud et Germaine by Gus Bofa © Marie Hélène Grosos-ADAGP.

Les Affaires sont les affaires: Le Marquis de Porcellet by Gus Bofa © Marie Hélène Grosos-ADAGP.

Le Foyer. Baronne Courtin by Gus Bofa © Marie Hélène Grosos-ADAGP.

Le Foyer. Le Baron Courtin by Gus Bofa © Marie Hélène Grosos-ADAGP.

Le Foyer. Mlle Rambert – Mme Pigeon by Gus Bofa © Marie Hélène Grosos-ADAGP.

Le Foyer. Robert D'Auberval by Gus Bofa © Marie Hélène Grosos-ADAGP.

Le Foyer. Abbé Laroze by Gus Bofa © Marie Hélène Grosos-ADAGP.

Le Foyer. Armand Biron by Gus Bofa © Marie Hélène Grosos-ADAGP.

Le Foyer. Les petites by Gus Bofa © Marie Hélène Grosos-ADAGP.

have filled their coffers with gold, yes, but who have also had an impact on everything … generated wealth everywhere … changed people's lives everywhere … Whereas in your day of glory, when you proclaimed the glories of your traditions, you robbed the people … you left them starving … What did you give them for nourishment? Rivers of filth in the towns and a little scrap of land to huddle on in the country … What did you give in exchange? You abused them and beat them, my dear Marquis … But look at me. I've given them roads … railways … electric light … hygiene … schools … And cheaply. All of it. A little less dramatic than a good hiding with a club, I admit … But all the same, not a bad deal from a bunch of brigands, eh?

MARQUIS: Mr Lechat, I cannot and will not deign to listen to these journalistic diatribes …

ISIDORE: Quite right! So you shouldn't! Enough philosophy for one day, I think … Besides, philosophical argument leads nowhere … And it nearly made us lose the thread of our conversation … Tell me, Marquis … Are you a gambling man?

MARQUIS: Not when I am bound to lose.

ISIDORE: That's true, yes, that's true! I am bound to win … Now … this little wager I have in mind … Let me put it another way … Suppose you go and ask one of those great politicians dressed in black robes … or white robes … or brown robes … or scarlet robes … The colour really doesn't matter! Those overdressed 'important people' who claim to lead the world and in whom you have such touching confidence. Suppose you went and asked any one of your 'confessors' and see if he hesitates for a second when given the choice of supporting Isidore Lechat – filthy rich to the tune of fifty million, a wicked socialist, anticlerical and excommunicated – or you, the poor, frail Duke of Maugis. *(Silence. ISIDORE stares the MARQUIS squarely in the eyes)* Yes … Suppose you asked for advice on what I have proposed to you – marriage and all that – and I dare you to tell me, in your heart and in your conscience, that he wouldn't answer you clearly and give his blessing: 'My son, my son … You must agree … You must go forth in the name of progress and in the name of St Mary!' *(Silence. The two men stare at each other)*

MARQUIS: *(Lowers his head, his tone less assured)* But it's impossible … *(Silence)*

ISIDORE: Ah! … *(Pause)* My dear Marquis … when you came here today … I had only one simple desire … to squeeze the life out of you with my bare hands … I'm being entirely frank now … you know that … I have told you quite plainly … I've rejoiced at the thought of taking Porcellet off your hands … For two years I've thought of it as mine … Yes, it's true … and in that drawer I have a map … Do you want to see it? It shows Porcellet as part of my own estate … Your name is scratched out and mine is emblazoned in its place … Funny, huh? … But … I don't know why … but somehow you've touched me … you've moved me … I mean it … Deep down … I am a kind man … People don't realize … but I *do* have a heart … And so … I was happy to find another solution … A middle way to keep everyone happy … A proposal which could satisfy my business interests, my own pleasure and would safeguard your own interests … *(The* MARQUIS *gives an ironic gesture)* Yes, yes … it's true … I came up with this idea … And it's really not such a bad idea … My daughter is a very attractive young woman … she has a certain charm … she's of good stock … she's not too ugly, the minx! … I defy you to try and find anyone equal to her … Try to find anyone as suitable as her to live in the Porcellet Mansion … She's a genuine princess, my dear Marquis!

MARQUIS: I would never question your daughter's qualities …

ISIDORE: Well? … Don't force me to reconsider my first plan again … Come on, talk to me! … Don't upset me now! *(Expansively)* I'm having a good day today … better make the most of it! …

MARQUIS: *(His voice less and less assured)* It's impossible … It's very, very difficult …

ISIDORE: Oh, come off it! You'll not be the first to agree to a union like this!

MARQUIS: That much is true …

ISIDORE: Well?

MARQUIS: My dear Mr Lechat, I don't want to seem ungrateful … But … there is … at the end of the day … a rather *personal* matter–

ISIDORE: *(Stares at the* MARQUIS *suspiciously)* Oh?

MARQUIS: Yes … You have been … in your time … accused of entertaining … some very controversial ideas … I am not a man to judge, but at the end of the day …

ISIDORE: That's how I've got where I am! Huh – if you to trace back every fortune to it's source … your own included, my dear Marquis … it's never a spotless affair. What really concerns you, what's really worrying you … is opinion … Public opinion, especially amongst your own social set …

MARQUIS: I do not subject my beliefs to public opinion …

ISIDORE:	Of course you haven't … But you're sensitive to it … Naturally so … Well, tell yourself this … Opinion only matters when it is expressed by those with money … No matter how noble and heroic a man may be, if he hasn't got a penny to his name, he's only fit to throw to the dogs … That's not my 'opinion', my dear Marquis … It's the wisdom of the world … Not fair, eh? Just look all around you.
MARQUIS:	(*Slowly and awkwardly*) I want to be sure … that the measures proposed to my cousin Bragard … will be … completely uncontroversial …
ISIDORE:	Yes … completely uncontroversial … all quite simple …
MARQUIS:	As for my backing in the elections …
ISIDORE:	Don't worry, my dear Marquis … Don't trouble yourself … It's a question of judgement …
MARQUIS:	Yes … quite so … but, my dear Mr Lechat … aside from politics … there is a question of *decorum* …
ISIDORE:	Political questions are the only questions that matter … You're covered by the Church …
MARQUIS:	Covered? … Covered? …
ISIDORE:	No doubt about it … In all honesty, you know it yourself … Don't fool yourself … A question of decorum, eh? Christ Almighty! … Obviously you'd like to see the father of your future daughter-in-law win a resounding victory … (*He laughs with a tone of bonhomie*) That's all quite proper … We're talking *family*, after all …
MARQUIS:	I have not discussed your proposal with my son.
ISIDORE:	Do you think I've spoken to my daughter? Children are put on this world to obey their fathers … And anyway, Marquis, did you consult with your son when, while he was away in Tonkin, you had to 'negotiate' something on his behalf? … Yes, I know the whole story … A rather 'shocking' marriage, shall we say? … Ha … ha …
MARQUIS:	Gossip … Slander …
ISIDORE:	That's still a possibility, granted … But in my experience screaming 'slander' very rarely gets anywhere … Besides, I know a little chap with a passion for hunting peacocks who would not make things as difficult as you have and who … believe me … would not be at all impressed with the idea of being ruined in the vain attempt to preserve the manner of life to which he has become accustomed, rather than a guaranteed life of peace and comfort … As for me, my dear Marquis … I won't bother you

much … I won't embarrass you by turning up on your doorstep … And I won't even ask you to get me membership at the Jockey Club … *(He laughs and rubs his hands)* Good God, no! I have other aspirations …

MARQUIS: *(With effort)* Very well … I'll go … and think about what we've discussed …

ISIDORE: No. I cannot let you leave here without everything written in stone. You have the opportunity to be like a widower … free in your actions … You need never look back … Just think of it! … There could be nothing better …

MARQUIS: But this is an extremely serious matter which mustn't–

ISIDORE: *(Interrupting abruptly in a harsh voice)* As we've agreed, you will keep possession of Porcellet … In addition I will give you two hundred thousand francs and pay off the debts you owe to other creditors … *(A short silence. The MARQUIS has stood up with his head lowered, and he stares at the pattern in the carpet)* My dear Marquis … *(The MARQUIS raises his eyes towards ISIDORE just as the latter prepares to ring the bell)* May I call in my wife and daughter now?

MARQUIS: *(With great effort)* Yes … Do so … *(He sits down heavily in a chair. ISIDORE rings and a Maidservant enters)*

ISIDORE: Go and inform my wife and daughter that the Marquis of Porcellet and I wish to speak to them. *(The Maidservant exits. The MARQUIS remains seated, his gaze rigid. ISIDORE strides around the room his hands in his pockets. Long silence)*

Scene Three

Enter MRS LECHAT. She looks troubled and stares anxiously at the MARQUIS and ISIDORE. GERMAINE enters after her. As soon as she enters, GERMAINE realizes that she has stumbled into a scene where something extraordinary has happened. When the women enter, the MARQUIS stands and salutes in silence. At this, MRS LECHAT's anxiety increases. ISIDORE goes over to his desk with a chilling expression of triumph on his face.

ISIDORE: Sit down, my darlings … His grace the Marquis of Porcellet has something to tell you … *(The women sit down. ISIDORE folds up the MARQUIS's file)* Marquis …

MARQUIS: *(With effort and a quiet voice)* Madam … on behalf of my son, Robert, Count of Porcellet, may I have the honour of asking for the hand of your daughter, Miss Germaine Lechat, in marriage? (*GERMAINE turns and stares fixedly at the MARQUIS*)

MRS LECHAT: (*Astonished and stuttering*) I ... er ... (*She cannot speak. She raises her hands and looks at ISIDORE, looks at the MARQUIS and looks at GERMAINE*) Really?

ISIDORE: Yes, of course! What's wrong with you? (*GERMAINE turns to look at her father with derision*) The Marquis has asked for Germaine's hand in marriage ... Are you deaf or something?

MRS LECHAT: Yes ... yes, I heard ... I am just a little startled ...

ISIDORE: A mother's joy, Marquis! Come on ... for Christ's sake pull yourself together, woman! (*To GERMAINE*) Come on, Germaine, you say something ...

GERMAINE: (*Standing*) I'm really flattered, sir ... I know what I am expected to say ... But I'm afraid I must refuse ...

MARQUIS: (*Standing*) You refuse?

GERMAINE: Yes, sir ...

ISIDORE: You're saying no?

GERMAINE: Yes.

ISIDORE: (*All that is vile and vulgar in ISIDORE's personality appear in his expression*) Listen ... Listen to me ... You cannot say no ... The Marquis has asked that you give your hand in marriage to his son ...

GERMAINE: And I say no ... (*To the MARQUIS*) And I must say that I wish my father had thought of consulting me first ... It would've spared us all the embarrassment of this awkward if not humiliating situation ...

ISIDORE: (*With a look of anger and a humiliated tone*) No ... no ... my dear Marquis ... My daughter has not understood ... she didn't hear the question properly ... She's in a state of shock, I expect ... Joy! Elation! Of course she will accept ...

GERMAINE: (*Bitter*) No, I refuse! How many times must I say it!?

ISIDORE: Oh, come on ... don't be hasty ...

MARQUIS: (*Awkward and troubled*) I presume, Miss Germaine, that you feel that Porcellet is not becoming? ...

GERMAINE: No, it's not that, sir ...

ISIDORE: Oh, for God's sake! What is this about?

GERMAINE: (*Sorrowfully*) The daughter of Isidore Lechat cannot marry the Marquis's son ... Because she is not available.

ISIDORE: Not available? What the hell are you talking about? You are available because your mother and I tell you that you are! *We accept the proposal!*

GERMAINE:	I am not available.
ISIDORE:	Why?
GERMAINE:	I can't say. Not here.
ISIDORE:	*(Menacingly)* Why? Why?
GERMAINE:	You want to know?
ISIDORE:	Yes …
GERMAINE:	I'm not available … because I have a lover! *(Stunned silence)*
ISIDORE:	What? What? What do you mean? No, no, Marquis, don't listen to her! *(Laughs bitterly)* You can see my daughter has a sense of humour … Yes, she's joking … She doesn't know what she's saying … A lover? My daughter? Ha, ha, ha! She's a fine one! *(He leers towards his daughter menacingly)* Say it again … I dare you! I dare you! Look your father in the eye and say it again …
GERMAINE:	I have a lover! Do you hear? A lover! A lover! How many times do you want me to scream it out at you!
ISIDORE:	You liar … She's lying … She's lying, I tell you … You see, Marquis, she doesn't know anyone … she never sees anyone … She's lying! *(Viciously to GERMAINE)* Listen, my little girl, you will stop this right now … Enough. Understand? You will not turn this into a farce … No one believes you, you see … Come on, come clean; tell us the truth now …
GERMAINE:	I chose my lover and I love him. He loves me too … He loves me … He's not some part of a financial deal … he's not some business transaction … He is my lover … We love each other … totally … *freely* … *(To the MARQUIS)* I can see you're surprised, Marquis … I admit it's unusual to meet someone called Lechat who is a free person, not a commodity to be bought and sold.
ISIDORE:	*(To MRS LECHAT)* What about you? Stood there like a doorpost! I normally can't shut you up! Can't you do something to shut *her* up!
MRS LECHAT:	*(Overwhelmed)* What do you expect me to say, damn it!
ISIDORE:	Well, is it true?
MRS LECHAT:	I've no idea, have I? *(Suddenly)* Oh my God … my God … my God! *(She sobs)* It was bound to happen! I knew it!
ISIDORE:	What? What was bound to happen?
MRS LECHAT:	*(Between sobs)* Nothing … I don't know … Something terrible!
ISIDORE:	*(Barges around bumping into the furniture)* My daughter's insane! So's my wife! They're both mad! *(The MARQUIS makes ready to leave)* Marquis … wait … wait … It's just a misunderstanding … I tell you it's a terrible misunderstanding! …
MARQUIS:	If I may be excused?

111

ISIDORE:	Yes. Maybe that is a good idea. I'll talk to her. *(Going over to the MARQUIS)* Oh, my dear Marquis … You work hard for your children … you amass a fortune of millions to make them happy … You have such dreams for them … and just look at it! I need to sort this out … Family, eh? I've seen other people manage to! *(Quietly to the MARQUIS)* I think I may have to make a couple more concessions, you know how it is … I will see you tomorrow, Marquis …
MARQUIS:	*(Very coldly with a haughty superiority)* It seems to me, sir, that we have nothing left to discuss.
ISIDORE:	*(Looking at the MARQUIS for a while before opening the door)* You think not?
MARQUIS:	Correct.
ISIDORE:	Ah …
MARQUIS:	Good day to you, sir! *(He is about to leave when ISIDORE catches his shoulder)*
ISIDORE:	What do you mean? You don't think it's still a viable business proposition?
MARQUIS:	Unhand me, please.
ISIDORE:	What … Our partnership's over then, is it? *(The MARQUIS is silent)* You really think so? … *(Silence)* Very well … You'll be hearing from my lawyers … tomorrow! …
MARQUIS:	Whatever you say! … *(He exits)*
ISIDORE:	*(Waving his fist after the MARQUIS)* Silly old fool! …

Scene Four

ISIDORE:	Alone at last, eh? *(He goes over to GERMAINE who watches his every move with a provocative air)* Don't look at me like that you little bitch … *(Menacing)* Get on your knees … While you are here beneath my roof you will do exactly what I ask of you … Understand? On your knees now. And I'll kick you out the door later. *(He grapples with her trying to force her to her knees. GERMAINE struggles and manages to wriggle out of his grasp)*
GERMAINE:	Calm down … I'm going to leave anyway … And don't think it's you who's forced me out … I am leaving by my own free

	will … This ridiculous farce you just put us all through has not even hastened my departure by a minute … I was going to leave anyway … I had made up my mind and my heart to leave this dreadful place …
ISIDORE:	*(Raising his arms)* Books! All those bloody books! Look what they've done to my daughter!
GERMAINE:	Leave my books out of this … It's not books that have driven me away from you … It's you … you yourself. Your daughter? What makes you think I could be your daughter? We've never spoken more than ten words to each other. And to what good too? You could never understand anything I said to you … and you and everything you say … fills me with disgust and rage …
ISIDORE:	*(Mocking tone)* Yes … yes, dear … I know … You hate me and my business … You despise business … But I notice you've never despised money, have you?
GERMAINE:	Did I ever ask for anything? I never wanted any of your money … your gifts … I never wanted *you*! I have never wanted anything to do with you!
MRS LECHAT:	*(Overwhelmed)* Germaine … You're talking to your father!
ISIDORE:	*(To MRS LECHAT)* You keep out of it! *(To GERMAINE, laughing scornfully)* Ha! Ha! Tell me who brought you up? Tell me who paid to have you fed and clothed?
MRS LECHAT:	*(Begging)* Isidore … You're talking to your daughter!
ISIDORE:	*(To GERMAINE)* Your possessions … your dresses … Where do you think they come from?
GERMAINE:	From the day I was old enough to understand, from the day I understood where all your money has come from … I have repudiated it … The perfume you've bought me I've tipped away because it burns my skin like acid … Understand? Because everything here … everything in this place … is stolen and miserable … You thief … You thief!
MRS LECHAT:	*(Crying)* Stop it! Stop it! You ungrateful child!
ISIDORE:	I told you to keep out of this. Anyway, she's a fool – she's too stupid to understand. *(He shrugs but his fists are clenched)* My God, the insult of it! … Talking to her father like that … *(Going to GERMAINE)* The nerve of you to talk like that … You dare say all that, you little bitch.
GERMAINE:	I've said nothing to be ashamed of …
ISIDORE:	What about all those lies you said in front of the Marquis?

GERMAINE:	I spoke the truth …
ISIDORE:	*(Disgusted expression)* A lover … a man! Surely that disgusts you, Miss Holier than Thou?
GERMAINE:	I'd rather give myself to a man I love than let myself be sold to one I don't.
ISIDORE:	Clever! Always so clever! Always thinking, aren't you! I've brought to heel better people than you, you know … I'll make you see reason, my poor little girl …
GERMAINE:	There's nothing you can do to me.
ISIDORE:	Really?
MRS LECHAT:	My darling, please! …
ISIDORE:	*(To MRS LECHAT)* You are such a pest! It's your weakness that's caused all this! I'm going to ensure she's a spinster all her life … *(To GERMAINE)* Where did you find this lover? Where have you hidden him?
GERMAINE:	Just wait … and you'll see.
ISIDORE:	Am I supposed to do what *you* tell me? Do you want me to throttle you? Oh, I'll make you talk alright … Tell me his name! …
GERMAINE:	*(Running to the open terrace door and shouting)* Lucien! Lucien!
ISIDORE:	*(Flabbergasted by this name. Silence)* Lucien? Which Lucien do you mean? Garraud? Surely not … That's ridiculous … Absurd!
MRS LECHAT:	I should have guessed.

Enter LUCIEN who arrives quickly from the terrace.

Scene Five

ISIDORE:	*(Standing in astonishment as he beholds LUCIEN)* It can't be you, can it? … *(LUCIEN is silent)* It's you? … *(Silence)* Well, well, well … Doesn't that just put a cherry on the cake … You know, it's *almost* funny … *(Suddenly lunges at LUCIEN with fists raised)* You swine! … You bastard! *(GERMAINE intervenes. LUCIEN pushes ISIDORE back)*
LUCIEN:	*(Calm yet forcefully)* Let's just calm down shall we, Mr Lechat? *(ISIDORE stops, mutters a few words to himself and moves away slightly)* I promise you that I can control myself … But I have to warn you that I will not tolerate any violence on your part …
ISIDORE:	*(Hoarse voice)* You too, huh? Trying to teach me a lesson as well, are you? You thief! You think you can come here and coax away

	my daughter from me? Very well … but you'll never see one penny of my money – oh yes, I promise you that!
LUCIEN:	Nobody wants your money …
GERMAINE:	And he knows it …
ISIDORE:	*(Ironically)* Yes, yes, that's right! … But seriously, what *are* your plans? … You two make your move … Then it all goes wrong … Next, forgive and forget, eh? To be one big happy family again … with the help of a few Lechat millions! Sorry, but you got your sums wrong …
LUCIEN:	You are very much mistaken, sir … I haven't done any 'sums' at all …
ISIDORE:	You don't fool me!
LUCIEN:	Germaine has utterly renounced her inheritance.
GERMAINE:	As long as I live, I renounce all your money …
ISIDORE:	Well, I'll ignore that … *(Staring at LUCIEN)* because *I disinherit her!* And don't think I'll change my mind … *(Pointing at GERMAINE)* She … she's a fool … doesn't understand anything … But you can understand … So don't think that I can't disinherit her … I can! On the one hand there's the law … but then there are lawyers and together we will ensure that that girl will see nothing of her inheritance … God knows, my lawyers and I have stitched up more difficult cases than *this* before!
GERMAINE:	I'm counting on it! Nothing would make me happier!
ISIDORE:	*(To LUCIEN)* And not one penny … Understand? You will never see one penny of mine!
GERMAINE:	Good! Good! I'm pleased to hear it!
ISIDORE:	Even if she should drag herself back to this house one day – and believe me, it won't take long – begging and pleading, scratching at my door in misery …
GERMAINE:	Misery? Go on then, cast me out into misery! I beg you! I implore you! Send me out into misery! At last it's something I can take from you! Set me free into misery!
ISIDORE:	What an idiot … and supposed to be a daughter of mine! And him … The only man I have ever loved! Of course! What a fool I have been! *(Close to LUCIEN)* Come on, Garraud … Be sensible now … Just think for a moment …
LUCIEN:	I have done enough thinking already, thank you …
ISIDORE:	You're not a fool … Come on now … what are you doing to do?
LUCIEN:	I'll find work …
ISIDORE:	What, for two hundred francs a month? Maybe a position that pays you two thousand? But then what? I know what

you're like. You are a *dreamer*. You don't know how to earn money.

LUCIEN: Money isn't everything, you know.

ISIDORE: Money isn't everything? God, he's talking like her now! You weren't always a fool like this! It's her – her stupidity has poisoned you! *(Close to LUCIEN again)* To think I had such plans for the girl! I had such tremendous projects riding on her! My daughter ... well, I suppose she's doing me a favour after all! Huh! The day I pulled you out of the gutter, I should have slit my own throat there and then! Have you forgotten that I pulled you out of the gutter, hmm?

LUCIEN: Mr Lechat ... I know all that I owe you ...

ISIDORE: And this is how you pay me back?

LUCIEN: I paid you back with my time ... my work ... my loyalty ... I gave you all of those ...

GERMAINE: And that was more than you should have given! He deserves nothing of yours, my darling!

ISIDORE: Shut up! I forbid you to call him that in front of me!

LUCIEN: *(He tries, gently, to make GERMAINE be silent)* But my thoughts ... my feelings ... I never abandoned those to you, Mr Lechat ... My love for Germaine has nothing to do with my career working with you ... I love Germaine with all my–

ISIDORE: *(Erupting)* Oh, I've had enough sweet nothings for one day, thank you very much! ... You want to go, then go, then go ... clear off ... disappear ... You want money? Very well ... name your price, name an honest price ... I'll pay ...

LUCIEN: You must be mad!

ISIDORE: You'll be the first man who ever succeeded in ripping Isidore Lechat off ... But never mind ... name your price.

LUCIEN: I'm losing my patience.

ISIDORE: It really isn't a case of money? No? You mean it really is a case of *love*? *(He stares at LUCIEN and then laughs in a sinister way)* You idiots! You had me fooled too, you know! What on earth did you want from me? I couldn't care less about the pair of you! Off you go! Go to hell for all I care! An idiot and a madwoman ... What a fine couple! Go and starve to death of hunger wherever you fancy ... That will be my revenge on you ... That will be my joy!

GERMAINE: Go, Lucien ... I will follow you soon ...

LUCIEN *exits.* MRS LECHAT *stands up, deeply sorrowful.*

Scene Six

ISIDORE barges around the room like a bull in a china shop, barging into the furniture and stamping his feet.

MRS LECHAT:	*(Pleadingly)* Please listen to me …
ISIDORE:	Ha! It speaks! At last … Someone steals your daughter from under your very nose and you sit there … saying nothing … doing nothing … sitting there like a sack of potatoes! …
MRS LECHAT:	Please listen to me, my dear …
ISIDORE:	Garraud! A bare-arsed peasant! A man of no means … Utterly worthless! *(As he passes his desk he punches it with his fist)* If he came in here again … I don't know what I'd do!
MRS LECHAT:	Listen … Losing your temper won't get you anywhere … There's no point talking to children in anger … no matter how much they're in the wrong … You're in no state to talk sensibly … Let me speak to her.
ISIDORE:	You've got nothing to say to that girl!
MRS LECHAT:	*(Rather imperiously)* How would you know? … Now, leave me alone with Germaine, just for one minute …
ISIDORE:	Huh! I like the sound of that! Off you go then … start whining to each other! Snivel in each other's arms! … But woe betides her if she's still feeling sorry for herself when I get back! … *(ISIDORE exits in a rage)*

Scene Seven

MRS LECHAT looks at her daughter with a face both overwhelmed and imploring. Eventually she reaches out to GERMAINE.

MRS LECHAT:	Germaine … Germaine, my darling! *(She takes a few little steps towards GERMAINE, her arms outstretched)* Germaine, my darling! … (GERMAINE *turns her head away and steps back slightly and makes a powerful attempt to hold back her emotions. She suddenly throws herself into her mother's arms)*
GERMAINE:	Oh, mother … mother! … *(They hug each other and both sob. A long embrace of sobs and crying.* MRS LECHAT *takes* GERMAINE's *head in her hands and showers it with kisses)*

MRS LECHAT:	You're not going to leave, are you? You're not going to leave me, are you? That would be … That would … That would be more than I could bear …
GERMAINE:	Please … it's all too late … all too late now …
MRS LECHAT:	(Kissing her) No … no … my darling … don't say it's too late … Not now … Not today … Everyone's being silly, that's all … Your father is being unreasonable … He's angry, that's all … but tomorrow … well … maybe a few days … I'll talk to him … yes, let me talk to him … I'll make him understand … I swear I will … and I promise that he will consent to your marriage … Mr Garraud …
GERMAINE:	(Her face has hardened at the mention of her father) He will not consent.
MRS LECHAT:	Wait and see … I swear … You'll see … Your father will consent …
GERMAINE:	Don't even mention that man to me.
MRS LECHAT:	Very well … As you wish … I won't mention him again … But you will stay here with me, won't you?
GERMAINE:	Please, mother, I beg you … Do not ask me to do something which it is impossible for me to do … I must go … I must!
MRS LECHAT:	No … no … it mustn't happen … Don't you see? You're my daughter … What about me? What will happen to me? All alone in this ghastly house? All alone … at my age … Just think! It will be the death of me! You see, Germaine … Can't you see? Please, have a heart … have mercy … Don't leave me here all on my own …
GERMAINE:	Come with us … You'll be happy with us …
MRS LECHAT:	No! I couldn't do that! Impossible! … Besides, I've lived with him all this time … It is only fit that I should die with him … I can't simply abandon him now … It would be a *sin* … I cannot do it … I simply cannot do it … (Pause) Yes … yes … I've learnt something today … I realize … that we didn't love you enough … my poor darling … We didn't love you like we should've loved you … We have been so wrong … Especially me … Yes, it's true … And I am so bitterly sorry … I really am! But you were a little at fault too … You were always so miserable with me … You always closed off your feelings and your thoughts from me … And that could sometimes infuriate me … That's why I have always been so strict with you … Because … Because I never really knew you … I only ever saw your coldness, not your true being, your soul … But I still loved you … And now … I love everything about you … and

	I will love you forever … I will always love you with all of my heart–
GERMAINE:	I also misjudged you … time and again … I didn't understand you either …
MRS LECHAT:	*(Rapidly)* Well, now that we do understand one another–
GERMAINE:	Too late …
MRS LECHAT:	Oh my god! Is it true? Oh, if only we had stayed in a happy little house somewhere … none of this would ever have happened … It's this beastly house, isn't it? All these rooms so cold and eerie … All this decadent wealth … all this money … That's the only thing that there is here … and it covers up the noise of our screaming hearts so that no one can even hear them … Oh God, it's nothing short of tragedy … The day I find my daughter is the day I lose her forever … *(She sobs)* I have so much I want to tell you … and … I don't know … I don't know … My head is so heavy … there is a mist before my eyes … *(She hugs her daughter firmly)*
GERMAINE:	Mother … let go …
MRS LECHAT:	No … no … don't go … my darling … Don't go … never leave me! I beg you! Go tomorrow … a few more days, that's all … Oh, don't leave me today … not today … Don't leave me all alone today …
GERMAINE:	I don't want my father to find me here … I don't feel full of hatred now … let me go … let me go without hate in my heart … *(She tries to struggle free)*
MRS LECHAT:	My god! My god! *(Flooding with tears)* Write to me … promise me you'll write … I beg you!
GERMAINE:	I promise …
MRS LECHAT:	And if you move to Paris send me your address as soon as you can …
GERMAINE:	Yes, yes … I promise …
MRS LECHAT:	I'll come and see you … I'll come and see you all the time … No one will know … I'll tell no one … But what if you're ill … my god … Heaven forbid! You'll have no money … And what about him? He's not a rich man … I can't imagine what you'll do. *(Remembering suddenly)* Those three hundred francs?
GERMAINE:	*(Poignantly)* No, mother.
MRS LECHAT:	Whenever you need anything, anything at all, write to me …
GERMAINE:	Goodbye. *(A long embrace. GERMAINE breaks free and very quickly she exits out of the room)*
MRS LECHAT:	Germaine … Germaine … Don't go! Please don't go! *(MRS LECHAT looks all around her. She is overwhelmed by everything surrounding*

her. Wearily, dazed and miserable, yet without a sound, she collapses into a chair. Silence)

Scene Eight

ISIDORE *enters with his head lowered, hands in pockets with a melancholy expression, looking around furtively.*

MRS LECHAT:	*(Without raising her head)* She's gone.
ISIDORE:	To hell with her.
MRS LECHAT:	*(Looking up at her husband)* Is that it? Is that all you can say?
ISIDORE:	*(Harshly)* What on earth do you want me to say?
MRS LECHAT:	She's gone … Can't you say something? Surely you can scream out something!?
ISIDORE:	Oh, leave me alone.
MRS LECHAT:	*(Standing up)* Very well … Enough is enough … I quite agree … It's too much to bear, it really is … And do you realize that everything that's happened is entirely *your fault*? … Did you hear what I said? It is entirely your fault … *(She makes to leave)*
ISIDORE:	Oh, I understand … You needn't put yourself to any trouble, my dear … Join her yourself for all I care … Goodnight …
MRS LECHAT:	*(Turns to face him)* Damn you! It would serve you right if I did walk out!
ISIDORE:	So everyone's abandoning me, eh? So be it! That suits me fine! We'd all be much happier! *(MRS LECHAT exits)*

Scene Nine

ISIDORE *sits at desk. He thinks for a moment, then shuffles the papers on his desk.*

ISIDORE:	Ah! My dear Marquis! *(Shrugs his shoulders)* You think it's over, do you? We shall see about that … The joke's on me, you know … *(Rests his elbows on his desk with his head in his hands. He seems distant from everything around him. A* SERVANT *enters quickly through the door, looking flustered and haggard)*
SERVANT:	Sir! … Sir! …
ISIDORE:	*(Without moving, his voice distant)* What is it? …
SERVANT:	*(With difficulty)* Oh, sir … something awful … something truly awful has happened …

ISIDORE:	*(Still not moving)* I am well aware of that and I forbid you to mention it … It's none of your business, damn it …
SERVANT:	Your son …
ISIDORE:	You mean my daughter, you idiot …
SERVANT:	It's not about your daughter, sir …
ISIDORE:	She's gone, yes, I know …
SERVANT:	No, sir, no …
ISIDORE:	What on earth is wrong with you? Are you a complete fool?
SERVANT:	You don't understand, sir … Your son … *(with effort)* Mr Xavier …
ISIDORE:	Well?
SERVANT:	He's been killed – an accident on the road …

ISIDORE *doesn't move. His head is buried in his hands. A very long silence. Finally, his hands drift away. He stares at the servant in astonishment.*

ISIDORE:	What did you say? …
SERVANT:	Mr Xavier is dead …

ISIDORE *bounds to his feet and seizes the* SERVANT *by the neck and begins to throttle him.*

ISIDORE:	What did you say? … You idiot! … What did you say? … *(He shakes him as the* SERVANT *attempts to defend himself)* You complete and utter imbecile! … I defy you to say that again! …
SERVANT:	Let me go, please, let me go …
ISIDORE:	*(Casts him away)* Tell me … Talk …

As the SERVANT *speaks, the eyes of* ISIDORE *increasingly fill with horror and his body weakens.*

SERVANT:	*(Struggling)* When he left Marecourt … he swerved in the road … and the automobile overturned … and Mr Xavier was thrown out of the car … and hit the wall of the café Gadaud … He was thrown out so violently … He was smashed against the wall … He died instantly.
ISIDORE:	*(Trembling and haggard, his mouth almost paralysed, his face contorted in apoplexy)* What? … What? … What? … *(His mouth gapes half open and he falls silent)*
SERVANT:	The Duke's son saw the accident … he came here on horseback … he brought us the dreadful news …
ISIDORE:	It … It … *(His lips mouth words which are inaudible)*

SERVANT:	They're bringing the body of your son back home, sir … It'll be here in ten minutes …

ISIDORE *cannot speak. He rips off his tie and tears open the button of his shirt partly revealing his chest as he does so. His mouth opens wide; he struggles for breath. His false neck collar has opened out and looks like two white horns by his cheeks. He staggers and the* SERVANT *helps him as he collapses heavily into a chair. Suddenly he bursts into tears, his body heaving with sobs.*

SERVANT:	Sir! … Sir! …
ISIDORE:	*(After a few moments he speaks with a frail voice that is hard to hear)* I've lost everything … in a single day … I've lost everything! *(Gasping for air)* And … my wife? …
SERVANT:	I don't know, sir …
ISIDORE:	Yes … yes … *(Pause)* In a single day! *(Pause)* Air! … Give me air! … I can't breath! … *(The* SERVANT *opens the window and leads* ISIDORE *over to it.* ISIDORE *gasps in the air with heaving breaths like a man who's been drowning)*
SERVANT:	Is that better, sir? …
ISIDORE:	Yes … that's … better … *(Pause. He continues to breathe in the air)* I'm better now … I'll be alright …
SERVANT:	Sir, you're in no fit state–
ISIDORE:	Yes … yes … I'm fine … Let me go … Just leave me alone now … *(He takes a few steps while the* SERVANT *tries to assist)*

Scene Ten

ISIDORE *takes stumbling steps. The door opens and* PHINCK *and* GRUGGH *walk in.*

SERVANT:	Sit down, sir … You're in a bad way, sir … please sit down … *(He brings a chair over to* ISIDORE. PHINCK *and* GRUGGH, *looking deeply concerned, stand either side of the chair)*
GRUGGH:	How dreadful!
PHINCK:	Please accept our condolences … our most heartfelt condolences …
ISIDORE:	Oh, my friends … my dear friends …
PHINCK:	Partners, Mr Lechat, please call us *partners* …
ISIDORE:	My dear partners …
GRUGGH:	So young!
PHINCK:	With so much potential … He had his whole life ahead of him!

GRUGGH:	It's utterly appalling, it really is …
ISIDORE:	I've lost everything … in a single day! …
PHINCK:	We want to offer you our condolences … but in the face of such a tragedy what can one possibly say …
ISIDORE:	In a single day …
GRUGGH:	Time. Only time can take away the sting of death! Oh my God …
PHINCK:	And such a handsome young man too … *(ISIDORE nods his head)* And … to think he was here, alive and well, just a few hours ago … so full of life … so happy … so charming …
ISIDORE:	My friends …
GRUGGH:	And you loved him so very much! Oh! You didn't deserve this!
ISIDORE:	*(Taking their hands)* My dear friends!
GRUGGH:	Be brave! You must be brave! You mustn't let this tragedy destroy you!
ISIDORE:	Oh … Oh … *(PHINCK and GRUGGH are speechless and look troubled, making a dumb show of sympathy. Silence)*
PHINCK:	Please forgive us … but we must interrupt your grieving for just a tiny moment …
GRUGGH:	Of course … we appreciate … that to talk of business … at a time like this … is extremely awkward … *(He pulls out some papers from his pocket)* And if we were not obliged to leave today you must understand that we would not … *(ISIDORE stares at PHINCK and GRUGGH. Instantly, GRUGGH puts two pieces of paper in front of ISIDORE)*
PHINCK:	The contract you agreed to sign with us … *(ISIDORE is silent)* Do you recall?
ISIDORE:	No … not today … please … Please, leave me alone right now … *(He continues to stare at PHINCK and GRUGGH)*
GRUGGH:	I am sorry, but we really must insist …
ISIDORE:	No … please … Not now …
PHINCK:	Sorry … but we *must* … *(GRUGGH produces more papers)*
ISIDORE:	*(After a silence with a terrible expression on his face)* Very well … Give them to me … *(They give him the papers)*
GRUGGH:	We have agreed to all your conditions …
PHINCK:	Every single one of them … *(ISIDORE reads the papers. His hand trembles. From time to time, he raises his hand to his neck. When he has finished reading he looks at PHINCK and GRUGGH with a terrifying expression. His voice is tense and trembling)*
ISIDORE:	You bastards …
PHINCK:	I'm sorry? …
ISIDORE:	You thieving bastards! …

GRUGGH:	But …
ISIDORE:	Taking advantage of my misery! … Exploiting my broken heart! … *(He stands up and walks over, unsteadily, to his desk)*
GRUGGH:	I don't understand …
ISIDORE:	Come here …
PHINCK:	Did we forget something? …
ISIDORE:	Come here … *(He places a piece of paper in front of both of them and gives a pen)* You will write here and here … *(He indicates with his finger)* Write this down! *(PHINCK and GRUGGH hesitate. ISIDORE speaks forcefully)* Write this down now! *(Dictates)* 'Mr Isidore Lechat … is in sole charge … of the financial direction … and commercial administration … of the business … of the business … And … Mr Phinck and Mr Gruggh … have expressly … and voluntarily … abandoned … all rights … in this regard …' *(PHINCK and GRUGGH stop writing and raise their heads)* Write this down! … 'Abandoned all rights in this regard … And will not be permitted … to contravene … any business plans, proposals or decisions … ' *(HOUSEMAID enters)*
HOUSEMAID:	*(Frightened)* Sir … They've brought in the body of Mr Xavier … Madam has collapsed … she's unconscious in the lounge …
SERVANT:	*(Imploring)* Sir! …
ISIDORE:	*(His voice has changed in tone again. To save himself from collapsing, he studies himself with both hands on the desk)* I'll be there in a minute … in a minute … *(HOUSEMAID and SERVANT exit)* 'any business plans, proposals or decisions … which are deemed by Mr Isidore Lechat … and him alone … to be of benefit … to the business … ' That's all … Now sign it … Here … *Sign it!* *(PHINCK and GRUGGH sign)* Now hand them over! …

ISIDORE takes the papers and scrutinizes them. He signs both copies and hands one to PHINCK in silence. ISIDORE folds his copy and puts in his pocket and without acknowledging PHINCK and GRUGGH he staggers towards the door, bumping into the furniture. PHINCK and GRUGGH looked stupefied, crushed and devastated. They watch ISIDORE pass by them without a word or gesture. They stand still and speechless in an attitude of terror. ISIDORE exits. Alone in the room, PHINCK and GRUGGH remain motionless and silent with wide eyes and open mouths, unable to look away from the door through which ISIDORE disappeared.

THE END

Charity

A Comedy in Three Acts
(*Le Foyer*, 1908)

ARMAND BIRON
BARON J. G. COURTIN
FATHER LAROZE
ARNAUD TRIPIER
CHARLES DUFRERE
CELESTIN LERIBLE
ROBERT D'AUBERVAL
LUDOVIC BELAIR
JEAN
FREDERICK
BARONESS THERESE COURTIN
MAIDSERVANT
MISS RAMBERT
MRS PIGEON
MRS RATURE
MRS PIVIN
MRS TUPIN
JULIE
FOOTMAN
SERVANT

Act 1

The study of BARON COURTIN. *It is well-furnished including, on the left, a portrait of Empress Josephine mounted above a modern sofa. On the right there is an English tea table with drinks on it. Centre stage is a large desk on which are several bronzes and numerous papers and dossiers. On the mantelpiece is a marble bust of Napoleon. On the right is a bookcase. Through the window, trees can be seen in the garden. There are several doors leading to other rooms in the mansion, including, stage left, a billiard room.*

Scene One

THERESE *stands by the table.* BIRON *stands further back.*

THERESE:	Would you care for some cognac, Biron? Or chartreuse? What would you like?
BIRON:	*(Approaching)* Cognac … yes, a good cognac … In a large glass, please.
THERESE:	Here.
BIRON:	Thank you. *(Examines the glass)* That great vintage of 1822, I trust?
THERESE:	But of course.
BIRON:	*(Holding out the glass at arm's length)* Behold! The peerless nectar of France! …
THERESE:	*(To* SERVANT*)* Take this tray of drinks into the billiard room … *(*SERVANT *takes the tray)* Wait! Don't forget the ice for Mr D'Auberval's kummel! *(*SERVANT *exits)*

Scene Two

BIRON:	He's lucky!
THERESE:	*(Her back to* BIRON*)* Who?
BIRON:	D'Auberval. *(Sarcastic)* He nearly didn't get his ice.
THERESE:	Would you like a cognac?
BIRON:	You've already poured me one!
THERESE:	Oh, silly me! *(Laughs)*
BIRON:	Quite irresistible.
THERESE:	Yes, it is good cognac, isn't it?
BIRON:	I was referring to our young friend … D'Auberval.
THERESE:	Mr D'Auberval.

BIRON:	Mm.
THERESE:	*(Going towards the settee)* I wouldn't know! …
BIRON:	Handsome chap … very handsome … *(Pause)* How old is he? Twenty-three?
THERESE:	Ridiculous! He must be at least twenty-six.
BIRON:	*(Humorously yet bitter)* Still too young for you …
THERESE:	Why don't you have a cigar? …
BIRON:	*(Looking into the billiard room)* There he is … playing billiards with Courtin … and he's losing, of course … Clever chap, that D'Auberval.
THERESE:	*(Sitting down)* Biron, if you only knew what a fool you're making of yourself.
BIRON:	Yes, yes, I know … as you said over lunch, I am a little old-fashioned … Not everyone can be a millionaire – a young millionaire with anarchistic principles, no less!
THERESE:	What are your plans for the summer?
BIRON:	Well, I thought I'd start off by spending some time with you, then stay with you a little longer and head into autumn, er, with you.
THERESE:	Sounds lovely.
BIRON:	Yes, I thought so.
THERESE:	What else?
BIRON:	Apart from that, I thought I might get to spend a little more time with you.
THERESE:	A tad monotonous, wouldn't you say?
BIRON:	*(Moving closer to her)* You see, I try and–
THERESE:	*(Pointing at the cigar box)* Cigar?
BIRON:	Thanks … *(He pulls an enormous cigar out of the box and a cigar kit from his pocket)* You don't mind if I smoke next to you like this, do you? *(He produces a cigar cutter)*
THERESE:	You don't have to sit *quite* so near to me …
BIRON:	*(Clipping his cigar aggressively)* Why are you so beastly to me! So very mean! *(Lights his cigar)* Does *he* smoke a lot?
THERESE:	I've no idea.
BIRON:	*(Mocking)* No idea! Likely story! *(Pause)* I remember you used to disapprove of smoking, and now you just disapprove of *me* smoking … Curious, don't you think?
THERESE:	Yes … *(Pause)* You haven't even told me what you're going to do this summer.
BIRON:	*(Smiling)* See a lot of you …
THERESE:	*Seriously.*

BIRON:	Oh God, the same as every summer! Deauville, Dieppe and then Aix, probably.
THERESE:	Aix? Taking the waters for your pains!?
BIRON:	*(Enraged, standing up awkwardly)* Yes! Perfectly true! You never miss a chance to say something horrible to me!
THERESE:	*(Conciliatory)* I'm sorry, I just–
BIRON:	And if my suffering allows it, I'll go to Engandine … *(Pause)* Are you going to Engandine?
THERESE:	No idea. The Count has many engagements this summer.
BIRON:	Huh!
THERESE:	Meetings about education policy and he's involved with the inquiry into marriage reform.
BIRON:	Oh, *that*!
THERESE:	And then there's The Haven, the charity home.
BIRON:	Oh yes, 'The Haven', that outrageous waste of money!
THERESE:	Money, maybe, I wouldn't know about that … But there are certainly other demands it makes on us … All the paperwork! All those pamphlets!
BIRON:	The man's insane. *(Sits down)*
THERESE:	You know, a charity home is far more demanding than a business!
BIRON:	I guess I'll have to wait until autumn.
THERESE:	No … I'm sure we can arrange something … We'll come to Deauville or Dieppe … That'll be something.
BIRON:	Well, today was a waste of time!
THERESE:	Biron, if you want us to remain friends …
BIRON:	*(Stands up)* What did I say? I can't say a word! Wonderful!
THERESE:	Come on, sit down. *(Looking towards the billiard room)* And keep the noise down.
BIRON:	*(Sits down and speaks quietly)* Do you even remember Deauville? And Aix? Women have very short memories, I must say!
THERESE:	It's been so long it'd be better to forget!
BIRON:	So long!? Deauville was hardly ten years ago! And as for Aix … *(Sadly)* I don't think I've got the courage to go back there … *(Dramatically)* Oh, Therese!
THERESE:	*(Finger on his lips)* Ssh!
BIRON:	Why can't I call you Therese now and then …
THERESE:	You promised …
BIRON:	What harm can it do? … To either of us? Oh, in the past ten years whenever summer's upon us … *(As he moves nearer to her she moves away in equal measure)* Oh, Therese … that afternoon … in Aix … by the lake …

THERESE:	I beg you …
BIRON:	*(Exultant)* You were so beautiful! A dress of white linen … *(He leans over, risking a gesture)* You were wearing stockings …
THERESE:	*(Moving* BIRON'*s hands away)* Enough!
BIRON:	*(Almost choking)* Stockings … Tight stockings … *(*THERESE *laughs,* BIRON *struggles to his feet and struts around)* Go on then, mock! Mock!
THERESE:	I don't want to upset you … But we agreed …
BIRON:	But I must have my memories! … *(Coming closer)* What will become of me if you deny me my memories … *(Sits down)*
THERESE:	*(Gently and almost cuddling him)* Biron … You know full well that you can be rude, egotistical, disrespectful, even violent at times … *(*BIRON *protests)* You know it's true … You also have good qualities too …
BIRON:	Really?
THERESE:	And I loved those qualities in you … I still love them … I loved you … and I always will … but in a different way now … *(*BIRON *tries to speak and* THERESE *closes his mouth)* Not another word, I beg you … It only makes things difficult … And it changes nothing. *(Stands up)*
BIRON:	I can't do it! … I simply cannot do it! … I can never stop wanting you! … It's insane to think that I could! …
THERESE:	*(Looking into the billiard room as* BIRON *comes over to her)* Will you be quiet! *(Sits down)*
BIRON:	The last six months have been hell! … I can't stand it anymore! …
THERESE:	Be quiet … Come here. Oh! If only you could get out of this awful habit of *shouting* all the time!
BIRON:	*(Quieter)* I can't help it if I'm miserable!
THERESE:	But at least try and act normal! Now sit down! *(Indicates a stool near the settee)*
BIRON:	*(Sitting down and speaking quietly)* Oh, Therese, I am so unhappy! … So terribly unhappy! …
THERESE:	Well think of happier times, I think I prefer that …
BIRON:	All those years, those wonderful years … So many joys … every decent pleasure known to man! …
THERESE:	Biron!
BIRON:	*(Smiling)* And even a few *indecent* pleasures, remember?
THERESE:	Biron! Biron!
BIRON:	Is there no way that I can win you back? No way I can rekindle the burning passion that used to rage like an inferno inside you?
THERESE:	The things you say! *(Laughs)*

BIRON:	*(Very excited)* Your lips … Your mouth … Your teeth, oh God, your teeth!
THERESE:	*(Very dryly)* I am going to lose my temper in a minute.
BIRON:	You are so cruel … yes … so cruel … And I adore you for it … Those eyes, so beautiful when they are full of rage … Oh, they remind me of something wonderful … You know, when you're … when you're about to lose your temper … *(Shakes his head)* Miaow! You're like a wildcat on heat! *(THERESE smiles and relaxes a little)* No, more like a beautiful pussycat … Oh, I know you so well …
THERESE:	You are impossible!
BIRON:	There's so much between us … So many things … and so many things we've shared … So many things that join us together – don't just brush them away like that! … *(Speaks very tenderly into her ear)* I was always nice to you … *(She pushes him away slightly)* Your every whim … Your every fantasy …
THERESE:	*(Without losing her calm)* Will you stop now?
BIRON:	That summer afternoon … in this room … it was so hot … we closed the shutters … *(THERESE has stood up and goes over to a desk)*
THERESE:	You're terrible … *(Her head in her hands)* You're *terrible* …
BIRON:	Terrible? Me? Why?
THERESE:	You get some terrible pleasure from making me blush!
BIRON:	*(Standing up)* Oh!
THERESE:	Yes, it's appalling! … Appalling! …
BIRON:	*(Approaching her)* I won't say another word … I promise … I'm sorry … *(He reaches for her hand)*
THERESE:	Seeing that you can't behave … *(She moves away)*
BIRON:	*(Following her)* I'm sorry …
THERESE:	We have no choice …
BIRON:	Please forgive me …
THERESE:	*(Firmly)* There's only one way we can see each other again …
BIRON:	*(Walking around)* I'm all ears! Tell me! This is most promising! Go on!
THERESE:	Travel.
BIRON:	Egypt? Japan? America? Go on!
THERESE:	Your yacht is moored in Marseille … *The Argo* … She's a lovely yacht … Take a cruise on her …
BIRON:	Hang on, without you? … *(Suddenly)* You'll come with me, right?
THERESE:	I don't like the sea.
BIRON:	You don't like anything these days! *(Comes over to THERESE)* Enough – let's talk about you.
THERESE:	Whatever for?

BIRON:	Last Thursday I saw you … in Rue de la Paix … You were in a cab …
THERESE:	So?
BIRON:	You! In a cab! *(Pounds the table)*
THERESE:	God! That frightened me!
BIRON:	It was dreadful! It was ridiculous!
THERESE:	Don't make me laugh!
BIRON:	A terrible mistake! No better way to proclaim to the world the fact that you've separated!
THERESE:	That's enough, Biron!
BIRON:	No … Let me finish … I'm not joking now … We're not children, for God's sake! … I swear this is a scandal! …
THERESE:	No!
BIRON:	Yes … For you … For me … For Courtin … I *adore* your husband … It's true! He's a fine man. He does have some odd beliefs. *(Points at a bust of Napoleon)* He thinks we can bring back the Empire! Ha! Some very odd beliefs … And there's this charity nonsense too …
THERESE:	That's his business!
BIRON:	And yours too! Yours more than anyone! And it means you have to travel around in a cab … A common life? A mediocre way of life for a lady like you? No! … You need luxury, precious things … I'd make it a priority … a duty … a joy! …
THERESE:	That's right, throw me promises off the top of your head!
BIRON:	It's not that!
THERESE:	Typical you!
BIRON:	No … Just think for a moment … Since you refused to accept anything from me anymore, it's awful … You've reduced your stables … your servants have gone … Less and less all the time … Your antiques and your jewellery …
THERESE:	*(Playing with her pearl necklace)* My jewellery? Really?
BIRON:	I've done enough shopping in my time to know true quality when I see it …
THERESE:	Oh, that's ridiculous … I've cleared a few things out, I admit …
BIRON:	*(Folding his arms)* And the Fragonard?
THERESE:	What?
BIRON:	The Fragonard that used to hang in the lounge.
THERESE:	The one you gave me?
BIRON:	It's gone!
THERESE:	You exasperate me! Do I have to hold myself to account to you!
BIRON:	Do you know where this is leading you?
THERESE:	Do tell me.

BIRON:	*Disaster.*
THERESE:	So be it … At least I'm *happy* …
BIRON:	Happy!? And what about me? *(THERESE laughs)* That's right, laugh! I suppose that D'Auberval's rich enough for you, eh?
THERESE:	*(Furious)* What!?
BIRON:	Nothing. Nothing. Nothing!
THERESE:	You're always the same! Utterly obsessed with money! I knew I should have slammed the door in your face!
BIRON:	Calm down …
THERESE:	Be quiet – everything you say is stupid or vulgar …
BIRON:	Therese …
THERESE:	Leave me alone … And don't you *ever* …
BIRON:	I promise … *(THERESE heads towards the billiard room)* Therese! Wait!
THERESE:	*(Ignoring BIRON she opens the door and calls through)* Are you still playing? Surely that's enough …

Scene Three

COURTIN:	We've just finished.
THERESE:	We were getting ready to send out a search party!
D'AUBERVAL:	*(Appears at the door and immediately follows THERESE)* Fancy a game? … Of course you do! … *(He takes her arm)*
THERESE:	Over my dead body!
D'AUBERVAL:	You don't enjoy billiards?
THERESE:	It fills me with horror – all games do, in fact.
D'AUBERVAL:	Ah, but is billiards a game or a sport?
THERESE:	I wouldn't know.
D'AUBERVAL:	*(Approaching BIRON)* What would you say – is billiards a game or a sport?
BIRON:	*(Points towards COURTIN)* One for the Academy.
COURTIN:	The Academy has no interest in sport – only games. And maybe exercise too.
D'AUBERVAL:	So what is billiards?
COURTIN:	A bit of both …
BIRON:	*(Interrupting)* Who won?
D'AUBERVAL:	I lost … Both games.
BIRON:	I knew it … You lack the authority to be a winner, young man. *(Stands and taps COURTIN on the shoulder)* Here is the master of everything!

COURTIN:	You're too kind!
THERESE:	Biron's full of kindness, my dear! *(She walks and* D'AUBERVAL *follows)*
COURTIN:	Not to worry – D'Auberval is making excellent progress.
BIRON:	*(Looking over* COURTIN's *shoulder at* THERESE *and* D'AUBERVAL*)* So I see.
COURTIN:	He could beat you before long, I'm sure.
BIRON:	We'll see about that …
THERESE:	*(Quietly to* D'AUBERVAL*)* Did you manage to talk to the Count about the summer job?
D'AUBERVAL:	Couldn't get a word in edgeways … All he talked about was charity, charity, charity …
THERESE:	Why do you persist in arguing with him?
BIRON:	*(To* COURTIN*)* Really? You think he's intelligent? I'm astonished!
COURTIN:	Yes, a little contradictory, a little naïve … but highly gifted.
BIRON:	He's read a few pamphlets and speaks loudly at parties … And suddenly he's an expert … A champagne socialist … The boy's a fool.
COURTIN:	He's more committed than you'd believe … What scares me about socialism is how all the young fall for it. Truly, my dear Biron, I have no idea what the future holds for these merciless youngsters.
BIRON:	Huh! The same thing that happened to us; they'll get old.
D'AUBERVAL:	*(Having been in a lively conversation with* THERESE*)* Tell me, Baron, isn't it true that The Haven will soon be ten years old?
COURTIN:	Not exactly … This is its eighth financial year … It will be in its ninth year come October.
D'AUBERVAL:	*(To* THERESE*)* You see, I was right …
THERESE:	I can hardly believe it …
D'AUBERVAL:	I'm an expert on The Haven! …
COURTIN:	Remember that first summer …
BIRON:	Yes, remember Deauville …
THERESE:	It was wonderful …
COURTIN:	We were in Deauville trying to think of a name …
BIRON:	*(To* THERESE*)* And you suddenly thought of one: The Haven!
THERESE:	You've got a good memory.
BIRON:	I have an *exceptional* memory.
THERESE:	A *ruthless* memory.
BIRON:	*(To* THERESE*)* So, The Haven was your idea? Yet you claim to be so indifferent to it!
THERESE:	I may have thought of the name – but the idea was certainly the Baron's.

COURTIN:	That's true. I insisted on it.
BIRON:	You can't disown it now … *(To D'AUBERVAL)* Courtin has written numerous books … But you wouldn't know them … They're too heavy for you … You'd prefer something lighter …
D'AUBERVAL:	Me?
BIRON:	No need to defend yourself – it's just your generation.
D'AUBERVAL:	On the contrary, only *old* men like light reading … *(THERESE laughs and BIRON walks away)* If I have a passion it's for sociology.
BIRON:	Sociology! How pretentious! *(Returns towards D'AUBERVAL)* Why on earth haven't you read Courtin's books then!
D'AUBERVAL:	I have. They're classics. Baron J. G. Courtin: *Napoleon the Charitable*, Perrin, 1888, one volume; Baron J. G. Courtin: *Charity and the Consulate*, Perrin, 1890, one volume; Baron J. G. Courtin: *The Worker Question*, Perrin, 1894, two volumes; Baron J. G. Courtin: *Organized Charity*, Perrin, 1896, one volume; Baron J. G. Courtin, member of the Académie française: *The Street and the Workshop*, Perrin, 1898; Baron J. G. Courtin: *A Pariah*, 1901; Baron J. G. Courtin: *Working-Class Feminism*, 1903.
COURTIN:	*(Smiling)* Correct in every detail!
BIRON:	Yes … *(To THERESE)* Not the only one with a good memory in this room … *(To COURTIN)* He knows every single *title*.
D'AUBERVAL:	And the contents too … *(To BIRON)* Shall I?
BIRON:	No! Please don't! …
COURTIN:	You can never say too much about the poor women who work so hard in Paris. *(BIRON takes his cognac and sits down)* Nothing can recompense the terrible injustices they've endured. Charity can never find enough opportunities to help. *(THERESE offers a cigarette to D'AUBERVAL)*
D'AUBERVAL:	*(Lighting the cigarette, quietly to THERESE)* He's off again …
THERESE:	*(Quietly)* Hush!
COURTIN:	In parliament and the newspapers … there is constant debate about the *workers* … The workers … But what has concerned me for a long time now is a particular *type* of worker … The woman … Not so much the married female worker but the vulnerable young woman …
BIRON:	Feather-brained little girls, more like!
COURTIN:	*(Serious)* Poor young women, sixteen to eighteen years old …
BIRON:	Even thirteen?
COURTIN:	Yes, there are some … These women are at a vulnerable age and need to be protected from the women they themselves are becoming … They need to be protected from the temptations of

the street … And the dangers of despair … And the lifestyle of their parents … They need somewhere safe … a home …

BIRON: A shelter … and there you have it: The Haven! *(Puts his glass down)* An ingenious way to corrupt adolescent girls … *(Laughs)*

THERESE: Oh!

BIRON: *(Wags his finger)* Very dubious …

THERESE: You are impossible! …

COURTIN: Don't worry, darling, Biron has a cruel sense of humour, but he means well …

BIRON: *(Ingratiating)* Exactly.

COURTIN: When we started to look for young women outside factories and shops, we were not the only ones interested in them … Things were difficult … But now we have our own workshops and more young women queuing at our door than we can possibly house … *(Goes over to BIRON)* But the problem is money …

BIRON: *(Moving away)* Money is *always* the problem …

COURTIN: Happily, we've been able to place our products in some major shops and with a number of suppliers … *(A MAIDSERVANT enters with drinks and coffee and exits)*

D'AUBERVAL: *(To THERESE)* Very clever … and you claim to be indifferent …

THERESE: Honestly, it's all the Baron's idea …

COURTIN: You've helped us a great deal … But it must be said that our girls have worked miracles … The fashion for sequins and lace has been most fortunate for the darling girls … And as for the embroidered collars, we haven't been able to keep up with demand …

D'AUBERVAL: That kind of work is dangerous for eyesight!

COURTIN: Teenagers have excellent eyes.

D'AUBERVAL: Which grow tired …

THERESE: The poor things!

COURTIN: But isn't it tremendous to see this kind of industry being generated between these poor children and their benefactors? … You rescue them and in return they dress you …

THERESE: But it's hardly a fair exchange, is it?

BIRON: Just like any exchange … There's always someone who gets *had!* *(Laughs)*

THERESE: Biron!

BIRON: So what? That's life, isn't it? Anyway, they're not in The Haven for fun, are they? The Haven is crammed with two hundred poor unfortunates who, rather than dying of hunger …

D'AUBERVAL: Work themselves to death instead.

COURTIN: *(Shocked)* Oh!

BIRON:	What would you like to see, my young sociologist? There will always be the rich and the poor.
D'AUBERVAL:	Because the rich *need* the poor …
BIRON:	Listen, socialism doesn't frighten me, you know! Ha! And I say that the *poor* need the *rich*! …
COURTIN:	*(To D'AUBERVAL)* Listen to him … *(To BIRON)* I'd add only this: the poor need the *good* rich … Take Biron, for instance, our successful, thrusting businessman … He has made himself a fortune …
BIRON:	*(Modest)* Oh …
COURTIN:	He's been most generous to us.
BIRON:	I can't deny it … I just give it away! …
D'AUBERVAL:	And what becomes of the money you give? A teaspoon of sugar to make the ocean taste sweet …
COURTIN:	We can't do everything, I admit … *(He goes over to his desk)*
BIRON:	No one can do everything … *(Sits down)* Obviously …
COURTIN:	But at least we can do *something* …
D'AUBERVAL:	Tokenism … The same old game … *(Sits near THERESE)*
COURTIN:	Chance governs everything in this imperfect world …
D'AUBERVAL:	What about *justice*? *(BIRON shrugs)*
COURTIN:	My dear boy, you'll find that you are merely deceiving yourself if you're counting on justice … You're young, enthusiastic … a dreamer … You'll find out soon enough that the human race is not ready to be ruled by justice … *(Supporting himself on his desk)* Happily, as far as charity's concerned, there is always resignation in the human spirit … *(Enter DUFRERE holding a paper)*

Scene Four

COURTIN:	*(Carries on ignoring DUFRERE)* Resignation is a most admirable quality in the dispossessed … Yes, we should be grateful that the poor are so resigned to their fate …
BIRON:	That's their strength! …
D'AUBERVAL:	Baron, don't you think that one day the poor will rise up against the charity, which has trapped them in misery in order to safeguard the wealth of the rich?
BIRON:	*(Shouts)* This is outrageous! … Besides, my eminent sociologist, the poor are poor precisely because they are *incapable* of rising up! … They don't even have time to think … Sweatshop labour puts a stop to that …
THERESE:	What a vile thing to say.

BIRON:	Ha! Ha!
COURTIN:	*(To BIRON)* Watch what you say … While the workers have no free time, others who do have it think for them and start to lead them … And that could lead us into serious danger …
THERESE:	*(Pointing out DUFRERE to COURTIN)* Darling …
COURTIN:	Slanderous to say that! *(Opens a dossier)* Look at this; this is the dossier that came with the prize the Academy awarded me. According to this, I am a miracle worker … I challenge you to put your finger on any one of these examples of sacrifice and deny it. Luckily, the poor are happy with their fate … they expect nothing …
BIRON:	Obviously …
COURTIN:	And do you know who troubles me most and yet strengthens my resolve? It's because there are people who are the most humble, uneducated … let's say the word … *illiterates.*
BIRON:	Listen to that D'Auberval!
COURTIN:	They achieve the most wonderful things …
BIRON:	Fine people!
COURTIN:	The people I fail to understand are not the socialists – they're just insane – but those radicals who lean towards socialism … many of them are rich …
BIRON:	Too rich!
COURTIN:	They have too much to say to the poor … Too much advice to give … *(Gestures like an orator)* You say there are too few schools – I tell you there are too many!
BIRON:	*(Applauding)* Bravo!
COURTIN:	It is ill-advised to let education spread … Knowledge is the beginning of wealth and wealth simply cannot extend to everyone … Education is a deathtrap. What is it, Dufrere? *(He takes the paper from DUFRERE)*
THERESE:	*(To DUFRERE)* Shall we leave you alone with the Baron?
DUFRERE:	Sorry, madam, but my office is too crowded …
BIRON:	We'll go … *(To D'AUBERVAL, who kisses THERESE's hand)* Young man, I have brought my car. If your principles allow, would you care for a lift?
D'AUBERVAL:	*(To THERESE)* Tomorrow, madam.
COURTIN:	Gentlemen, remember to be punctual. We must be at The Haven before two o'clock …
THERESE:	184 Rue de la Chapelle, Mr D'Auberval.
D'AUBERVAL:	Yes, I know …
COURTIN:	No one can arrive after the Duchess.
BIRON:	The Duchess?
COURTIN:	The Duchess of Saragossa. *(D'AUBERVAL exits)*

BIRON:	*(To* THERESE, *who reluctantly accepts his kiss on the hand)* Twenty-six years old, eh? *(*THERESE *shrugs and* BIRON *exits)*

Scene Five

COURTIN:	*(To* DUFRERE*)* First of all it's Ludovic Belair …
DUFRERE:	Shall I bring him in?
COURTIN:	Yes … he's a right bore … I must get rid of him …

THERESE *takes a book and exits left as* DUFRERE *exits right.*

SERVANT:	Mr Ludovic Belair!

Scene Six

BELAIR:	*(Shakes* COURTIN's *hand and heads over to designated chair)* While I was waiting in your antechamber, my lord …
COURTIN:	So sorry to keep you waiting …
BELAIR:	Not at all, my lord! It is I who must apologize for taking up your precious time … *(Sits)* Anyway, as I was waiting I found myself with two nuns, an old man, children, wet nurses and the poorest of women … I couldn't help but remember someone you wrote about in your most edifying book *Organized Charity* … Saint Vincent de Paul …
COURTIN:	Sir …
BELAIR:	And I blushed when I thought of the purposes of my visit, disrupting your magnificent work …
COURTIN:	I'm here for everyone.
BELAIR:	But here I stand – sit – before the man who orchestrates the very *conscience* of society …
COURTIN:	*(Smile)* Yes … I believe Anatole France said something like that in one of his more satirical moods …
BELAIR:	Anatole France? Oh, I hadn't realized.
COURTIN:	Enough! None of us has the right to deny anyone their due. To me that is the most important principle of anyone voted to the Academy.
BELAIR:	Mrs Labellevigne has informed me of all the kind things you've said about my humble little volume, and I am here to thank you, my lord. It is thanks to you that my work has been so warmly received.

COURTIN:	Your book has genuine merit, as does all your work … It has taught me a great deal … You have won many admirers!
BELAIR:	*(With difficulty)* Well …
COURTIN:	You have many influential admirers in journalism and in society, and if you win the Cornard-Cabasson prize I will have a hundred thank you letters to write to members of the government, not least in my own department …
BELAIR:	I'm rather confused, my lord …
COURTIN:	Why? One gets the friends one deserves. *(Silence)*
BELAIR:	The Cornard-Cabasson prize, you say?
COURTIN:	You don't rate that one?
BELAIR:	No, my lord! It's a wonderful prize … I wouldn't dare–
COURTIN:	Look. If you do win, it is not just because of your friends in high places, and neither is it solely a matter of talent. No. I'd be delighted to see recognition going to the young champion of ideas so dear to friends of the status quo.
BELAIR:	Yes …
COURTIN:	And knowing your ideas I advise you to steer clear of a tendency in your writing … You may not even be aware of it …
BELAIR:	*(Humble)* Yes, I know, some of my descriptions of passion may be rather too–
COURTIN:	Not that. I'm talking about your tendency towards *satire*. Writers should really avoid that. In ridiculing the morals of our time you open the door to revolution …
BELAIR:	Heaven forbid!
COURTIN:	I know it's enough to warn you. Nothing is more important for social stability than keeping quiet about society's little problems … Even more important than doing good deeds is silencing evil … Yes, silencing it … Prevent it, if you can … But at least try not to dwell on the bad things in society …
BELAIR:	*(Astonished)* That's a maxim I won't forget.
COURTIN:	Good. Take it to heart. *(Stands)*
BELAIR:	*(Standing)* So I can count on your support for the prize, my lord?
COURTIN:	Absolutely. *(Shakes BELAIR's hand)*
BELAIR:	Thank you, my lord … *(Heading towards the door)* Oh, if I may be so bold, may I invite you to write an article for a series I am preparing for the *Figaro*? It'll be called 'Men of Charity' or 'Charitable Organizations' …
COURTIN:	That'll be difficult for me!
BELAIR:	There's no rush. Later in the year will be fine. Charity is only newsworthy come winter …

COURTIN:	Fine …
BELAIR:	Thank you again, my lord …
COURTIN:	Remember – silence evil! *(DUFRERE appears at the door. BELAIR bows and shakes DUFRERE's hand and exits)*

Scene Seven

COURTIN:	Do you know him?
DUFRERE:	Yes … A victory for the conservatives!
COURTIN:	What do you mean?
DUFRERE:	We go way back … We worked on the *Libertarian Review* together.
COURTIN:	You're joking! Oh well, it's good to see people can change so dramatically …
DUFRERE:	Ha! It won't last … *(Shows the list)* We're already behind schedule. There are ladies here to see you from the cloakroom at St Martin's, from small donations, from the soup kitchens and from The Haven too … Do you want to see them or shall I get shot of them?
COURTIN:	No, it's alright … I've put them off for three weeks now … Let them in …

DUFRERE exits and brings in four women who enter nervously, shake hands with COURTIN and sit down.

Scene Eight

COURTIN:	Ladies, how can I help?
MRS PIGEON:	We've handed this week's receipts to Mr Dufrere … *(The women look sad)* Unfortunately, we've not had a good week, sir.
COURTIN:	Oh dear, ladies.
MRS RATURE:	We're all upset. *(All agree)*
MRS TUPIN:	People only want to give for their own neighbourhood.
MRS PIGEON:	There are too many causes – every day a new one!
MRS PIVIN:	Most are daylight robbery – there should be a law!
MRS PIGEON:	People spend their money on new fashions like automobiles!
MRS PIVIN:	Lotteries!
MRS RATURE:	The miners' fund!
MRS PIVIN:	International disaster relief!

COURTIN:	No one appreciates better than I how difficult your task is … Nor how noble is your task … Don't be downhearted … You must find *new* ways …
MRS PIGEON:	*(Sighing)* But every day, sir? … None of our ideas work for long. First we worked with housemaids … I sold ribbons and lace.
MRS TUPIN:	And they love my novels, the racier the better …
MRS PIGEON:	But it's not them who have the real money.
MRS RATURE:	When you think how rich some of the people are who open their doors to you and present you with one whole penny …
MRS PIVIN:	Open their doors? Lucky you! People are always 'out' when I call.
MRS RATURE:	Better call at mealtimes then.
MRS PIVIN:	They eat out too.
MRS TUPIN:	*(Sadly)* And there are some *beastly* concierges …
MRS PIGEON:	But I must tell you, sir … There's a real success story in the suburbs … Women beggars and their children are making little clay ornaments … It's lovely for the little darlings – they get the benefits of charity, a grasp of economy and have the chance to play with the things they've made for a little while … I've brought an example, sir … The heart of Jesus Christ.
MRS TUPIN:	Oh, that's lovely! *(The* LADIES *stand and take turns admiring the pottery object)*
COURTIN:	A child made this? Who would've thought it! Wonderful!
MRS PIGEON:	They also make soldiers, sheep, dolls … *(The impressed* LADIES *sit down again)*
COURTIN:	Ladies, remember my system. You should target occasions where people feel generous – weddings, births, marriages, funerals … *(The* LADIES *approve)* First communion …
MRS TUPIN:	*(Ecstatic)* First communion!
MRS PIGEON:	People are more generous at funerals than when they're happy … *(She sighs and raises her arms)*
COURTIN:	Ladies, charity is like cooking … You need a recipe! You must talk to people – face to face!
MRS PIVIN:	Talk to people? But where? When?
COURTIN:	Charity is an art – it is the art of *giving* … *(*MRS PIVIN *disagrees)* But it also the art of *making others* give. Let us say that you have certain information relating to someone you speak to … *(The* LADIES *listen carefully, frequently in agreement)* Little secrets, shall we say … There's no harm in *alluding* to these little secrets – discreetly, of course!
MRS RATURE and MRS TUPIN:	Yes …
COURTIN:	Tastefully.

MRS PIGEON:	Of course, *most* tastefully …
MRS PIVIN:	*(Pulls a face)* There's *one* lady I know …
COURTIN:	Sometimes people need a little *encouragement* to be generous … *(DUFRERE enters)*
DUFRERE:	Miss Rambert has arrived.
LADIES:	*(Whispering)* The manager of The Haven … The manager of The Haven …
DUFRERE:	She is pressed for time …
COURTIN:	We're all family here … Show her in … *(DUFRERE exits)* Do your best, ladies … in the name of charity! *(The LADIES agree. Enter RAMBERT)*

Scene Nine

RAMBERT:	Baron Courtin … *(She quickly greets the LADIES who disperse quietly and form a group upstage)* Baron Courtin, I've come to see if you have any instructions …
COURTIN:	Thank you, but I think everything's ready … *(He leads her downstage)* Is The Haven clean?
RAMBERT:	Immaculate.
COURTIN:	Are the girls washed?
RAMBERT:	Each one was scrubbed clean before bed last night.

The LADIES admire the décor.

COURTIN:	Perfect.
RAMBERT:	It was no easy task … Remember we only have three old bathtubs, and they are often unusable and–
COURTIN:	Is everyone clear on how they must behave in front of the Duchess?
RAMBERT:	Yes. And after breakfast tomorrow we will run through it again. Some are clumsy and unsightly but some look good enough to eat!
COURTIN:	Do they all understand that they must talk correctly?
RAMBERT:	Perfectly.
COURTIN:	What about their hair? The Duchess has told me she despises hair in bunches …
RAMBERT:	She has nothing to worry about.

The LADIES' chattering has grown in volume; COURTIN gestures for quiet.

COURTIN:	I don't need to tell you how much I want to be sure that we make the right impression … Not just because of the Duchess …

RAMBERT:	Sir …
COURTIN:	The whole committee will be there and the newspapers …
RAMBERT:	Rest assured, sir. Nothing will go wrong.
COURTIN:	You are a most capable woman …
RAMBERT:	*(Quietly)* Sir … Do you think we could be alone for a moment? …
COURTIN:	Ah … Ladies! I mustn't delay you any longer. Remember, we're really counting on you tomorrow at two o'clock … *(The LADIES bow)*
MRS PIGEON:	And those little Jesus hearts, sir?
COURTIN:	We'll see about that on Saturday … Goodbye, Ladies! Thank you! *(They leave slowly, one at a time)*

Scene Ten

COURTIN:	Is it something serious?
RAMBERT:	There's a bit of a problem at The Haven.
COURTIN:	Oh?
RAMBERT:	Quite a serious matter actually.
COURTIN:	Tell me.
RAMBERT:	One of the wardens, Miss Barandon, locked a girl in a cupboard and forgot all about her …
COURTIN:	*(Stunned)* What?
RAMBERT:	She left her there all day – and all night!
COURTIN:	But that's crazy!
RAMBERT:	As soon as Miss Barandon remembered, the girl was rescued but she was unconscious …
COURTIN:	This is awful!
RAMBERT:	And despite our best efforts, she died …
COURTIN:	*(Terrified)* She's dead?
RAMBERT:	Yes.
COURTIN:	This is dreadful … *(He walks, his head lowered)*
RAMBERT:	Luckily we were able to remove the corpse from Miss Barandon's room without anyone seeing …
COURTIN:	You are sure that no one …
RAMBERT:	No one. Mrs Antoinette, the concierge, kept a lookout.
COURTIN:	Locking a child in a cupboard all day and all night! *(Raises his arms)* Unbelievable! Absolutely dreadful! Who was the child?
RAMBERT:	Caroline Mezy.
COURTIN:	Caroline Mezy? *(He gestures that he does not know her)* Parents?
RAMBERT:	A mother.

COURTIN:	In Paris?
RAMBERT:	She used to be … A bit of a 'man hunter' … She's fled to the country now – who knows where.
COURTIN:	Did anyone ever visit the girl?
RAMBERT:	Never, luckily.
COURTIN:	How could anyone lock a child in a cupboard and forget about it!? It's atrocious. People will say we're monsters.
RAMBERT:	*(Calm)* It's standard disciplinary procedure.
COURTIN:	Fine procedure, I must say!
RAMBERT:	Approved by the committee – two hours in the cupboard.
COURTIN:	Two hours! Four hours even! But twenty-four hours?
RAMBERT:	It was an accident. Accidents will happen, even in The Haven.
COURTIN:	An accident? *(Changes tone)* That's true … *(Changes tone again)* But we are horribly responsible …
RAMBERT:	The child did have some history of heart problems … The doctor won't be in the least *awkward* …
COURTIN:	Awkward? This is serious … *(Urgently)* What about Father Leroze?
RAMBERT:	He doesn't know anything.
COURTIN:	He didn't take her last confession?
RAMBERT:	She was unconscious.
COURTIN:	Did anyone administer the last rites?
RAMBERT:	What for?
COURTIN:	A dead body in The Haven – without the due process of religion! Just think! And me in my position!
RAMBERT:	You never know what the chaplain will be like – nervous, babbling, stressed …
COURTIN:	So what!?
RAMBERT:	He would have upset the whole house, all the neighbours … That would have been a sight!
COURTIN:	This is appalling! And what about tomorrow? Whatever will we do?
RAMBERT:	It will be fine, believe me. I have taken care of everything. *(Pause)* There is one matter though …
COURTIN:	What? Tell me!
RAMBERT:	*(Timidly)* Could I ask for … a little money …
COURTIN:	More money? I've no idea what you do with it! I gave you some only last Saturday.
RAMBERT:	*(Scornfully)* Three hundred francs!
COURTIN:	*(Unimpressed)* We will talk about this on Monday …
RAMBERT:	I desperately need it for tomorrow morning … At least fifteen hundred francs … *(COURTIN raises his arms)* You realize that every week … *(Firmly)* I have to pay the wages with my own money …

COURTIN:	Alright …
RAMBERT:	I'm not out of pocket but …
COURTIN:	Understood … Tomorrow morning … *(Raises his arms and walks)* A cupboard! A girl locked in a cupboard! *(LAROZE appears at the half-open door stage right)*
RAMBERT:	*(Noticing LAROZE, quietly)* Not a word to the chaplain, sir, I beg you … Otherwise all is lost!
COURTIN:	Don't worry. *(LAROZE enters)*

Scene Eleven

LAROZE:	Hello Baron! Oh – and Miss Rambert! *(He looks over at her rather coldly)*
COURTIN:	The big day tomorrow, Father … I expect you wish it was all over?
LAROZE:	I cannot disagree, Baron, I cannot disagree! … I must say I am rather uneasy about this inspection …
RAMBERT:	Inspection?
COURTIN:	*Visit* … An important visit, true, but a straightforward visit all the same …
LAROZE:	Much too official to be a mere visit … I am rather anxious, I can't deny it …
COURTIN:	Rest assured everything will be fine.
LAROZE:	No doubt our friend here has assured you of that … But we cannot be too vigilant …
RAMBERT:	Wise words, Father … I was only just saying to our patron how impressively vigilant you yourself are …
LAROZE:	*(With gentle irony)* Why thank you, Rambert, you are simply too kind! But, please, don't embarrass me … *(Discreetly to COURTIN)* I must speak to you alone. *(He walks towards the window)*
COURTIN:	Rambert, your time is so precious I really mustn't delay you any longer …
RAMBERT:	That's quite alright … I say, Father? *(LAROZE merely cocks his head towards her)* Would you care for a lift back to The Haven?
LAROZE:	Thank you so very much, my dear … but I have some other business to attend to …
RAMBERT:	I could always–
LAROZE:	*(Very fast)* It'd be completely out of your way.
RAMBERT:	Very well. *(LAROZE turns away completely)* Will we at least see you for dinner, Father?

LAROZE:	Of course.
RAMBERT:	Baron.
COURTIN:	*(Takes her hand)* See you tomorrow. *(RAMBERT exits)*

Scene Twelve

LAROZE:	At last! She can't bear to leave me alone with you for an instant! … Baron, I simply had to come and see you … My conscience demands it!
COURTIN:	Oh! Has something happened?
LAROZE:	*(Sitting down)* Nothing at all …
COURTIN:	*(Sitting down)* Well then?
LAROZE:	I don't want to worry you, but many things need improving at The Haven …
COURTIN:	*(Nonchalantly)* Of course they do … But what are you worried about? Tomorrow is bound to be a resounding success!
LAROZE:	That's exactly what's worrying me. *Success.*
COURTIN:	Don't be ridiculous!
LAROZE:	I'm not. Rambert's management is far from satisfactory. She is not a good manager. In fact, she's a *dreadful* manager. There are debts – spiralling debts. It's a total mess! *(Wrings his hands)* Food, medicine, everything!
COURTIN:	I know. *(Pause)* It's not Rambert's fault … The Haven is expensive to run and I am sorry to say that the generosity of our benefactors does have its limits.
LAROZE:	Yes, yes, but it's not only that.
COURTIN:	Well?
LAROZE:	Rambert is not reliable … She can be far too lenient … It makes her seem indulgent and over-familiar – it is completely out of place … I assure you it's not just a clash of personalities …
COURTIN:	Of course not …
LAROZE:	She is lacking in judgement … She spoils some of them; she's too soft on some of them …
COURTIN:	There are some pretty tragic cases–
LAROZE:	I know, but all these 'cuddles' and the preferential treatment … Children notice these things …
COURTIN:	Petty jealousies … You shouldn't listen to gossip!
LAROZE:	I beg you to believe what I have seen with my own eyes … Things that have made me shudder … And at other times Rambert is inexplicably draconian!

COURTIN:	There are some hardened cases–
LAROZE:	That's no reason to beat them half to death!
COURTIN:	Oh come on! …
LAROZE:	I've heard them crying … Children are always crying there. It's ghastly! How can it be justified? There are all manner of bizarre punishments … and equally bizarre rewards … Rewards given out in the evening – *far too late* …
COURTIN:	What are you trying to say?
LAROZE:	*(Seriously)* I am bound by confession. *(Silence)*
COURTIN:	Rambert has some quirks, I admit, but the children never complain …
LAROZE:	Oh!?
COURTIN:	Not much anyway … Besides, I have no time for little girls' petty grumbles and whining … I have other worries, chiefly financial …
LAROZE:	Quite so, Baron …
COURTIN:	I'm counting on the Duchess to make a considerable donation tomorrow … I have major plans …
LAROZE:	I see … Would this be anything to do with the man who visited you at The Haven last winter? *(Struggling to remember)* Mr …
COURTIN:	Lerible! Celestin Lerible!
LAROZE:	That's it! My memory! Mr Lerible … He seemed like a good chap!
COURTIN:	Don't be so sure … *(Brighter tone)* We shall see!
LAROZE:	Try and make a real success of things, Baron, before it's too late!
COURTIN:	You talk as if all is lost!
LAROZE:	No! But in all honesty, if I may, you sometimes make the mistake of closing your eyes to things … and you let people convince you that everything will work out fine …
COURTIN:	But everything *will* work out fine, Father.
LAROZE:	May God hear you, Baron … But don't leave everything in His hands … *(THERESE appears at the door to the billiard room. She wears a hat and scarf and carries an umbrella)*

Scene Thirteen

THERESE:	Oh, I'm sorry!
LAROZE:	*(Walking towards her with open arms)* My dear countess! I am your humble Servant!
THERESE:	*(Takes his hand)* It is so good to see you, Father. I've been to The Haven so many times, yet I never seem to catch you there.

LAROZE:	*(Caressing her hands while* THERESE *attempts to disengage from him)* It's even worse for me – seeing so little of you!
THERESE:	I was very busy myself – all winter! … I hope I'm not disturbing you?
LAROZE:	Disturb us? Not at all; I was just explaining to–
COURTIN:	We've been running through tomorrow's arrangements … *(Rubbing hands)* Everything will be fine …
LAROZE:	*(Startled)* Fine? *(COURTIN gestures)* Yes, indeed, everything will go swimmingly! … Well, I'd better take my leave of you … Thank heaven I had chance to see you! And I hope we may see you at The Haven before long; you are The Haven's mother, after all! Come and see us soon.
THERESE:	*(Dryly)* Certainly. *(She moves away)*
LAROZE:	You are most kind and charming! I will hold you to that promise. I am your most humble Servant. Don't trouble yourself, Baron. Goodbye. *(He bows several times and exits)*

Scene Fourteen

COURTIN:	That's not like you … You're normally so charming …
THERESE:	I *was* charming.
COURTIN:	Ha! He's done nothing to harm you, poor chap! He thinks the world of you!
THERESE:	He should mind his own business … *(She makes to leave)*
COURTIN:	You're a hard woman …
THERESE:	The way he grasps my hands like that … I hate it! It's obscene! *(She opens the door)*
COURTIN:	Leaving already?
THERESE:	Yes … *(Closes the door)* Or have you got something to say?
COURTIN:	I thought you were going out.
THERESE:	Oh, I don't fancy going out today … It's far too hot … Stifling heat … *(She sits)* Is Saturday looking busy?
COURTIN:	Like every Saturday.
THERESE:	I envy you! So many things going on … I am *so* bored …
COURTIN:	Why don't you do something?
THERESE:	What? Like you?
COURTIN:	It wouldn't hurt you to do something for the less fortunate sometime … It would be good for you. Charity is good for the health!

THERESE:	I'd love to give happiness to the world! Joy by the handful! … But unfortunately I am not the least interested in your work …
COURTIN:	How come!? You used to be so *committed* …
THERESE:	I was carefree then … Not a care in the world …
COURTIN:	You worry yourself too much … Live a little! *(Pause)* That little D'Auberval's an idiot – all his theories and his pessimism … This is his fault, partly – he does you no good.
THERESE:	I don't know what you mean … What do you prefer? That I spend time with the ever cheerful Armand Biron!?
COURTIN:	Biron …
THERESE:	*(Aggressively)* And stop calling him 'little D'Auberval'! His name is D'Auberval! Robert D'Auberval!
COURTIN:	I'm sorry, darling, it's just that Biron always–
THERESE:	Oh, how he annoys me! God, I hate him!
COURTIN:	Since when?
THERESE:	Pardon?
COURTIN:	Biron's very jealous. D'Auberval's thirty years younger and is always very presentable …
THERESE:	Yes, he is …
COURTIN:	*(Jeering)* So what!? Biron has many fine qualities and is extremely intelligent … …
THERESE:	I don't expect a man to spend too much time at the mirror, but that's no excuse to look like Biron … Have you seen his trousers?
COURTIN:	Er, yes?
THERESE:	They are hilarious! They are always too short! *(Laughs)* I don't know how he does it! But they are always too short! *(Laughs)* And he thinks he's elegant!
COURTIN:	I'm grateful to him …
THERESE:	God! It's pathetic how he imitates you!
COURTIN:	He's just trying to aspire to nobility–
THERESE:	Pah! *(Laughs and falls into chair)*
COURTIN:	Don't be cruel, my dear … I don't think that middle-class aspirations are ridiculous … It's quite flattering really!
THERESE:	And his optimism! There is nothing more nauseating than the optimism of an endlessly cheerful man!
COURTIN:	It doesn't bother me … And let me tell you something … I think it's disgraceful to see how Biron is treated …
THERESE:	What do you mean?
COURTIN:	Earlier … After lunch … D'Auberval can be quite tactless … He's immature … I don't like to see that sort of thing from a guest …
THERESE:	*(Dryly)* Have you told him this yourself …

COURTIN:	No, my dear, but I must say that you have done nothing to correct D'Auberval's manners ... *(THERESE smiles)* Yes, your habit of laughing at everything he says!
THERESE:	Why can't Biron understand that he visits us too often? That it's never a pleasure to see him?
COURTIN:	Do you really hate Biron that much?
THERESE:	I'd relish the chance to send him packing once and for all!
COURTIN:	He's an old friend ...
THERESE:	*(Aggressively)* Whenever you ask a favour of him he is simply impertinent!
COURTIN:	I think your problem is that you've grown impatient with him since you started to notice his faults. You used to love his sense of humour! You used to sing his praises!
THERESE:	He laughs too much.
COURTIN:	You've only noticed that since you stopped laughing with him.
THERESE:	What do we gain by being friends with him?
COURTIN:	He's a powerful man. Influential friends are very useful. They can help protect you from danger ...
THERESE:	To listen to you, one would think we're in grave peril!
COURTIN:	I wonder what he's been telling you ...
THERESE:	Nothing very precise ... Wasn't that deal he proposed a bit dubious?
COURTIN:	Put it this way: I refused to be patron unless he was on the committee.
THERESE:	Sounds wise ... Well? What else do you have to fear?
COURTIN:	Nothing. Absolutely nothing. Do you think I should have anything else to fear?
THERESE:	No. It's just Biron and his beastly insinuations.
COURTIN:	Calm down ... *(Lightly)* My situation, my fortune such as it is, is nothing next to Armand Biron's millions ... One of his manias is to think someone poverty stricken if they don't spend money like mad!
THERESE:	That's so true ... He thinks it's a disgrace to be seen in cab!
COURTIN:	Sorry?
THERESE:	Nothing.
COURTIN:	*(Lightly)* Biron's not a bad chap at all, really ...

FOOTMAN enters with a card on a plate.

COURTIN:	*(Takes the card)* Oh! My God! He's here! Announce him – announce him at once! *(FOOTMAN exits)* Darling ...

| THERESE: | I'm on my way! *(She exits quickly stage left.* COURTIN *turns to the door beaming)* |
| FOOTMAN: | *(Announces)* The Minister for Public Aid! |

Act 2

The same location.

Scene One

DUFRERE *stands by the mantelpiece, his arms behind his back.* CELESTIN LERIBLE *is sitting, timidly, at the edge of a chair and looks around the room. A noise is heard from offstage and* LERIBLE *leaps up.*

DUFRERE:	No, Mr Lerible … It's not the Baron.
LERIBLE:	I must say this is very annoying … Have you any idea why the Baron wants to see me? *(DUFRERE shrugs)* Is it to do with The Haven? *(DUFRERE shrugs again)* Yes! *(Distressed)* Things are in a pretty bad way …
DUFRERE:	Indeed?
LERIBLE:	Everyone's talking about it …
DUFRERE:	That's just gossip, Mr Lerible.
LERIBLE:	Yes, yes indeed! *(Pause)* You're a discreet chap, Mr Dufrere … Sensible too! … I saw Mr Biron yesterday …
DUFRERE:	*(Interested)* Really?
LERIBLE:	Yes! Just in passing, that's all … *(Noticing* DUFRERE's *interest)* Nothing! *(Looks at the clock)* Two o'clock already! … I do have another appointment, you know … This is *most* annoying!
DUFRERE:	The Baron will be here at any moment … *(LERIBLE fidgets around the room)*
LERIBLE:	So annoying, I must say! *(Pause)* Could make a pretty penny selling this lot off … Oh, I only said that to, er, express my admiration … *(Goes over to a sofa and rubs it with the back of his hand)* I know this piece of furniture like an old friend … It belonged to Pamard before he went bankrupt, didn't it?
DUFRERE:	I believe so …
LERIBLE:	Biron snapped it up for nothing! A museum piece like this!
DUFRERE:	You'd have liked it?

LERIBLE:	I would've liked the lot! … Poor old Pamard … I warned him … He was too quick to sell … *(He walks around agitated)* I wonder what he wants with me? I think the Baron was very disappointed the other day …
DUFRERE:	Oh?
LERIBLE:	Yes, when the Duchess visited The Haven …
DUFRERE:	Well?
LERIBLE:	She didn't give a thing! *(Raises his arms)* Five hundred francs!
DUFRERE:	Yet more gossip!
LERIBLE:	No! No! Charity is a very difficult business these days. *(Looks at the clock)* No, Mr Dufrere, I cannot wait any longer … Please convey my apologies to the Baron … Very annoying, I must say.
DUFRERE:	The stock exchange, eh?
LERIBLE:	I don't like to go there … It's for big businessmen … Not me … And besides, I don't trust all those Jews … They're too quick for my liking …
DUFRERE:	You mean you don't dabble in stocks and shares? Come off it!
LERIBLE:	Never … Well … I buy the odd thing … Shares that seem like a bargain … and …
DUFRERE:	Yes?
LERIBLE:	I wait patiently.
DUFRERE:	*(Roars with laughter)* You *wait patiently*!? *(Invites* LERIBLE *to sit down)*
LERIBLE:	No … I'm afraid I simply can't … The Baron will be in touch, I'm sure … *(He exits followed by* DUFRERE. THERESE *enters stage left. Seeing the room empty she enters quickly and turns suddenly when* DUFRERE *reenters stage right)*

Scene Two

THERESE:	Well?
DUFRERE:	The Baron's still not back.
THERESE:	You're certain?
DUFRERE:	Absolutely.
THERESE:	What time is it?
DUFRERE:	Ten minutes past two … Perhaps the Baron is dining out for lunch?
THERESE:	Never without letting me know.
DUFRERE:	There's nothing to worry about, madam. The Baron has been delayed at The Haven … That's all. You understand that since that anonymous letter was received – about that dead girl …

THERESE:	The poor child died from a weak heart. That's all. It was no one's fault. The doctor has–
DUFRERE:	But it's not about Caroline Mezy. It's about Louise Lapar …
THERESE:	All that nonsense about beatings? Absurd! Those girls are making it up! They have such an appetite for fantasy!
DUFRERE:	That may be, but that letter has worried the Baron … There may be an investigation …
THERESE:	Mr Dufrere … Other things concern me … But for a while now I've noticed the Baron becoming increasingly anxious and preoccupied … He's become quite a changed man … *(Amicably)* I know the confidence he has in you, and I know that you deserve it …
DUFRERE:	*(Bows)* Madam. *(JULIE enters stage left)*
JULIE:	Excuse me, madam, it's a man from the department store …
THERESE:	Tell him that we've had enough donations today …
JULIE:	*(Insistent)* But madam …
THERESE:	Tell them we're not interested …
JULIE:	But, madam, it's an *inspector* …
THERESE:	Oh. Tell him to wait. Thank you, Julie. *(Pushing JULIE towards the door)* Tell him I'm out … and so is the Baron … Tell him to call again sometime … *(JULIE exits)* I wish he'd come back!
DUFRERE:	He will, madam. *(Silence)*
THERESE:	I know the Baron holds you in absolute confidence. But you must let me know if we're in any kind of trouble.
DUFRERE:	Of course, madam.
THERESE:	But what is he so worried about? I'm afraid to ask him. I dare not ask him about money … He seems so anxious about it … Why?
DUFRERE:	All sorts of reasons … The election was expensive … The running of the house … Madam, if you would excuse me–
THERESE:	*(Friendly)* Come now! … *(Change in tone)* We've made savings …
DUFRERE:	A house like this is expensive to run.
THERESE:	But the Baron is well informed at the stock exchange …
DUFRERE:	Not entirely. A couple of times he's followed Mr Biron's advice …
THERESE:	Mr Biron?
DUFRERE:	Yes, and it hasn't worked out particularly well.
THERESE:	How bad are we talking?
DUFRERE:	We invested in the Pacific Railroad Company, and the price has dropped quite–
THERESE:	Oh, it's useless! *(Lamenting)* What on earth does he want with a railway in America!?
DUFRERE:	*(Smiling)* He bought *shares* …

THERESE:	Shares, railways, toy trains! These are all Biron's stupid ideas to squander our money!
DUFRERE:	He's given very good advice in the past …
THERESE:	*(With contempt)* In the past! *(Turns to face DUFRERE)* Why isn't he back? This is so annoying! *(Pause)* What about The Haven?
DUFRERE:	*(Reserved)* I wouldn't know about The Haven. The Baron keeps it to himself. But I suppose that it's a similar story …
THERESE:	And that Lerible? Do you think he'll help …
DUFRERE:	*(Shakes head)* Mm …
THERESE:	But he's a good friend of Biron, isn't he?
DUFRERE:	Business acquaintance, more like.
THERESE:	*(Sarcastic)* Well that's great. *(Anxious)* There are times when everything is simply awful! *(FOOTMAN enters and hands THERESE a card)* And sometimes things are just wonderful! *(To FOOTMAN)* Please tell Mr D'Auberval to come in … *(FOOTMAN exits)*
DUFRERE:	*(Bows)* Madam.
THERESE:	Thank you so much, Mr Dufrere … We'll discuss this again sometime … *(Exit DUFRERE. LERIBLE sits down with a book in one hand and a mirror in the other. Enter JULIE)*

Scene Three

THERESE:	What now?
JULIE:	He's still here, madam.
THERESE:	Who?
JULIE:	That inspector.
THERESE:	What do you want me to do about it?
JULIE:	But madam …
THERESE:	Why can't people leave me alone! *(JULIE makes to leave)* Julie … Is my hair in order?
JULIE:	*(Adjusts THERESE's hair)* You're beautiful, madam … *(JULIE exits. FOOTMAN brings in D'AUBERVAL)*

Scene Four

THERESE:	Good afternoon, you little tease.
D'AUBERVAL:	Tease? Why–
THERESE:	Because you did not turn up last night.

D'AUBERVAL:	You didn't get my message?
THERESE:	No.
D'AUBERVAL:	No?
THERESE:	No.
D'AUBERVAL:	That is so infuriating!
THERESE:	*(Laughs)* Let me see … your message said … *(She pulls out a note from her book)*
D'AUBERVAL:	*(Playful)* Oh! You're very good at telling fibs …
THERESE:	Not really – only when I'm making silly little jokes … What about you? Are you ready?
D'AUBERVAL:	To do what?
THERESE:	To tell fibs of your own … *(Points at the note)* You wrote here that the sole purpose of your evening was to be … with *me*. *(Pause)* Well?
D'AUBERVAL:	*(Embarrassed)* I've come to explain. *(He sits near her)*
THERESE:	So where were you?
D'AUBERVAL:	I was at the club.
THERESE:	This club of yours … A blonde or a redhead?
D'AUBERVAL:	Please don't joke … I'm so unhappy!
THERESE:	My poor dear! Why?
D'AUBERVAL:	*(Embarrassed and hesitantly)* Why didn't you tell me? …
THERESE:	Pardon?
D'AUBERVAL:	Why didn't you tell me the truth? … Am I really nothing to you?
THERESE:	What do you mean?
D'AUBERVAL:	Don't pretend … please … I know all about it … all about your problems … And to think that I never realized! *(Gallantly)* I cannot bear to think of you being unhappy … I will do anything to help you! Oh, if only I had a fortune to give you!
THERESE:	*(Embarrassed but dignified)* Thank you, my dear … That's most kind … But what gives you the right to talk to me like this? … *(Dryly)* When I need money I simply ask my husband. And if he can't provide, then I go without.
D'AUBERVAL:	Forgive me – I've upset you.
THERESE:	Confused me, more like.
D'AUBERVAL:	I didn't have the right … Forgive me!
THERESE:	*(Stares at him)* Somebody has been saying unpleasant things about me, haven't they? At your club last night, somebody said something? …
D'AUBERVAL:	Yes.
THERESE:	Who?
D'AUBERVAL:	Does it really matter–

THERESE:	Yes, it really matters. Who?
D'AUBERVAL:	General Fain was there …
THERESE:	Huh!
D'AUBERVAL:	And D'Auberive … Veneur … Steiner … D'Epiais.
THERESE:	Anyone else?
D'AUBERVAL:	No.
THERESE:	People I don't even know … Or hardly know anyway … And they were talking about me?
D'AUBERVAL:	Believe me, they were not in the least malicious … but …
THERESE:	Yes?
D'AUBERVAL:	They talked about you like they would about other women.
THERESE:	Does it really upset you when people talk of me as if I'm just an ordinary woman? *(She gives him her hand and he kisses it)* So what did they say?
D'AUBERVAL:	It will upset you. It's about the financial difficulties of the Baron. They think he's bankrupt. Madam, they *pity* you …
THERESE:	Tell them they can pity whoever they like. But not me. I am not to be pitied. *(Pause)* Come on. That's not everything, is it?
D'AUBERVAL:	No … *(Extremely awkward)* What really upset me was that they kept saying a certain name in the same breath as yours …
THERESE:	*(Calmly)* Biron.
D'AUBERVAL:	*(Shocked)* Oh!
THERESE:	*(Calmly)* Do you think this is the first time such slanders have been bandied about? I know I shouldn't have spent so much time with Biron. It's my husband's fault … Besides, Biron is a wonderful friend – he has done so much for us … People are so mean-spirited!
D'AUBERVAL:	Quite wicked!
THERESE:	Imagine if such a thing was–
D'AUBERVAL:	Don't say it!
THERESE:	You know I actually regret that what they said about us being bankrupt is not true! Do you think I like all this luxury? Heavens, no! I feel like … I feel like I'm a prisoner … *(Cheerfully)* Sometimes I dream of living in a tenement somewhere … Far away from this world … Everybody would leave me alone … Everybody except one person …
D'AUBERVAL:	Who?
THERESE:	*(Very close to D'AUBERVAL)* You.
D'AUBERVAL:	*(Sadly)* I think you'd avoid me too.
THERESE:	One cannot avoid people that one … loves …
D'AUBERVAL:	Loves?

THERESE:	More than one's own happiness …
D'AUBERVAL:	Not at all! I want to lie down at your feet!
THERESE:	*(A little sadly)* My poor dear! Don't mistake me for something that I'm not … You frighten me sometimes … Yes … I am just a woman, an ordinary woman … *(FOOTMAN enters and hands THERESE a card)* Tell him I will see him presently … *(FOOTMAN exits)* You must go now …
D'AUBERVAL:	I will … when I've seen who's here …
THERESE:	No, you must go … You're being impolite now …
D'AUBERVAL:	*(Stands)* I'm sorry … I'm being beastly! I will go – after I've kissed your hand four times! *(Kisses her hand)* One!
THERESE:	Oh, you child!
D'AUBERVAL:	Two!
THERESE:	You are *naughty* …
D'AUBERVAL:	Three!
THERESE:	Off you go now!
D'AUBERVAL:	Four! *(He looks at THERESE who is silent)* Now I can go … *(He heads towards the right-hand door)* There's a lady in Paris whom I adore with every fibre of my being!
THERESE:	*(Laughs)* If I see her, I'll tell her!
D'AUBERVAL:	Will it make her happy?
THERESE:	More than you'll ever know.
D'AUBERVAL:	Goodbye! *(He heads the right-hand door)*
THERESE:	That's the wrong door, my dear! Go that way … *(Indicates billiard room)*
D'AUBERVAL:	I'm quite flustered … I can't think why!
THERESE:	Listen, my dear, I don't what you're worrying about … Mrs Durand D'Avranches has come to see me …
D'AUBERVAL:	Sorry … I am such a pest! *(He exits. THERESE goes to the window, opens the curtains and rings the bell. BIRON enters)*

Scene Five

THERESE keeps her back to BIRON before suddenly turning around.

THERESE:	Why can't you leave me alone!? Is it too much to ask? After what I said to you at the theatre last night? Here you are again! Do you want to start a scandal? What do you want? What do you want!?
BIRON:	*(Timidly closes the door)* Can't we just talk like friends for a moment?
THERESE:	But we are not friends! You *persecute* me!

BIRON:	But I can't stop thinking of you! I can't live without you! I'm desperate! I'm scared of what I might do! ... Tell me what should I do?
THERESE:	*(Ferociously)* How about leaving me alone!? *(Changes tone, close to tears)* Biron, leave me alone, I beg you ... *(She wipes her eyes)*
BIRON:	I can see your tears ...
THERESE:	They are tears of *rage*.
BIRON:	Listen ...
THERESE:	*(Pacing around)* No ... You listen to me! You can see the state I'm in! I'm a nervous wreck! It is unbearable – for you too, if you're honest! It's best if we don't see each other ... Maybe I will change ... in time ... But for now ... Leave me alone. *(Increasingly nervous)* Please go ... I don't want to see you anymore ... I bump into you in restaurants, in the theatre, in shops, in streets ... Everywhere! I don't know how you do it ...
BIRON:	*(Smiling)* It's all prearranged ... You know what I'm like ...
THERESE:	*(Enraged)* Yes I do!
BIRON:	Instead of being angry, you should be touched. How can I make you see?
THERESE:	You can help me by doing what I say; get out of here ... and get out of my life!
BIRON:	But I simply *must* see you.
THERESE:	It will do you no good!
BIRON:	But I cannot live without seeing you!
THERESE:	*(Exasperated)* Do you want me to run out of the door? Do you want me to kill myself!?
BIRON:	*(Humble)* Do you really hate me so much? *(Silence)* Shall we sit down? ...
THERESE:	What's the point? Alright ... It's ridiculous to march around like this ... Sit down.
BIRON:	Don't you want to sit–
THERESE:	*Sit down.*
BIRON:	*(Sits on a pouf)* Are you sure you won't sit down too?
THERESE:	*(Sits down on the sofa)* I had decided that I wouldn't let you come and see me – never again ... But let's end this properly, once and for all.
BIRON:	Very well! Don't worry ... Let's sit and have a nice talk ... I am just a good friend, that's all ...
THERESE:	Yes, I know your idea of 'friendship'! You don't understand the meaning of the word ... Anyway ... I'm not well ...
BIRON:	*(Energetically)* You're ill!?

THERESE:	Ssh … I just need to rest. I need some time to myself.
BIRON:	My poor, poor darling!
THERESE:	So you're going to lavish me with pity too, eh?
BIRON:	I'm sorry?
THERESE:	Nothing … I have all sorts of worries …
BIRON:	Tell me! You shouldn't keep secrets from a friend like me! You know that I am a friend worth having!
THERESE:	Because you're rich?
BIRON:	No …
THERESE:	*(Standing)* I will never accept another thing from you.
BIRON:	What do you propose to do?
THERESE:	I will change my life.
BIRON:	No one can change their life …
THERESE:	I said I will *change my life.*
BIRON:	A lady like yourself? Impossible!
THERESE:	You'll see …
BIRON:	At your age!
THERESE:	So I'm old, am I?
BIRON:	You are not old, Therese! I adore you!
THERESE:	If I became old, you wouldn't love me anymore … But others would … You have never understood the youth that is inside me! The lust for life within me!
BIRON:	And the stupidity inside that head of yours! *(Pause)* I also know that you will come back to me.
THERESE:	Ridiculous!
BIRON:	You will come back to me, Therese. You will come back to me because you will not be able to stop yourself.
THERESE:	You think so?
BIRON:	Yes. And because I love you … *(THERESE roars with laughter)* Because I want you and need you more than anything I've ever had in my life …
THERESE:	Oh, I know this speech! I've heard this one before!
BIRON:	Therese …
THERESE:	The same words … The same gestures … They worked once upon a time, but this time, you have lost me.
BIRON:	No I haven't.
THERESE:	You won't set me free?
BIRON:	No.
THERESE:	No? *(She laughs nervously)*
BIRON:	That's right, laugh! … After all, you won't be laughing for long … *(Standing)* Whatever I wanted, I *had* …

THERESE:	*(Violently)* Everything has its price, but I'm no longer for sale!
BIRON:	*(Shrugs and grins malevolently)* Oh, we'll see about that …
THERESE:	You will drive me insane … *(Close to him)* Just go … Are you deaf? … Go! *(BIRON backs away)* Can't you see that I'm kicking you out!
BIRON:	You're losing your mind! *(BIRON exits, colliding into DUFRERE as he does so)*

Scene Six

DUFRERE:	*(Calling towards the door)* I beg your pardon! Hey!
THERESE:	Leave him. *(Silence)*
DUFRERE:	The Baron's back, madam. He'll be here any moment – he's just talking to a journalist …
THERESE:	Heavens, no! I'm in no state to see him! I'm going out … I won't be long … *(Exits door stage left. DUFRERE adjusts a chair that THERESE moved on her way out)*

Scene Seven

Enter COURTIN followed by FOOTMAN, who takes COURTIN's coat, walking stick and hat. Exit FOOTMAN.

COURTIN:	What? She's not here?
DUFRERE:	I believe she's gone out.
COURTIN:	But you said she was desperate to see me.
DUFRERE:	She was, honestly …
COURTIN:	This is most annoying! I'm due to see Miss Rambert … I wanted to see the Baroness beforehand … She gives excellent advice …
DUFRERE:	Miss Rambert? Won't she be at The Haven?
COURTIN:	I was there all morning. But no sign of Miss Rambert. I waited until three o'clock. I left a message telling her to come here *at once*. *(Pause)* What a day! The things I've learnt today are *unbelievable* … But I saw this coming … There was more than an element of truth to that letter …
DUFRERE:	What? Beatings?
COURTIN:	*(Protesting)* Beatings! Beatings! *(Changes tone)* That fact is that they have been using the cane … And I've been told some stories …

DUFRERE:	*(Smiling ironically)* Father Laroze has finally broken the sanctity of confession?
COURTIN:	*(Protesting)* No! *(Changes tone)* Well … He told me who I should talk to … There are things that are quite unrepeatable … The way the cane was used …
DUFRERE:	The children were stripped naked?
COURTIN:	Not *entirely* …
DUFRERE:	Witnesses?
COURTIN:	The witnesses were very precise … They made things sound even worse …
DUFRERE:	I see. What about Louise Lapar? Was she really hurt badly?
COURTIN:	She's in bed now … She's hurt … Badly hurt … There are bleeding welts across her shoulders and back … She's got a fever and is delirious … I'm worried about her … *(Silence)*
DUFRERE:	And the allegations about the food?
COURTIN:	When one person complains about that, everything else follows: 'The workshops are filthy … We're worked too hard … We're exhausted … There's no fresh air … ' All workshops are like that!
DUFRERE:	But …
COURTIN:	'The dormitories are cramped and disgusting … There's nowhere to wash … ' It's true. But it's the same story with charity homes the world over! And I admit, if you've spent a lifetime working in charity like I have, you do get blasé … *(Pacing)* But what am I supposed to do without money! I need money! *(Silence)*
DUFRERE:	Has a formal complaint been made?
COURTIN:	No … Not yet anyway … Since Caroline Mezy died there have been all sorts of malicious rumours … But when there was talk of exhumation and a full post-mortem … I decided to visit the Police Commissioner …
DUFRERE:	Oh?
COURTIN:	He's a charming fellow … He said to me 'No need! No need for that at all!'
DUFRERE:	So the doctor's verdict was final: 'Cause of death – heart attack'. They deferred to his judgement.
COURTIN:	Yes, but that doesn't mean they trust him!
DUFRERE:	Because he works for The Haven?
COURTIN:	No! Because of his political beliefs. 'We've got our eye on him', said the Commissioner. Absurd!
DUFRERE:	But you are in the clear?
COURTIN:	Completely exonerated, my friend … It is over … The Commissioner said something interesting. He said, 'I remember

	when we used to do what the Home Secretary wanted. Nowadays we do what the *newspapers* want. As long as the papers are happy we won't set foot in The Haven … ' It makes me think of that horrid little journalist I was just speaking to …
DUFRERE:	Maybe you were nervous? A bit short-tempered?
COURTIN:	No! I tried to make an excellent impression; I received him in the gallery and I especially wore a hat and carried my best walking stick … But he was *so* impertinent …
DUFRERE:	He probably didn't want to seem intimidated. I know him, actually, he's a good chap really but he does have the irritating habit of thinking that the revolution is nigh!
COURTIN:	He rubbed me up the wrong way immediately with his phrase 'charitable enterprise' … The Haven a 'charitable *enterprise*', I ask you!
DUFRERE:	Nobody reads his paper, anyway.
COURTIN:	So what? Whether they're read or not, newspapers are our masters, apparently. *(Silence)* Where the hell is that beastly Rambert? You know, I really should get shot of that woman. She'd make a good scapegoat … That would quell any remaining rumours …
DUFRERE:	You're the boss.
COURTIN:	Indeed I am. *(Enter LAROZE)*

Scene Eight

LAROZE:	Is she here?
COURTIN:	Not yet.
LAROZE:	Unbelievable! The little minx! *(Changes tone)* Have you seen any journalists?
COURTIN:	I have just seen one.
DUFRERE:	I think we should brace ourselves for some bad press …
LAROZE:	*(Scandalized)* How dare they attack a charity! Anyway, everyone loves charities … There is never bad news about charity.
COURTIN:	Don't be so sure, Father! If you could have heard that little jackanapes! According to him, all charities should be done away with!
LAROZE:	*(Raises his arms)* Do away with charity! Absolutely preposterous! *(Crosses his arms)* And what does he suggest we do instead?
COURTIN:	Introduce the concept of justice.
LAROZE:	Justice!? No such thing in this world. What about the poor?

COURTIN:	Do away with poverty too.
LAROZE:	*(Holds his head in his hands)* It's the end of the world! *(Changes tone)* Baron, I beg you, you must dismiss Rambert at once … Write to every newspaper that she's been dismissed … She's gone! Then the newspapers will be happy …
FOOTMAN:	*(Appears at right-hand door)* Miss Rambert. *(COURTIN gestures that she should be admitted)*
COURTIN:	This will be a cosy little chat … *(To DUFRERE)* Go and see if the Baroness is back. *(Exit DUFRERE)*
LAROZE:	Be firm, Baron, you must be firm.

Scene Nine

COURTIN:	Ah, we meet at last!
RAMBERT:	I was just waiting outside …
COURTIN:	And I've been waiting all morning.
RAMBERT:	I was busy, you know what Wednesdays are like. *(COURTIN shrugs)* The Father knows, don't you?
LAROZE:	I wouldn't know, madam. I concentrate on my own business, thank you very much.
COURTIN:	I assume you understand why I have called you here?
RAMBERT:	Not really, no. *(LAROZE fidgets, RAMBERT looks at him and shrugs)*
COURTIN:	*(Ferociously)* Do you know the distance between the beds in your dormitories, madam?
RAMBERT:	*(Stunned)* What?
COURTIN:	Twenty centimetres. How many bathtubs do you have?
RAMBERT:	I don't understand …
COURTIN:	*(Calming a little)* It's true … These are trivial next to other matters … Much more serious matters … *Scandalous* matters …
LAROZE:	Utterly horrifying matters!
COURTIN:	I saw Louise Lapar …
LAROZE:	You can't deny it!
RAMBERT:	Do you think I deny it? On the contrary, I take full responsibility.
LAROZE:	For everything?
RAMBERT:	For everything.
LAROZE:	Even burying that poor child without due ceremony. Poor, poor Caroline!
RAMBERT:	*(To COURTIN)* Is this about Caroline Mezy?
COURTIN:	No, that was a tragedy … But all the others? All the others you have maltreated?

RAMBERT:	Poor children are not the same as the fine young ladies you are accustomed to, Baron.
COURTIN:	In theory.
RAMBERT:	You cannot bring up these children like you would the daughters of millionaires or aristocracy. At very best these girls will become domestics or workers. They must be prepared for the realities of their adult life.
COURTIN:	By beating them?
RAMBERT:	Sometimes there is no choice. Not all of these girls are 'little angels' I'll have you know …
COURTIN:	And forcing others to watch?
RAMBERT:	As a warning and to set an example. This is my system. Punishments and rewards. Religion has always done exactly the same thing: here is Heaven, *there* is Hell. Society too with its prisons and penalties on one side and a variety of medals and honours on the other …
COURTIN:	*(Sardonically)* And the guillotine? A system too, eh?
RAMBERT:	Precisely.
COURTIN:	Well, Miss, I think it's time you practised your 'system' elsewhere.
RAMBERT:	*(Calmly)* Nothing would make me happier.
LAROZE:	That's settled then! *(Silence)*
RAMBERT:	Just think what *I've* put up with … The gossip … The slander … The stress … *(Stares at LAROZE)* The jealousy … The spying … I've had quite enough.
COURTIN:	Miss–
RAMBERT:	Not enough staff, not enough money … Nobody's ever paid. Arguments with suppliers every single day of the week. I'm bullied and insulted in front of the children … I'm as good as spat on in the street–
COURTIN:	Look–
RAMBERT:	Last week you promised me fifteen hundred francs … Did I get it? Of course not!
COURTIN:	You know that–
RAMBERT:	And you promised us something from the Pari Mutual donation – one hundred thousand francs! And we did not receive a single penny. *(Silence)* Yes, it is time that I went.
COURTIN:	*(Friendly)* If I can help you in anyway–
RAMBERT:	*(Dignified)* Thank you.
LAROZE:	Might I suggest that you go as soon as possible. Tomorrow if at all–

RAMBERT:	Tomorrow? I am not a criminal. *(Stares at* COURTIN*)* I will not be treated like a thief. *(Silence)* Anyway, it all depends.
COURTIN:	*(Raising himself up)* Indeed?
RAMBERT:	*(Energetically)* I will not have it said that I in anyway compromised the financial situation of The Haven.
COURTIN:	*(Friendly)* Let's just say we had a difference in opinion on how things should be run. Believe me, I will not cast the slightest shadow of doubt over your probity.
RAMBERT:	I am sorry but such guarantees are not enough. I am desperate to leave The Haven, but I will only do so when the debts are paid and the books are balanced. Understand? Until then, I am not leaving.
LAROZE:	You're not leaving?
RAMBERT:	No.
COURTIN:	Are you threatening us?
RAMBERT:	No – merely making some reasonable conditions.
COURTIN:	You'd better watch your step … After everything you've done … Do not force me to take legal action against you …
RAMBERT:	*(Gentle)* I beg you … Do not let The Haven get involved in a court case … For your sake more than my own.
COURTIN:	*(Furious but controlled)* What did you say? How dare you–
LAROZE:	*(To* COURTIN*)* Please … *(To* RAMBERT*)* How do you know that the financial situation–
COURTIN:	*(To* LAROZE*)* It's none of her business! The financial situation of The Haven is *none* of her business!
RAMBERT:	I think that Father Laroze understands me very well. Until the books are balanced, I remain your Servant.

RAMBERT *bows to* COURTIN *and exits, ignoring* LAROZE. COURTIN *watches her leave, then falls heavily onto a sofa.*

Scene Ten

LAROZE:	She didn't say goodbye to me. But at least she's going, eh? That's the important thing.
COURTIN:	*(Near collapse)* But she's not going yet …
LAROZE:	Whether she likes it or not, she is going!
COURTIN:	She can still cause us all sorts of trouble … She knew full well what she was saying, the minx …

LAROZE:	Call her bluff. Put The Haven in order!
COURTIN:	But how? It's not as if I only started thinking about this today, you know!
LAROZE:	But let her stay another week and the newspapers will be full of it. You simply must balance the books.
COURTIN:	But how?
LAROZE:	The Lord works in mysterious ways – you must have faith! The Catholic Church has connections …
COURTIN:	*(Ironically)* Just what we need – a blessing from the Pope. *(Walks around and opens the left-hand door)* Therese! Therese! *(Closes the door)* Why isn't she back yet?
LAROZE:	Maybe you should consider a radical solution. Maybe you should even consider inviting, Lord forgive me, wealthy Protestants or Jews to sit on The Haven's committee …
COURTIN:	You fool! Who cares about religion!? You're meant to help me and calm me down … But all you do is exasperate me talking such rubbish!
LAROZE:	*(Hurt)* Very well. If you don't want me to try and help …
COURTIN:	Oh, my friend … *(Enter DUFRERE)*

Scene Eleven

COURTIN:	The Baroness?
DUFRERE:	No. Mr Arnaud Tripier.
COURTIN:	Arnaud Tripier? You're sure?
DUFRERE:	*(Reads the card)* J. B. Arnaud Tripier, former member of parliament. *(COURTIN stares at the card)*
LAROZE:	More problems?
COURTIN:	Arnaud Tripier!
LAROZE:	Sorry, should I have heard of him?
COURTIN:	He crawls from the mud whenever there's a crisis in parliament. He's like the government's special envoy whenever there's a whiff of dodgy business. You don't think he's been sent to talk about The Haven?
LAROZE:	Don't jump to conclusions.
COURTIN:	But why's he here?
LAROZE:	With this government? Who can say?
COURTIN:	Surely they wouldn't dare!
LAROZE:	This government? They have no respect for anyone. *(DUFRERE exits. LAROZE takes his hat)*

COURTIN:	What? Are you going?
LAROZE:	A man from the government …
COURTIN:	You're going to abandon me …
LAROZE:	Me here, dressed in these robes? It'd only make things much worse for you. *(Bows and exits)*

Scene Twelve

COURTIN goes over to the mirror and smoothes his hair nervously and looks at the bust of Napoleon.

FOOTMAN:	Mr Arnaud Tripier! *(TRIPIER enters briskly)*
TRIPIER:	Senator! *(He shakes COURTIN's hand effusively)* I have the honour to bring you some most important news. *(COURTIN nods carefully and indicates a seat)* Thank you! *(Sits and removes his gloves)* As you are aware, our friends at the Senate are keen to begin discussions on education reform …
COURTIN:	*(Vaguely)* Oh?
TRIPIER:	You know how it is, we're near the end of session and the government wants to–
COURTIN:	I'd be quite happy to speak in the debate. I have some strong opinions on the government's so-called education policy …
TRIPIER:	*(Pretending to be amazed)* Really? You're willing to speak in the debate? Oh, that would be absolutely tremendous! Quite admirable!
COURTIN:	*(Forcing a smile)* Is it really so amazing?
TRIPIER:	*(Very amiable)* You wouldn't want to deprive parliament of what will undoubtedly be a tremendous speech.
COURTIN:	When I address parliament it is not for any selfish reasons or vanity … I stand up and speak on behalf of principles that I believe in … Values and opinions that are true and just … I stand up in the name of the great tradition of French liberalism … *(Simply)* Anyway, why wouldn't I want to speak?
TRIPIER:	*(After the slightest hesitation)* Quite so … Quite so … *(Pause)* It's quite beastly, isn't it? This is strictly between you and I, yes? As I was saying, it's quite beastly that our government seems utterly incapable of understanding a man like you.
COURTIN:	Oh?
TRIPIER:	Who do ministers listen to, these days? People who believe in the government's mission? No. The real voice of Paris? No. They listen to the lawyers and doctors from their own constituencies.

So provincial. *(Pause)* The kind of people who attach great importance to stories of little girls being beaten …

COURTIN: Ah.

TRIPIER: They call that a scandal? What utter rot! All this infernal fuss over the death of some child in a charity home. Ridiculous! So provincial! Anyway, how can you possibly make an omelette without breaking a few eggs, eh?

COURTIN: But …

TRIPIER: *(Lyrically)* The Fatherland has its martyrs; Religion has its martyrs … *(Smiles)* Why shouldn't Charity have some martyrs too, eh? Yes?

COURTIN: I don't quite follow. What connection can there possibly be between problems that may have recently surfaced in charity homes and the debate on government education policy!?

TRIPIER: *(Amicably)* None at all. *(Pause)* But because it will ultimately be the government's decision whether to conduct an inquiry into this business or not, it is assumed that you will be keeping a low profile.

COURTIN: What business?

TRIPIER: The Haven, of course.

COURTIN: Oh, how simplistic, how heavy-handed can they be!?

TRIPIER: Idiots. The lot of them. The new morality of modern democracy, eh? They might as well grab you by the arm and say to your face 'Keep your sanctimonious opinions on education to yourself and we will make sure that the scandal is whitewashed … ' Dirty business, politics these days!

COURTIN: *(After a moment's thought)* They can say what they like. Shame on them who are determined to turn a tragedy into a scandal!

TRIPIER: Yes … *(Losing the pretence of sympathy)* The government would also like an explanation of how a rather large donation was spent – a hundred thousand francs from Pari Mutual, I believe? …

COURTIN: Excuse me! No charity organization can be at the beck and call of government like this! I have nothing to fear – this is simply a point of principle. No government should have the audacity to intervene in a charity like this … I suppose they want me to vote for their abominable reforms?

TRIPIER: Not at all! They simply want you keep out of the debate.

COURTIN: *(Ironically)* Indeed?

TRIPIER: Yes, take a vacation. Maybe you should be ill? Every citizen has the right to be ill.

COURTIN: But no one has the right to be dishonoured. When you have a name and reputation like mine! A member of the Académie française! I

	belong to and represent the most sacred values of French culture! How dare they sully my honour like this! *(He walks in agitation. Silence)*
TRIPIER:	*(In a penetrating tone)* Senator … Do you remember Leverrier?
COURTIN:	Leverrier? A total crook! A con man!
TRIPIER:	Was he? He was quite an influential man in his day.
COURTIN:	Hmm.
TRIPIER:	He was an MP. A minister for a while. *He was one of theirs.* And they destroyed him, ruthlessly.
COURTIN:	Quite right too! He was a crook!
TRIPIER:	When they want to dispose of someone …
COURTIN:	*(Marches around, covering his ears)* I am not Leverrier! I am not Leverrier! How dare you! I am not Leverrier!
TRIPIER:	Do you mind? Leverrier was a friend of mine. I had dinner with him the day before he was arrested. Yes, *the day before. (Pause)* Three weeks later he was in prison …
COURTIN:	Watch what you say, you! You will regret threatening me! *(Despite his efforts he totters against a chair)*
TRIPIER:	*(Assisting COURTIN)* Baron Courtin.
COURTIN:	*(Shoving TRIPIER away, his voice strained)* Let go. I'm fine. I've had a tiring day. I haven't eaten. I am exhausted. Leave me alone.
TRIPIER:	I am so sorry. I didn't realize. I'll go.
COURTIN:	Leave me alone.
TRIPIER:	I'll see myself out. *(Very close to COURTIN)* A word of warning; this government can be quite ferocious. If I were you, I'd go and see them. Go and see the First Minister himself. He'd be more than happy to have a chat with you today. *(He touches COURTIN on the shoulder, COURTIN shudders)* But tomorrow … *(Enter THERESE)*

Scene Thirteen

THERESE:	Oh, excuse me! You wanted to see me?
COURTIN:	Yes, I wanted a word. May I present Arnaud Tripier …
TRIPIER:	*(Bows)* I have already had the honour of meeting you!
THERESE:	*(Turns to TRIPIER after scrutinising COURTIN for a moment)* I beg your pardon, sir, I don't quite–
TRIPIER:	In the Italian Embassy at Christmas.
THERESE:	But of course!

TRIPIER:	My dear Baroness and my dear senator … Please remember that nothing would honour me more than being your most humble Servant. *(Exits)*

Scene Fourteen

THERESE:	*(Hurries over to* COURTIN*)* What on earth has happened? What is it?
COURTIN:	This is terrible.
THERESE:	What?
COURTIN:	For The Haven … And for you … for me … a scandal … *(Paces around)* Scandal and ruin.
THERESE:	What do you mean? You're in such a state! Is it because of that anonymous letter?
COURTIN:	Will you be silent? Will you be quiet?
THERESE:	Your tone frightens me.
COURTIN:	I don't have time to find delicate words. Did Dufrere tell you that I was at The Haven all morning?
THERESE:	Yes.
COURTIN:	You can't imagine the things I saw there. But that is not the problem.
THERESE:	Well?
COURTIN:	When I arrived home there was a stupid journalist here, and I was foolish enough to let him interview me.
THERESE:	But, darling, it was not you who locked that child in the cupboard …
COURTIN:	It's not just that …
THERESE:	You're not the one who has been beating the children …
COURTIN:	It's not that either … I don't know why you pester me with such trivial things … Sit down … In short, they are threatening an inquest … You saw that Arnaud Tripier?
THERESE:	I didn't like the look of him …
COURTIN:	Please! Have you any idea what they will uncover if they start an investigation at The Haven?
THERESE:	No – tell me.
COURTIN:	They will discover that we are bankrupt.
THERESE:	Well, we'll just have to raise the money … People will always give to charity …
COURTIN:	You idiot! You're as bad as Father Laroze! He believes in miracles too!
THERESE:	*(Shocked)* Oh!

COURTIN:	Saints! Miracles! The power of prayer! *(He collapses into a chair)*
THERESE:	*(Goes over to him)* You're losing me now … The church … Arnaud Tripier … I mean, if The Haven is really in such trouble, let's just close it down. Simple as that!
COURTIN:	*(Raises his arms)* Simple as that! *(Stands and paces again)*
THERESE:	Darling, let's be honest, The Haven is not the only thing in your life. There's your political work, the Académie française. Good Lord, there's enough to keep you busy … Enough prestige! … *(Changes tone)* Don't look at me like that … You frighten me … Tell me, what is it?
COURTIN:	It's difficult to explain … You don't understand financial matters … Well … The money that has gone from The Haven …
THERESE:	Yes?
COURTIN:	I took it. But I don't have it anymore … Do you understand?
THERESE:	*(Turning her eyes away slowly)* I think so … Yes …
COURTIN:	Good. *(Sighs)* What was I supposed to do? We'd had a few very hard years. We needed the money … There were opportunities on the stock market … I took a chance …
THERESE:	Darling, you don't need to justify anything to me … But why didn't you tell me this before? *(Resolute)* We absolutely must return that money.
COURTIN:	It's an enormous amount.
THERESE:	So what? We must raise that money. *(She goes to the mirror and removes her hat)*
COURTIN:	I tell you it's a huge amount of money. Probably three hundred thousand francs …
THERESE:	I don't care. We must raise it, whatever the sum. Don't forget we have many friends …
COURTIN:	Like who? And with this timescale? And Rambert knows everything and will go public any minute!
THERESE:	We'll see about that.
COURTIN:	And the government! Those swine! They'd love to drag my name in the mud!
THERESE:	No – governments always prefer to avoid scandal whenever possible, anything to maintain the status quo.
COURTIN:	Just one story in the paper and they'll have me locked up!
THERESE:	Don't be so ridiculous! *(She looks at him, alarmed)* Just think straight now … *(Loudly)* We have no choice other than to find the money. Understand? Now, just calm down … *(Sits)*
COURTIN:	*(Ironic)* Oh, how admirable you are!

THERESE:	Just listen to me for a moment. The Marchioness of Ormailles? She's your aunt. She doesn't have any children. She adores you. She approves of The Haven.
COURTIN:	I've already thought of her. That amount is beyond her means.
THERESE:	Baron Glancz?
COURTIN:	He'd want to know every detail. And if he refused … I couldn't afford being compromised like that.
THERESE:	What about your brother, Robert?
COURTIN:	He's in America.
THERESE:	Damn, of course he is! Mrs D'Avranches?
COURTIN:	Three hundred thousand francs? You must be joking! I've thought of everyone, I tell you! It's impossible.
THERESE:	Will you stop marching around! You're making me nervous!
COURTIN:	What we need is someone we can talk to, openly. A friend. *(He slows and stands in front of THERESE)* Yes, a friend. I've had an idea. Are you thinking what I'm thinking?
THERESE:	No. And I hate charades. Do tell me.
COURTIN:	We need a friend. A friend we can both trust.
THERESE:	*(Quickly cries out)* Biron?
COURTIN:	Well? *(Silence)*
THERESE:	*(Very assertively after being fixed by the gaze of COURTIN)* You want me to … *(COURTIN nods)* Never!
COURTIN:	*(Gently)* Now don't be a child about this … You've turned to him a hundred times before … You now know the desperate situation we're in … And you hesitate?
THERESE:	Never … Never …
COURTIN:	This is crazy! Just think! If you don't trust me on this … It's the end. I warn you.
THERESE:	Never!
COURTIN:	Do I have to beg you? Do I have to get on my hands and knees?
THERESE:	Listen to me – it's impossible.
COURTIN:	*(Animated)* Why? Why? Why? Why are you so stubborn?
THERESE:	Try to calm down … Please understand … It's impossible … do not ask me to do the impossible. Try and understand.
COURTIN:	You are just being ridiculous. Childish!
THERESE:	*(Lowering her eyes, her voice quiet)* Let's not talk about this anymore … It will get us nowhere. *(Looks at COURTIN)* Understand? Let's just leave all of this behind us!
COURTIN:	I can't do that! That's absurd! And it would be suicide!
THERESE:	I beg you. Start writing again – finish your book on Empress Josephine. That would be wonderful!

COURTIN:	That's far, far away I'm afraid.
THERESE:	Don't say that, please … With a little effort you can rebuild your life …
COURTIN:	*(Violently)* In prison I suppose!
THERESE:	*(Panicking)* Prison! Let's go, let's go at once, far away as possible!
COURTIN:	*(Grabs* THERESE's *hands brutally)* Shall we take little D'Auberval with us?
THERESE:	*(Enraged, shaking her fist)* You! You embezzler! Taking money which did not belong to you!
COURTIN:	If truth be known, money should be used! It should be made to work for you!
THERESE:	You sound like Biron. By all means use money but you must be prepared to either give it back or go to prison!
COURTIN:	Baron Courtin will not go to prison for petty cash.
THERESE:	No, Baron Courtin will lie, steal, make the most disgusting proposals … But he will not go to prison, oh no! That would be most unbecoming!
COURTIN:	For your own stubbornness, your idiotic pride, you condemn me. And I've let you live as you wish. I've let you do what you want. *(Lowers his head)* A hundred times I've wanted to throw you out the door … I've had the *right* to throw you out! You're nothing but a–
THERESE:	*(Very quickly)* I've heard that before! *(Silence)* You're right … It's true … But what are you? Begging me, threatening me, forcing me back into the arms of a lover whom I despise to get your money for you!
COURTIN:	*(Races over to* THERESE *with his hand raised)* You'd better shut up! *(He goes to slap her; she protects her face with her hands.* COURTIN *lets his arms down)* You can lower your hands. I will not touch you. Do what you want. *(He goes slowly over to a sofa and collapses. He holds his head in his hands. Silence)*
THERESE:	*(Turns to* COURTIN*)* My darling … This is so dreadful …
COURTIN:	*(Without looking at* THERESE*)* No, it's me who is dreadful. My darling … *(*THERESE *goes towards him)* Why did I say those things to you? What made me do it? It feels like I'm falling in an avalanche … It feels like everyone is running up to me and pushing me, shoving me … And I don't have the strength to fight back … I'm lost … and ashamed … I'm lost … *(Cries)*
THERESE:	*(Sits beside him and holds his hands)* Don't turn away from me … Look at me … We're in this together … *(Silence)*
COURTIN:	What should I do?
THERESE:	I'll go. *(Stands up)*
COURTIN:	No, please … don't … I don't want you to …

THERESE:	*(Tearfully, kneeling on the sofa)* Yes, I will … He'll save us. *(Exalted)* Yes … I swear he will … The human heart is kind … He will save us!

Act 3

BIRON's *apartment. It is decorated with eighteenth-century furniture. There are two doors on the left, one of which reveals a bathroom and the other* BIRON's *bedroom. On the right a door leads to the entrance hall and there is also a Dubarry mirror on a gold stand. A Falconet clock rests on a desk. The apartment is bathed in sunshine.*

Scene One

As the curtain rises, JEAN *walks across the room holding a pair of boots. He sees* COURTIN *enter and seems surprised.*

JEAN:	Baron! My master wasn't expecting you this morning … You're early, sir …
COURTIN:	*(Holding some newspapers in his hands)* Tell your master it's rather important.
JEAN:	Of course. One moment please … *(Exits left.* COURTIN *looks through the newspapers.* BIRON *appears at the bathroom door; he has not finished dressing and also carries newspapers)*

Scene Two

COURTIN *shows the newspapers to* BIRON.

BIRON:	I've read them. *(Laughs)* Flagellation, indeed! Flagellation at The Haven! Anyway, I thought such things were becoming rather popular these days … *(Goes over to a table and starts flicking through various papers)* Can I find what I'm looking for? … What about that Rambert, eh? She hasn't had a dull moment by the looks of it! Journalists queuing around the block!
COURTIN:	*(Irritated)* Enough!
BIRON:	Don't be like that, old boy … *(He kisses his fingertips)* I want to show you something.
COURTIN:	*(Irritated)* Please!

BIRON:	In every newspaper and magazine the press agency account is reproduced. *(Holds out a magazine to* COURTIN*)* This one's rather amusing … They talk about selling tickets to come and watch … I trust you'll save a front-row seat for me, old pal!? *(Laughs)* Only joking … I hate these magazines … The servants like them, mind … *(*COURTIN *hands the magazine back to* BIRON*)* Seriously, my friend, is this what's bothering you?
COURTIN:	No … None of them mention any names specifically apart from 'a political personage'. There are plenty of those, mercifully!
BIRON:	Well?
COURTIN:	It's not what they've said that bothers me. It's what they *haven't* mentioned but I know.
BIRON:	What?
COURTIN:	A judge has been named to lead an inquiry.
BIRON:	Are you sure?
COURTIN:	Pretty much.
BIRON:	Pretty much? Look, old chap, a judge is either named or not – there's nothing 'pretty much' about an inquiry. What have you heard?
COURTIN:	Priou overheard something at the chamber …
BIRON:	Priou's no fool. What did he say?
COURTIN:	He came over to see me. We talked until very late. I didn't sleep a wink. You know how he smokes! Anyway, we reached an important conclusion. We agreed that you are the only person that I should confide in.
BIRON:	*(Importantly as he does up his shirt)* Yes, very wise … A good move on your part … So tell me, what did Priou hear?
COURTIN:	Apparently the Attorney General held a long meeting late last night … about The Haven!
BIRON:	Really? I see … *(Interested)* Do you mean to say there's some truth to what that Rambert said?
COURTIN:	No – just childish nonsense. It can all be explained away …
BIRON:	Well, what are you worried about?
COURTIN:	Nothing – and everything! An inquiry is an inquiry, a scandal whatever the result … My name will be in all the papers … It will be quite a circus, mark my words!
BIRON:	Yes, yes, quite. Do you want me to have a word with the Attorney General?
COURTIN:	That would be wonderful. Didn't he used to be your lawyer?
BIRON:	Yes. Not any more, obviously. But he's got plenty of favours he owes me … More than you'd believe …

COURTIN:	Could you telephone him? Maybe see him today?
BIRON:	I'm going to the chamber today, anyway. I'll see him there. After that, I'll meet you at the Senate …
COURTIN:	Ah, no, not there …
BIRON:	Don't be silly, dear boy! You must go to the Senate. You must show your face there! Baron Courtin at the height of his powers, eh!
COURTIN:	Maybe you're right … Yes … I'll see you at the Senate … My fortune is in your hands, Biron … *(He shakes his hand)*
BIRON:	You're trembling. Your hands are icy.
COURTIN:	It's true, I'm a bit nervous …
BIRON:	*(Importantly)* Chin up, old boy! I swear I won't let you down …
COURTIN:	You promise? *(Sighs)*
BIRON:	I've sorted out trickier things than this with him, I can tell you …
COURTIN:	I think the government means business. They sent Arnaud Tripier to see me …
BIRON:	Tripier? Why didn't you tell me?
COURTIN:	I forgot. I can hardly think straight …
BIRON:	What did he say?
COURTIN:	He warned me, in no uncertain terms, not to intervene in the government's education debate …
BIRON:	Blackmail, eh? *(Joyfully)* Excellent!
COURTIN:	Really?
BIRON:	Now tell me … Did you agree to his demands?
COURTIN:	*(Defensively)* Well …
BIRON:	Under duress? You must tell me. It's important.
COURTIN:	Yes, he forced me, the swine! Forced me to sacrifice my principles!
BIRON:	Very good … Very good indeed …
COURTIN:	I admire your optimism, I must say!
BIRON:	It's important that you caved in, dear boy … *(COURTIN walks away)* Besides, I know what is what with my old friend the Attorney General … I'll take things from here … There will be no judge to lead the inquiry … There will be no inquiry at all.
COURTIN:	Biron, thank you so much. You are the first person to make me feel more optimistic. Priou really worried me. Well, I have a few people to see this morning …
BIRON:	I'll get dressed … *(Takes COURTIN's hand)*
COURTIN:	Don't let me keep you. *(COURTIN heads stage right, looking hesitant and troubled)*
BIRON:	*(Heading stage left)* Everything will be just fine!
COURTIN:	*(Near the door)* I won't telephone you, Biron … I'll wait until I see you …

BIRON:	At the Senate.
COURTIN:	Don't keep me waiting.
BIRON:	As soon as I've seen my old friend at the chamber … Come on, old boy, I'm your friend … *(Opens the door)* Jean, Frederick, I want to get dressed. *(He turns and sees that COURTIN has moved away from the door)* What is it?
COURTIN:	I haven't told you everything that's worrying me.
BIRON:	*(Approaches COURTIN)* Make yourself comfortable; it's a nice chair that one.
COURTIN:	*(Sitting down, looking around)* Can we talk freely?
BIRON:	*(Sitting down, very interested)* Of course, old boy … If you only knew what these four walls have heard in their time, you wouldn't hesitate! *(Silence)*
COURTIN:	Biron … I only came here to tell you about the judge …
BIRON:	Yes?
COURTIN:	*(Embarrassed)* But you've been so kind, so chivalrous … I feel I must take you into my confidence … once again.
BIRON:	*(Suspicious)* I see.
COURTIN:	I'm sorry, shall I–
BIRON:	*(Coldly)* No. Carry on.
COURTIN:	You see … I have so many problems … *(BIRON is sullen, COURTIN embarrassed)* Problems never happen one at a time. They all happen at once! *(Silence)* The Haven … My beloved Haven … That labour of love! Well … We're facing a crisis … Not the first time, of course! … But, yes, we are facing a crisis … *(BIRON fidgets)* I want to ask your opinion …
BIRON:	For God's sake … get on with it …
COURTIN:	Unless we get some help … The Haven will be forced to close down … All my efforts will be down the drain … I cannot bear the idea … *(Silence)* All it would take is a generous man, a man of noble heart … a man like you, Biron …
BIRON:	Listen … Courtin. I don't want to be unduly harsh … I can see the state you're in … But you've never asked me for a penny … So how can you have the nerve to ask me, as an afterthought like that, for a fortune for that bloody charity?
COURTIN:	Biron, I'm surprised at–
BIRON:	It's disgraceful, it really is! It's high time you stopped fooling yourself, bleating on about that tiresome waste of time: 'The Haven! The Haven!'
COURTIN:	*(Standing)* The Haven is an extremely beneficial institution! It is noble and humane!

BIRON:	Tosh!
COURTIN:	You yourself said, 'The Haven is the embodiment of acceptable socialism!'
BIRON:	Did I say that?
COURTIN:	Yes …
BIRON:	Well I must have been joking! The truth is, I'm sick of The Haven and I don't even have anything to do with it! The Haven is nothing but a joke! The Haven is *nothing*. I'd rather you built a stable for racehorses than that home for destitute young women … At least racehorses would do some good for the world – and wouldn't be such a waste of money!
COURTIN:	*(Raises his arms)* Racehorses!?
BIRON:	Between you and me … The Haven has been beneficial for *you* … Being the patron of that thing has not harmed *you* or your reputation in any way … Good for you! But please don't pester me with the damned thing – it will make anyone serious about money laugh in your face! *(Silence)*
COURTIN:	*(Slowly)* But what if The Haven had debts that simply must be paid and I had no way to pay them …
BIRON:	*(Almost happily)* Really? Do you mean? … *(COURTIN lowers his head)* At last, I think I understand …
COURTIN:	*(Almost begging)* You are my best friend …
BIRON:	I understand … How much?
COURTIN:	*(Hesitating)* I can't quite say … about … three hundred thousand …
BIRON:	Strewth!
COURTIN:	I'm being completely honest now–
BIRON:	That's a lot of money.
COURTIN:	Not for you, it isn't.
BIRON:	No. I can't. Anyway, between you and me, I have a few financial issues of my own right now …
COURTIN:	*(Bitter)* You wouldn't even notice it! …
BIRON:	How the hell did you let things get into such a state!? Are those girls paupers or princesses? Three hundred thousand francs! *(Stares at COURTIN)* You must be rich if this is the kind of sum you trifle with!
COURTIN:	No more jokes, I beg you …
BIRON:	No, I'm serious. You only give that kind of sum to someone incredibly rich …
COURTIN:	Someone who doesn't really need the money, I suppose?
BIRON:	Exactly. You never lend money to someone who really needs it.
COURTIN:	So that's how you justify refusing to help a friend?

BIRON:	I didn't say that …
COURTIN:	When the inquiry begins …
BIRON:	There will be no inquiry.
COURTIN:	Not yet … but maybe … And you won't help a poor soul like–
BIRON:	You're not a poor soul, Baron Courtin.
COURTIN:	It is dreadful that you can treat me like this – a friend and a respected member of society!
BIRON:	I am sorry. I am very sorry. But I do not have three hundred thousand francs at *your* disposal.
COURTIN:	But you've got so much money! You're rolling in money!
BIRON:	Of course I've got money. A lot of people have got money. But that doesn't mean they give away sums like that – for nothing! On a whim! You're like a child. No wonder you're broke!
COURTIN:	*(Dignified)* I'm not ashamed of that …
BIRON:	kNo. Just try and understand that it is not possible. To throw away money like that doesn't make sense. Anything over ten or fifteen thousand francs is no longer money; it's *business. (He moves away)*
COURTIN:	Off you go! Play the businessman! Did you know that everyone used to say that you never do favours for anyone – and it was I who always leapt to your defence! I told everyone about how you have helped me!
BIRON:	*(Turning)* Excuse me, that is not the same thing …
COURTIN:	*(Furious)* Enough! Can't you shut up! *(Silence)*
BIRON:	You forced me to say such nonsense.
COURTIN:	*(Goes towards BIRON)* My fault, eh? *(Raises his arms)* That is so insulting!
BIRON:	Look … Words are just words … Let's forget it … *(Following COURTIN)* Is this the time to lose your temper? Just think of the situation you're in … *(Changes tone)* You must find a way to survive this.
COURTIN:	*(Turning to BIRON, imperiously)* My dear Biron, just because you've seen me in a weakened state … I'm not on best form this morning … And just because I made the stupid mistake of asking you a favour … Don't let it fool you. My kind have been around for centuries – long before your type earned your first grubby coin – and we know very well how to survive …
BIRON:	Oh, Courtin, enough rhetoric, please! You're very good at insulting people, but don't you realize that no one listens to you? No one even gives you a second glance! And do you know that everyone makes fun of you!? *(Changes tone)* Go on, take off your hat.
COURTIN:	*(Embarrassed)* But I'm going …

BIRON:	Come on … This is idiotic. For the pleasure of playing the hero you could throw it all away … *(COURTIN takes off his hat)* Besides, you are not alone … *(Timidly)* Does the Baroness know? …
COURTIN:	She knows everything.
BIRON:	Oh dear – the poor lady!
COURTIN:	Poor Therese!
BIRON:	Poor Therese!
COURTIN:	*(Bitter)* She wanted to come and see you this morning.
BIRON:	Really?
COURTIN:	*(Still bitter)* She thought she might be able to touch the heart of a friend … *(Shrugs)* She told me that you were no longer interested in her … I just wanted to spare her the humiliation.
BIRON:	What humiliation?
COURTIN:	I didn't want to ask anything of you … But I suddenly felt so affectionate towards you, it was stupid of me … But I don't regret it …
BIRON:	You stopped her coming here?
COURTIN:	Yes …
BIRON:	And you let us argue like that! You are more of a fool than I thought! *(Pause)* Look, come back here for lunch at … one o'clock. Maybe we can find a way to help you after all …
COURTIN:	One that will cost me most dear …
BIRON:	Will you stop?
COURTIN:	*(Dramatically)* If that is really the case, I know what I must do …
BIRON:	*(Loud)* A stupid thing to say! *(Calm)* You wouldn't do it anyway.
COURTIN:	I'll find a way … I'll muster up the courage … I will prove that you're mistaken. *(He heads towards the door)*
BIRON:	See you at one o'clock.
COURTIN:	Farewell! *(Exits)*
BIRON:	I'll be waiting! *(Pause)* What a performance! Pure melodrama! *(Pause)* He'll be back. *(He rings a bell. JEAN appears)* At last!

Scene Three

JEAN:	*(Rubbing his hands on his shirt)* Sorry, sir, I was just helping Frederick and Martin empty the swimming pool …
BIRON:	*(Jovial)* Wonderful! *(Changes tone)* I must get dressed. *(JEAN opens the bathroom door)* I don't need your help this morning.
JEAN:	Very good, sir.

BIRON:	No … I want you to telephone Paul and tell him to get the car ready. You're both going to make a little trip. *(JEAN picks up the telephone and calls)* I want you to be ready to go in the next fifteen minutes. I want you to go to Mr Lerible's house …
JEAN:	*(Mumbling)* Mr Lerible …
BIRON:	You know where he lives? Good. I want you to go there and bring him back here. As quick as you can. Don't let me down.
JEAN:	*(Self-satisfied)* Rest assured, sir, I won't.
BIRON:	Excellent! *(Sings)* 'Lerible's a jolly good fellow, Lerible's a jolly good fellow, Lerible's a jolly good fellow! Which nobody can deny!'
JEAN:	You're in a wonderful mood today, sir!
BIRON:	*(Heading towards the bathroom he suddenly stops)* Oh, is there anyone else waiting to see me?
JEAN:	Not really, sir. The message boys from the stock market have gone.
BIRON:	*(Poetically)* Ah, the message boys from the stock market have gone …
JEAN:	Your tailor's still here though.
BIRON:	Get rid of him.
JEAN:	Mr Martinon as well.
BIRON:	Get rid of him too – in the nicest possible way …
JEAN:	*(On his way out)* Oh – I forgot, sir. The Marquis of Roche Pluvignon Gransac telephoned. He wants to see you today.
BIRON:	Yes, yes, I know. He gets on my nerves that rag and bone man! Tell him tomorrow. Come on, or I'll never get ready! *(Pause)* Oh, when you're back call Mr Perlier and tell him that he can pop in at five o'clock for my signature. Tell him to call London and Berlin himself, but tell him that I am expecting an important call from Brussels at half past five. Most importantly, tell everyone that I am not to be disturbed today. Understand?
JEAN:	*(Rather sadly)* You're expecting someone, sir?
BIRON:	*(Playfully)* I do hope that fits in with your schedule!
JEAN:	A lady?
BIRON:	None of your business!
JEAN:	Sir, I'm just worried that you'll cause awful trouble for yourself again–
BIRON:	Enough! Call Frederick.
JEAN:	*(Rings the bell)* I only say if for your own good, sir; you're not fifty anymore you know … *(FREDERICK enters)*
BIRON:	*(Shrugs and then sees FREDERICK)* My best frock coat!
JEAN:	*(Scandalized)* A frock coat? At eleven o'clock? In one's house?
BIRON:	Last Saturday Courtin was in his frock coat at ten o'clock!

JEAN:	Baron Courtin was going to a wedding. *(To* FREDERICK*)* Please prepare sir's *lounge suit.*
BIRON:	*(To* FREDERICK*)* And my patent leather moccasins – the new ones! *(*FREDERICK *exits)*
JEAN:	You know very well that they're not comfortable, sir …
BIRON:	Since when do I need your opinion? *(At the bathroom door)* Just go and get Lerible. *(*BIRON *goes into the bathroom and can be heard singing '*LERIBLE*'s a jolly good fellow … ' again)*
JEAN:	*(Picks up the telephone)* Is the car ready? … Well hurry along? … What? … Oh? And since when do I need your opinion? *(He hangs up and rearranges the furniture. The doorbell chimes, twice.* JEAN *opens the door and bows very low as* THERESE *enters)*

Scene Four

JEAN:	Baroness? It's you! *(Bows again)*
THERESE:	Hello, Jean.
JEAN:	Please forgive my lapse in courtesy, Baroness, it's just such a delight to see you here again.
THERESE:	That's quite alright, Jean.
BIRON:	*(Offstage)* 'Lerible's a jolly good fellow, Lerible's a jolly good fellow, Lerible's a jolly good fellow! … ' *(*THERESE *turns her head towards the noise)*
JEAN:	Yes, that'll be sir, Baroness … He's dressing … And singing … He's very happy …
THERESE:	Please tell him I'm here.
JEAN:	At once, Baroness … *(He enters the bathroom)*

Scene Five

THERESE *looks around the room.*

BIRON:	*(Suddenly appears with his arms wide open and he walks unsteadily towards* THERESE*)* Oh! Oh!
THERESE:	*(A fixed smile)* Yes. It's me.
BIRON:	I am so happy …
THERESE:	You can gloat over your victory.
BIRON:	*(Protesting)* Oh!
THERESE:	Try to be kind.

BIRON:	I wouldn't dream of gloating … I am just so perfectly happy … *(He takes her hand but* THERESE *pulls away and swiftly places a small table between them)* Perfectly happy …
THERESE:	It's always so pretty here … *(She kneels on a chair and looks at a painting)*
BIRON:	*(Gazing at her from behind)* You'll see … It will be just like before … *(*THERESE *turns around quickly)* Therese … My sweet Therese …
THERESE:	*(Pleading)* Please … It's difficult to say what I need to say … Don't make things impossible for me … *Help me* … *(Suddenly very formal)* Biron, are you my friend?
BIRON:	Am I your friend? *(He clasps her hands)*
THERESE:	*(Extricates her hands quickly)* I'm being serious now … Biron, how much do you know?
BIRON:	*(Arrogantly)* I know everything!
THERESE:	Oh God! Even about …
BIRON:	*(Joyously)* Everything! Everything! *(*THERESE *sits)* And I have done for a long time … *(He sits close to* THERESE*)* What can I say? I did warn you, after all …
THERESE:	Yes, you did. And I'm here … I'm here to ask you to save us.
BIRON:	Of course … *(Stands)* I will … I will do anything you want *(He moves nearer to her. She recoils a little)* Everything that needs to be done, *will* be done … *(He moves away)* Courtin came to see me just now.
THERESE:	Just now?
BIRON:	*(Turns to face her)* Yes … Just now … *(*THERESE *fidgets)* You mean you didn't know?
THERESE:	No.
BIRON:	*(Closing in on her)* You didn't know he came to see me?
THERESE:	No … No …
BIRON:	*(Scrutinizes her)* Oh, come on now!
THERESE:	*(Ironically)* Oh yes, this is the Biron I love so much! The trusting, valorous gentleman!
BIRON:	Oh!
THERESE:	I'm telling the truth … No, stay where you are! You know I find it impossible to lie! Look what you've done – you're going to make me cry … *(*BIRON *moves further away)* Why can you never believe me? *(*BIRON *comes closer)* Tell me; why did he come and see you?
BIRON:	My God!
THERESE:	What did he ask of you? Tell me.
BIRON:	He told me about the judge, that's all.
THERESE:	Judge? What judge? What will they do to us!? *(She starts crying)*
BIRON:	*(Sits near her and takes her hands)* Come on …

THERESE:	They want to destroy us!
BIRON:	Come on, Therese … Calm down … *(Caresses her hands)* You'll stain your beautiful gloves … Nothing is going to happen …
THERESE:	*(Crying)* They'll send him to prison …
BIRON:	Don't be silly!
THERESE:	And he's so scared! …
BIRON:	*(Rubs her shoulders)* You're trembling … Look, nothing's going to happen, I promise you … Have I ever let you down? … *(THERESE shakes her head)* Well?
THERESE:	*(No longer crying)* Is it true? Everything's going to be alright?
BIRON:	Yes … Yes …
THERESE:	Everything will be alright.
BIRON:	Yes …
THERESE:	You've no idea how I've suffered since he told me everything … I couldn't sleep all night … I was sobbing and sobbing … *(Changes tone)* Look at my nose – it's bright red … Don't laugh … No, *do* laugh … I deserve it … *(A sob)* Oh, I'm so happy now … *(Joyfully)* So you'll save us? I knew you would! *(She goes over to the mirror)* It's such a large amount of money, you see! *(She powders her nose)*
BIRON:	*(Sighing)* You can say that again … *(Sighs again, reflectively)* Quite a price to pay …
THERESE:	*(Turning to face him)* Too much?
BIRON:	Well, maybe … But don't you worry about it … Come and sit beside me … *(Moaning a little)* Therese … Let me have a little morsel of you … *(He takes her arms)*
THERESE:	*(Seriously)* Stop. Don't spoil everything. Don't ruin everything you've done for us.
BIRON:	*(Letting go of her)* Sorry?
THERESE:	*(Exultant)* Save us out of the goodness and generosity of your heart! Ask for nothing in return!
BIRON:	*(Comically)* I'm not asking for anything in return. I just want you to sit beside me …
THERESE:	No. If you're expecting something in return for your 'generosity' then I'm not interested … *(Sharply)* You must give up on me.
BIRON:	*(Startled)* What?
THERESE:	You must forget that we ever–
BIRON:	You've got to be joking! Forget!? Forget my reason for living!?
THERESE:	You won't do it?
BIRON:	Ah! What you demand is impossible!
THERESE:	*(Bitterly)* So *that's* your idea of friendship!?

BIRON:	I've told you before … I can't … It's *inconceivable*!
THERESE:	*(Shouts)* Do you really think I came here to haggle over the price like a–
BIRON:	This is ridiculous … It's one extreme or the other with you … Look … I am *not* demanding anything … But … At the same time … *(Bitter)* You come here, into my house, as pretty as ever … Worried … I heard your voice … You want something from me … And I'm in paradise! … You knelt down on the chair with your back to me … And you expect me to *forget*!
THERESE:	*(Gently)* If it's necessary to do so, yes …
BIRON:	*(Angry)* Ah!
THERESE:	And if I beg you to?
BIRON:	Save you just to lose you!? Never!
THERESE:	*(Exultant)* But you won't lose me … You'll have my heart forever in the noblest, purest way!
BIRON:	*(Shakes his head)* Oh! What nonsense …
THERESE:	Then you don't know the joy of sacrifice … The joy of sacrificing something for someone you love … *(Smiles ecstatically)* The pure joy of turning shameful pleasures into something so noble!
BIRON:	*(Trying to laugh)* The shameful pleasures are more than enough for me …
THERESE:	*(Shuddering)* Biron!
BIRON:	*(Moaning)* Therese … I am not a saint, a poet, a hero … I'm a man … *(He sits down, deflated)*
THERESE:	*(Sitting near him)* Listen … Listen … *(She lowers her eyes and speaks quietly)* D'Auberval loves me. He loves me like a fool …
BIRON:	*(Enraged)* Oh does he indeed!? Well, let me tell you; you're the only fool in that relationship!
THERESE:	*(Calmly)* I have never given him any cause for hope …
BIRON:	He only has to look at you to see that *you're* besotted with *him*!
THERESE:	If you agree to forget about me … I swear I will not see him again …
BIRON:	Never?
THERESE:	*(Trembling voice)* Never … *(Sighs)* Or at least until I am over him … *(Weeps)*
BIRON:	Well that will guarantee that you will never get over him … *(Silence)* But tell me … What are you going to do?
THERESE:	We're going to leave. As soon as the Baron is able to.
BIRON:	Where will you go?
THERESE:	*(Growing in happiness)* We must change our life. We must change ourselves. I won't leave him. I cannot abandon him.
BIRON:	Good! And then what?

THERESE:	He'll work. With me by his side. I will give him courage. I have wronged him in so many ways. I will make it up to him. You don't understand what a good man he is, inside. He can be so kind and generous. *(Smiles)* That great man is a child at heart!
BIRON:	*(Grumpily)* We're all children at heart!
THERESE:	What he did ... was just a moment's weakness, that's all ... And I understand ... I thought about it all night long ...
BIRON:	Instead of getting a good night's sleep!
THERESE:	My plans carried me away in happiness!
BIRON:	Yes, I know those sorts of plans ... They seem wonderful in the middle of the night ... But in the cold light of day ... It all collapses ... All those marvellous ideas can be seen for what they really are: impossible and ridiculous.
THERESE:	I see nothing ridiculous in my plans.
BIRON:	That'll be because you're half asleep. Do you honestly think that when you set up home in some rural backwater or stuck on a mountain somewhere that you will do anything other than cry your eyes out? *(THERESE bursts into tears)* There you go! And anyway, do you think that Courtin could stand it either? And what about little D'Auberval? What will you do with him when he comes visiting?
THERESE:	Armand!
BIRON:	Do you think he won't come sniffing around after you? Until he finds some other mature woman to chase around!
THERESE:	Armand! Some men love one woman for their whole lives.
BIRON:	And this is the way you give up on him!? *(Silence)* Do you think I'm asking you to do that? ... Do you think I'm asking you to make a sacrifice? ... In case you've forgotten what you used to say, let me remind you ... Follow your desires! Do whatever your heart commands you to do! *(THERESE smiles)* You're smiling now! The crisis you're in will pass – I've told you that. And tomorrow, when it's all over, you will once again be that delicious woman whose desire knows no limitation ...
THERESE:	Am I that woman?
BIRON:	Always. *(Silence)* Anyway, he's not so bad, that little D'Auberval ...
THERESE:	Not so bad? He is adorable!
BIRON:	Well he's young isn't he ... He would be ... And you want to break his heart?
THERESE:	Is it my fault?
BIRON:	Who else forced you to torture him? ... Who else forced you to torture me.

THERESE:	*(Stunned)* You?
BIRON:	Yes! I must mean nothing to you …
THERESE:	You know that I love you dearly …
BIRON:	*(Caressing her arms)* You see … It's always me you run to … It's always me you confide in … Your pleasures … Your pain … When you cry, I'm the one who consoles you … No one in the world has …
THERESE:	… ever loved me like you do.
BIRON:	More than you'll ever know! And no one knows how to give you pleasure like I do …
THERESE:	Stop talking about my pleasure … *(She weeps)*
BIRON:	Don't worry about that … And, please, stop crying … Let's just do what you want to … Let's go somewhere … Paris doesn't need you at the moment …
THERESE:	Well …
BIRON:	Nor Courtin …
THERESE:	That's true!
BIRON:	Nor me. Let's leave.
THERESE:	Where?
BIRON:	Let's take the yacht somewhere.
THERESE:	Really?
BIRON:	Yes, *The Argo*! Let's go! *(Forcefully)* What are we waiting for!?
THERESE:	But Courtin couldn't possibly …
BIRON:	Oh, he can. *(Closer to her)* And I tell you what … You can invite whoever you want … Loads of people … Or no one … Maybe just a certain young man …
THERESE:	Oh, you make me feel so ashamed … *(Weeps)*
BIRON:	Oh, come on now, you will love it … *(In her ear)* And you know that whatever gives you pleasure drives me crazy …
THERESE:	Why are you so obsessed with my worst instincts?
BIRON:	Oh, don't you worry about me!
THERESE:	You are incorrigible. *(Smiling)* So when do we go?
BIRON:	In the time it takes us to get to Marseille.
THERESE:	But I haven't packed.
BIRON:	You need only bring yourself. *(Holds her hands)* Do you remember our trip on *The Argo* three years ago?
THERESE:	*(In reverie)* Yes … Trieste at dawn … The sun glistening on the Adriatic …
BIRON:	That night in Amalfi? Dancing on the bridge? And afterwards …
THERESE:	*(Puts her hand on BIRON's lips)* Ssh … Oh, I cannot resist you …
BIRON:	Therese! Therese, my darling!

THERESE:	I am so weak!
BIRON:	No, you're just regaining your senses …
THERESE:	I can see that I'm going to betray my heart once more …
BIRON:	Don't be silly! You are going to be true to your heart once more, that's all! *(Emphatically)* We will explore your every whim!
THERESE:	*(To herself)* You poor thing … *(Changes tone)* Oh, I am so tired … I feel tipsy … Drunk … Don't laugh … I feel like I've drunk the sweetest wine … And the sun is so bright …
BIRON:	*(Delighted)* Oh, Therese! *(He goes to embrace her)*
THERESE:	*(Stopping him)* It's frightfully late … I must leave … Help me … *(BIRON takes her hands and supports her)*
BIRON:	*(Kissing her hands)* My darling! Darling!
THERESE:	*(Wriggling free)* Something's changed in this room. What is it?
BIRON:	The Dubarry mirror … It used to be over there …
THERESE:	No, not that. Something on the desk.
BIRON:	You're quite right … The Falconet clock … *(In her ear)* It used to be in the bedroom, remember? …
THERESE:	*(Laughs)* I simply must go!
BIRON:	I must let you go because I have so much to do *for you. (Rings the bell)* But come back soon …
THERESE:	Shall I meet you back here? *(JEAN enters)*
BIRON:	Of course. *(To JEAN)* Lerible?
JEAN:	Indeed, sir.
BIRON:	Excellent!
JEAN:	Shall I escort you out, Baroness?
BIRON:	That's quite alright – off you go. *(JEAN exits. BIRON rubs his hands)*
THERESE:	That ghastly little Lerible is here to see you, is he?
BIRON:	*(Giggles)* Yes.
THERESE:	That little worm is here? … *(BIRON nods, still laughing)* Is he having lunch here? *(BIRON shakes his head)* Will you have finished by two o'clock?
BIRON:	Well before … meet me at two. But I've got a few things to do now – things I must do in order to get Courtin, and The Haven, off the hook!
THERESE:	Thank you so much.
BIRON:	You can count on me … If that little worm doesn't take all your worries off your back, no one will! Mark my words! *(Kisses THERESE's hand)* I'll see you later. *(THERESE exits. BIRON rings the bell and a FOOTMAN enters)*

Scene Six

BIRON:	Tell him to come in. *(FOOTMAN bows)* But before that … help me get these shoes off, will you? *(FOOTMAN assists. He puts some old shoes on. LERIBLE enters. BIRON holds his hand out over the head of the FOOTMAN who is tying up BIRON's laces)* Good to see you, Lerible, old chap!
LERIBLE:	Hello, Mr Biron, you wanted to see me?
BIRON:	I want to see if you are a man, Lerible.
LERIBLE:	Sorry? *(BIRON grabs him by the coat)*
BIRON:	What if I offered you the chance to take over The Haven?
LERIBLE:	Oh, I wouldn't–
BIRON:	*(Jovial)* Oh come on! It would pay off the money that's owing to you … Guaranteed. And you'd get to keep all that it produces … The hard labour of all those kids slaving away … *(LERIBLE smiles)* I knew it! You'd simply love to do it!
LERIBLE:	But we can't talk about this without Baron Courtin, surely?
BIRON:	Don't worry yourself about him … I'll deal with him … *(Looks at the clock)* Any minute now in fact … Come on, man, make your mind up.
LERIBLE:	But do you think he'd agree to it?
BIRON:	You know what the aristocracy is like … Minds on higher things … Not interested in the financial side of things … Or its potential, eh? *(Sniggers)* What's important is that we see eye to eye … I need your agreement now.
LERIBLE:	*(Feebly)* The truth is that I'm not so interested in it now … No, really … *(Scratches his head)* Is The Haven really viable? …
BIRON:	If it hasn't been it's Courtin's fault … He only knows how to *give* … What do you expect? He's never done a real day's work in his life!
LERIBLE:	Yes, there's no muck on his hands alright …
BIRON:	He's very proud too. Arrogant even. *(Very cheerfully)* Come on, you old goat … Just think of it … Regardless of the business side of things … Think of the prestige … Wouldn't you like to see something on your lapel … Celestin Lerible, Légion d'honneur! I can see it right there … *(Silence)*
LERIBLE:	And what will you get out of this? Money? Perhaps. I'm not sure. You certainly didn't drag me over town at breakneck speed in your car for this? I couldn't care less about Baron Courtin, that's true. But you? Could it be that poor Mr Lerible will give his time and energy for nothing …

BIRON:	How can you say such a thing?
LERIBLE:	Very well. I'll do it … with some collateral from you … Fifteen thousand francs …
BIRON:	Now that's just being greedy.
LERIBLE:	But you're the one who seems to be keen to haggle … For The Haven, something that you, too, have been most interested in the past …
BIRON:	I'm in a good mood today, I can't deny it! But that doesn't mean I'm in the mood to gamble …
LERIBLE:	All interesting business ventures are a gamble at first.
BIRON:	(Grimaces) But can you guarantee that my money will be safe? I can give you the money but I do not want to lose it …
LERIBLE:	(Smiles) I distinctly remember saying this to you before, Mr Biron: business is a lottery … And sometimes you can hit the jackpot!
BIRON:	Quite. Very well. You won't regret this. (Looks at the clock) Courtin will be here any minute now … (Doorbell chimes) What did I tell you!?
LERIBLE:	(Anxious) Where should I go?
BIRON:	Stay here.
LERIBLE:	Don't let him say anything nasty to me, will you? You know what he's like. (Excited) He needs me now! …
BIRON:	(Laughs) Don't worry about that! (FOOTMAN enters)
FOOTMAN:	Baron Courtin …
BIRON:	Send him in. (FOOTMAN exits) Come with me … (He leads LERIBLE to the bathroom)
LERIBLE:	What are you doing? Where are you taking me?
BIRON:	(Shoving LERIBLE into the bathroom and following him) In with you … You need to simmer down a little …

Scene Seven

FREDERICK:	(Opening the door and allowing COURTIN in) Sir will be with you presently. (Exits. COURTIN wanders around the room. He is decidedly jaunty. BIRON enters and gazes in delight at seeing COURTIN so happy)
COURTIN:	(Turning) Biron! I have excellent news! Excellent! And I've come to see you, in person, to tell you … Everything is going to be just fine.
BIRON:	(Stupefied) Oh? How come?
COURTIN:	There was a cabinet meeting this morning. About The Haven.
BIRON:	I see.
COURTIN:	They have decided that they do not want to cause me any embarrassment. I am far too important, you see.

BIRON:	*(Astonished)* So that's why you are as happy as a child! *(Seriously)* And what about The Haven?
COURTIN:	What about it?
BIRON:	The money.
COURTIN:	*(Embarrassed)* Oh … yes … the money …
BIRON:	You forgot that, I take it … *(Roars with laughter)* Never mind! I have sorted that out for you myself!
COURTIN:	*(Delighted)* But how?
BIRON:	You shall see. *(He opens the bathroom door.* COURTIN's *eyes follow him in wonder.* LERIBLE *is revealed on the threshold, looking worried)*
COURTIN:	*(Quietly to* BIRON*)* Lerible?
BIRON:	Lerible. *(To* LERIBLE*)* Come on, there's a good chap. I believe you want to say something to Baron Courtin. *(*BIRON *rubs his hands)*

Scene Eight

LERIBLE:	*(Coming closer)* Yes … Yes, indeed … But the Baron has heard it all before … The same proposal, the same conditions …
COURTIN:	That scam–
BIRON:	Listen to him.
COURTIN:	That scam that I refused! The scam that would kick me out of The Haven forever!
LERIBLE:	Not at all …
BIRON:	No, Courtin … With this proposal you will remain the official patron.
LERIBLE:	Yes, you will continue to be part of The Haven.
COURTIN:	*(To* LERIBLE, *pompously)* Using my name, my honour, my reputation as a front for your unscrupulous activities! No, thank you! Emblazoning your prospectus with my name … *(With a booming voice)* Patron: Baron Courtin, member of the Académie française, senator …
LERIBLE:	Don't forget the Légion d'honneur.
COURTIN:	This is a joke, surely?
BIRON:	What a performance!
COURTIN:	I refuse!
BIRON:	Virtuoso stuff! You should be on the stage!
COURTIN:	I refuse!
BIRON:	*(Calmly)* Listen to me, Courtin. You have no choice. *(*COURTIN *walks awkwardly)* Do you hear me? I'm sticking my neck out for you, you know! *(Follows him)* I am *rescuing* you! *(Silence)* Enough.

Pull yourself together. *(Silence.* COURTIN *stands still)* Come on, Courtin, be reasonable now …

COURTIN: *(Bitter)* I am not thinking of myself. I am of no consequence. But what about The Haven? *(To* LERIBLE*)* To make the fortunes you dream of … You can work those little girls to death, you know! You can kill them!

LERIBLE: Of course I know that–

COURTIN: You have to *nourish* them too … They can be very difficult too …

LERIBLE: Just like people who can't pay their debts.

COURTIN: You must understand that they are indispensable! The good work of The Haven is indispensable!

LERIBLE: Rest assured, Baron. Believe it or not, I do have principles. The essence of life is work. The children will continue to work, and they will continue to love their work …

COURTIN: You're not hoping to make a fortune out of it?

BIRON: Don't worry yourself about that …

COURTIN: I just want to warn you that it's impossible …

LERIBLE: *(Smiling and calm)* Baron, I owned a prison in Nantes …

COURTIN: A prison? You owned a prison?

LERIBLE: Yes … Well … I was the governor … I got the prisoners to make furniture out of sticks and straw … Cheap, affordable furniture … The profits subsidized the costs of running the prison … Not so different to The Haven, hmm? *(*COURTIN *fidgets)* My two predecessors were ruined … Some years were better than others, but I always, without fail, made a profit …

BIRON: I never knew that! Are you still involved with it?

LERIBLE: No. They decided to turn it into a humanitarian prison. No extra punishments permitted. I knew it was time to leave then.

BIRON: You see, Courtin, this is exactly the kind of man The Haven needs!

COURTIN: *(Sits down, anxious)* Oh, I'm so worried … I'm worried it'd be a mistake … The Haven is a charity. Do you understand what charity is?

BIRON: Yes. But I will admit that charity is not my business …

COURTIN: *(Standing, disapprovingly)* Charity is never a business …

LERIBLE: The fact is …

COURTIN: Charity is a pleasure, a luxury … Charity is a duty … Through charity we set an example to the world …

BIRON: Yes, yes, very good. Very inspiring. But the most important thing in the world is balancing the books, Baron …

COURTIN:	That is the cynical attitude which is sweeping away the very foundations of society.
BIRON:	Courtin … Just because the kids will work a little harder doesn't mean that it's the start of the revolution!
LERIBLE:	We understand the nature of revolution nowadays … And we all know who ultimately has to pay the price – and it's *not* us …
BIRON:	Look, it's getting late … Let's sign as soon as possible … What do you think, Courtin?
COURTIN:	*(Sitting down)* Nothing.
BIRON:	Lerible … Could you draw up a little contract …
LERIBLE:	Yes, of course …
BIRON:	*(To COURTIN)* When shall we meet?
COURTIN:	Whenever you want …
BIRON:	And where?
COURTIN:	Wherever you want …
BIRON:	Very well … Tomorrow … Here … At ten o'clock … Agreed? Good …
LERIBLE:	*(Bowing)* Until tomorrow, Baron … *(BIRON leads LERIBLE to the door. LERIBLE suddenly points at his own lapel and speaks to BIRON)* You really think so? Just here?
BIRON:	Yes, dear boy … Every year five or ten of my closest associates receive that greatest of honours … *(LERIBLE exits. BIRON heads over to COURTIN who is sitting, solemnly)* Well, Courtin, I do believe I have saved you. Chin up, man, for Christ's sake! *(Exits)*

Scene Nine

COURTIN stands and takes a few steps then sits down again, exhausted. Enter THERESE.

THERESE:	Oh, you're alone?
COURTIN:	As you can see.
THERESE:	Are you waiting for Biron?
COURTIN:	No … *(Silence)* I'm not waiting for anything anymore.
THERESE:	Isn't everything sorted? …
COURTIN:	Yes. It's sorted alright.
THERESE:	Is it a good plan?
COURTIN:	Couldn't be better.
THERESE:	*(Sits beside him)* My darling … *(Silence)* Only children believe in miracles … I came to realize that myself, when it was almost too late! *(Silence)* Money's to blame – money poisons our very existence …

COURTIN:	*(Despair)* Money … *(Silence)* But what can we do, Therese?
THERESE:	We must find other pleasures in this world …
COURTIN:	You are such a dreamer …
THERESE:	Yes, I am …
COURTIN:	*(Standing)* And meanwhile the real world slips away from us … *(THERESE wipes her eyes. BIRON barges in rubbing his hands)*

Scene Ten

BIRON:	*(To THERESE)* Has he told you? It's all arranged … *(To COURTIN)* Has she told you? We're off!
COURTIN:	*(Surprised)* We're off?
BIRON:	Yes!
COURTIN:	We're going away?
THERESE:	*(Sadly)* I think so. *(She sits down)*
COURTIN:	But where?
BIRON:	On the yacht! The Adriatic! You, me, her and that little fellow she likes so much …
THERESE:	*(Quickly)* We haven't quite decided who's coming yet!
BIRON:	Yes, that's true … *(To COURTIN)* It's up to her … But what's important is that we get going at once!
COURTIN:	But I couldn't possibly … I have things to do …
BIRON:	You have *nothing* to do … You can leave it all behind you … Lucky you!
COURTIN:	*(Bitterly)* But the Académie française …
BIRON:	*(Laughs)* Don't worry about that!
COURTIN:	My report.
BIRON:	What report?
COURTIN:	My recommendations for awards.
BIRON:	Bring it with you. Write it on the yacht … You'll have plenty of peace and quiet … Sun beds too … Let's go to Venice! Yes, Venice! You'll do some wonderful writing there, I know you will!

BIRON *offers his arm to* THERESE. *They leave and* COURTIN *follows.*

THE END